STILL AT LARGE

A Casebook of 20th Century Serial Killers Who Eluded Justice

STILL AT LARGE

A Casebook of 20th Century Serial Killers Who Eluded Justice

by

Michael Newton

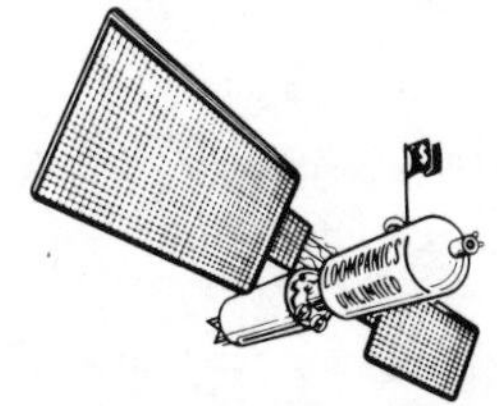

Loompanics Unlimited
Port Townsend, Washington

This book is sold for informational purposes only. Neither the author nor the publisher will be held accountable for the use or misuse of the information contained in this book.

Still At Large: A Casebook of 20th Century Serial Killers Who Eluded Justice

Published by:
Loompanics Unlimited
PO Box 1197
Port Townsend, WA 98368
Loompanics Unlimited is a division of Loompanics Enterprises, Inc.
1-360-385-2230
E-mail: loompanx@olympus.net
Web site: www.loompanics.com

Cover illustration by Mark Lang

ISBN 1-55950-184-7
Library of Congress Card Catalog 98-86892

Contents

The wily lunatic is lost if through the narrowest crack he allows a sane eye to peer into his locked universe and thus profane it.

Colette, "Freedom" (1966)

Acknowledgments

As always, I owe primary thanks for assistance on the research for this volume to friend and fellow author Dave Frasier, at Indiana University in Bloomington. Others who provided valuable input during 20 years of sporadic research include, alphabetically:

J. Richard Abell, Cincinnati (Ohio) Public Library

Mary Allely, San Diego (California) Public Library

The Blade Library Staff, Toledo (Ohio)

Detective Donald Bradley, Cleveland (Ohio) Police Department

David Cappoli, Librarian, Los Angeles (California) *Herald-Examiner*

P.W. Dukes, Librarian, Detroit (Michigan) *Free Press*

Ellie, at alt.true-crime

Jeanne Engerman, Washington State Library

Patricia Garneau, Librarian, Edmonton (Alberta) *Journal*

Eleanor Geheres, Denver (Colorado) Public Library

Diana Hunter, Librarian, *Atlanta Journal & Constitution* (Georgia)

Margaret Martin, Cleveland (Ohio) *Plain Dealer*

Charles Memminger, Honolulu (Hawaii) *Star-Bulletin*

Antonio Mendoza, of the indispensable Internet Crime Archives

Heath Meriweather, Miami (Florida) *Herald*

Davis Merrit, Jr., Wichita (Kansas) *Eagle-Beacon*

Marcia Morelli, New Castle (Pennsylvania) Public Library

Marcy Ruff, also at alt.true-crime

Judy Savage, Santa Barbara (California) Public Library

Bess Sheller, Director, Carbon County (Wyoming) Library

Carol Thomas, Librarian, Wilkes-Barre (Pennsylvania) *Times-Leader*

Harold Wilson, Seattle (Washington) Public Library

Introduction

Everybody loves a mystery. Across the board, without exception, we are captivated, titillated, and invigorated by encounters with the unexplained. Witness the popularity of modern television programs like *The X Files, Unsolved Mysteries,* and *Sightings.* It explains why some of us prefer to think that Adolf Hitler is alive in South America, instead of buried in a Russian grave; why most of us are more intrigued by Sasquatch than by African gorillas; why the average skywatcher would rather spot a UFO than catch a falling star.

We love the ones who got away.

In the beginning, there was Jack the Ripper, a gaslight ghoul who slaughtered London prostitutes in 1888, taunting authorities with mocking notes and bits of pickled viscera. Although, in fact, he claimed a mere five victims — and the poorest of the poor, at that — Jack's crimes terrorized Europe's largest city. They made headlines from Moscow to New York, and drove a string of copycats to butcher working girls in Russia, Texas, even Nicaragua. (Like their mentor in Great Britain, all the imitative Rippers managed to remain at large.)

Today, if we may trust the faceless experts laboring behind the scenes on *Jeopardy,* more books and articles have been published, more movies, plays, and operas produced about Saucy Jack than any other single criminal in history.

What can explain such popularity? Despite published claims that London's Ripper was the "first known serial killer," he actually missed that dubious honor by some 1,200 years. In terms of prolificacy, his meager body count would hardly qualify for front-page coverage in the era of Theodore Bundy,

John Gacy, and Jeffrey Dahmer. Why, then, does the Ripper still clutch our imagination in a stranglehold?

Because *he got away.*

There is no end to theories in the Ripper case, the list of suspects ranging from unknown Jewish slaughtermen to Masonic plotters, demonologists, even the Prince of Wales. In London, guided walking tours of the Ripper's not-so-happy hunting ground are sold out seven nights a week, year-round, come fog or freezing rain. Tourists from every corner of the globe are anxious to retrace the Ripper's footsteps, stand where he stood, drink a pint at the same pub where two of those he murdered plied their seamy trade.

If Red Jack had been captured, tried and hanged in 1888, he would be nothing but a footnote in the history of crime. Instead, by eluding Scotland Yard, he passed into legend and achieved grim immortality.

In that, sadly, the Ripper has not been unique.

While no official body catalogs such information, my personal files on the subject of serial murder (including more than 1,400 cases from 5th-century Rome to the present day) reveal that some 18 percent of all known serial killers — nearly one in five — evade capture and remain forever unidentified. That figure is sufficiently unnerving in itself, but I must warn the reader that my list is doubly incomplete. First, it is certain that my search of public records, spanning more than 20 years, has missed an unknown number of serial murder cases, including some that remain unsolved. More to the point, while self-styled experts are quick to offer estimates on the number of serial killers at large in any given year, their calculations are necessarily limited to *known* operators — that is to say, the killers who leave bodies in their wake. As for the others — those like Gacy, Dahmer, Dean Corll, Juan Corona, whose murder sprees are unsuspected by police until they make some critical mistake and land in jail — no estimates are possible.

The mysteries we cherish in these cases commonly owe less of their appeal to who the killers were than why they killed... or why they *stopped.* Why would a homicidal maniac retire, when he has managed to elude police for months or years on end? Death is an explanation frequently advanced, whether in terms of suicide, disease, or an untimely accident. The wily psychopath is, after all, a mortal being, equally susceptible to cancer, car wrecks, even homicide. Likewise, a psycho-stalker may be sidelined by some crippling injury or ailment. It is possible, in certain cases, that a killer may have been committed (voluntarily or otherwise) for treatment in a mental institution. Such is one theory suggested for Cleveland's **"Mad Butcher of Kingsbury Run,"** and Connecticut "Bra Strangler," Benjamin Miller, who spent time in a private sanitarium before police finally arrested him in 1972. Yet another possibility — especially when there is a protracted lull in killing, after which the murderer returns to start afresh — may be incarceration on some unrelated charge. Many serial killers pursue lives of crime on the side, with offenses ranging from petty theft to rape and robbery, any one of which may land them in jail.

And yet...

Suppose some killers simply have the wherewithal to say, "Enough!" and quit the game before they are identified. What then? Our minds rebel at the idea, presuming that a man or woman "sick" enough to kill repeatedly without apparent motive must lack fundamental self-control, and thus keep hunting until killed or captured by police. It works that way in movies and on television, after all... but real life dishes up some rude surprises, now and then. If Jack the Ripper and his progeny can simply stop at will, retiring undefeated while police grope blindly in the dark for clues, what happens to the rest of us? Who is secure?

More to the point: *Who's next?*

Still at Large collects case histories of 186 20th-century serial killers who, by one means or another, managed to avoid arrest and punishment, although their crimes were recognized by the authorities. (Forty-odd additional cases were omitted, due to insufficient information.) Three cases — those of **Belle Gunness, Bela Kiss,** and **Carl Menarik** — stand out for the fact that while the killers were identified, they *still* eluded justice, two by faking their own deaths, one by escaping from the lunatic asylum where he was confined. Another case, unique in my experience, involves the Cleveland **"black widow"** killer who, while arrested on charges of multiple murder, was never publicly identified, her case "lost" in the criminal justice system without explanation or adjudication. As for the rest, they played the Ripper's game with variations, passing into history as nameless, faceless predators whose bloody tracks begin and end in mystery.

Some of the killers treated here, like Jack the Ripper, craved publicity and chased it actively in letters to police or journalists.

"How many do I have to kill," one strangler whined, "before I get some national attention?"

Others acted out some private ritual with victim after victim — posing bodies, bathing those they slaughtered, keeping trophies, even mailing severed organs to police. It should not be supposed, however, that such actions indicate a secret wish to be identified and captured. That could be accomplished by surrender (like Mack Edwards in 1970), or even by suicide (like Carmelo DeJesus in 1973). Conversely, those who get away with murder for a lifetime typically display great ingenuity in covering their tracks. Some, like the **"Truckstop**

Killer," troll for victims nationwide, while others voluntarily confine their hunting to a smaller area — even a single public building — but they all display a kind of evil genius for evading capture. Time and time again, they kill and slip away like shadows on a foggy night.

As in all but one of my nine previous crime encyclopedias, entries in ***Still at Large*** are arranged alphabetically. This posed an obvious problem, because only three of the subjects described here have been identified by name, but the difficulty was overcome as follows: Where an unknown killer has been tagged with a popular nickname in the press — ranging from the **"Ax Man of New Orleans"** to the "**Zodiac**" — that sobriquet is used. In other cases (the majority, in fact), where no nickname exists, entries are designated either geographically (e.g., **Alameda County murders**) or by type (e.g., **Latino murders**). Confusion is avoided in the case of duplicate headings (e.g., **Gay murders**) by inclusion of locality and date (e.g., **Taxi cab murders — New York [1980]**). Murders confined to a particular institution are, whenever possible, identified by the name of that institution (e.g., **Riverdell Hospital**). **Bold type** is employed to denote subjects with their own discrete entries in the text.

Every effort has been made to keep the text of ***Still at Large*** as accurate and up-to-date as possible. That said, I would appreciate notification of any errors or omissions. Any reader with more detailed knowledge of the cases here contained — or any unsolved cases that have been omitted — is invited to contact the author in care of Loompanics Unlimited, at P.O. Box 1197, Port Townsend, Washington 98368.

Alameda County Murders — California (1983-84)

In the 12-month period between December 1983 and late November 1984, four teenage girls were killed in Alameda County, California, on San Francisco Bay. The crimes were grim enough, inciting fear in every parent at the time of their occurrence. Worse, the case remains unsolved today.

Kelly Jean Poppleton was the first victim, murdered in December 1983, at age 14. On April 5, 1984, Tina Faelz, also 14, was stabbed to death while using a popular shortcut under a freeway, near the Alameda County fairgrounds. The same month, Julie Connell, 18, disappeared from a local park; her lifeless body was discovered six days later, casually discarded in a field. Lisa Monzo, 18, was last seen alive on November 27, walking through the rain near Nimitz Freeway. Reported missing on November 28, her strangled body was recovered four days later.

At this writing, nearly 15 years after the final slaying in the series, authorities report no suspects in the case. Raw statistics indicate that most successful homicide investigations are concluded within 48 hours of the crime. As years go by, it seems unlikely that the Alameda County slayings will be solved — except, perhaps by the confession of a prisoner arrested on some unrelated charge.

"Alphabet" murders — New York (1971-73)

This troubling case draws its popular name from the initials of three young victims in Rochester, New York, raped and murdered over a three-year period.

Carmen Colon, 11, was the first to die, in 1971. Wanda Walkowicz was next, in 1972, and the killer's victim for 1973 was 10-year-old Michelle Maenza. The "alphabet" angle was further emphasized when each victim's body was dumped in a nearby town whose name began with the same letter as the dead girl's first and last names — Carmen Colon in Churchville, Wanda Walkowicz in Webster, and Michelle Maenza in Macedon. Police spokesmen noted that aside from similarity in age (all three victims were 10 or 11 years old), each girl was also from a poor Roman Catholic family, and each had recently suffered from problems in school. The latter items lead detectives to suspect a killer working for some social service agency, whose job might give him access to such information, but despite the grilling of 800 potential suspects, lawmen came up empty.

Six years had elapsed from the last murder, before Rochester police named their prime — and *only* — suspect as serial slayer Kenneth Bianchi. Better known to Californians as one-half of the "Hillside Strangler" team, blamed for the murders of 10 Los Angeles women and two more in Bellingham, Washington, Bianchi was a Rochester native who moved west in January 1976, teaming up with cousin Angelo Buono to win infamy on the West Coast. It took Bianchi's 1979 indictment for multiple murders to put Rochester police on his trail, belatedly noting that his car resembled a vehicle reported near the scene of one "alphabet" murder. In fact, while some New York authorities remain convinced of Bianchi's guilt in the earlier killings, he has never been charged. In early December 1995, an imprisoned murderer claimed to know the identity of the Rochester's "alphabet" killer, but that information — like the Bianchi lead before it — failed to produce an indictment in the case.

9

Ann Arbor hospital murders — Michigan (1975)

In six weeks time, between July and August 1975, 27 patients at the Veterans Administration hospital in Ann Arbor, Michigan were stricken with respiratory arrests that left them unable to breathe without mechanical aid. Some patients suffered more than one attack, 11 dying by the time physicians realized the incidents were inexplicable as natural phenomena. Investigation proved that 18 of the patients — nine of them deceased — had received unprescribed doses of Pavulon, a synthetic form of curare sometimes used by anesthetists as a muscle relaxant.

Federal agents summoned to investigate the case reported that most of the respiratory arrests occurred in the hospital's intensive care unit, during the afternoon shift. All the victims had been fed intravenously, and agents concluded that Pavulon was pumped into the feeding tubes, because injection in the larger IV bottles would effectively dilute the dosage. Examination of relevant work schedules focused suspicion on two Filipino nurses, 31-year-old Leonora Perez and 29-year-old Filipina Narciso. Both denied involvement in the crimes, but Perez was fingered by survivor Richard Neely, 61, as the nurse who entered his room — and then ran away — when he called out for help in the midst of a near-fatal respiratory arrest.

Indicted on five counts of murder, nurses Perez and Narciso were convicted in July 1977, those verdicts overturned on appeal five months later. Charges were dismissed against the pair in February 1978, and no new suspects have been named, despite the government's insistence that at least five persons (and perhaps 11) were deliberately murdered by some unknown member of the VA staff. No motive was suggested in the case, and it — like the identity of the elusive murderer — remains a mystery today.

Apulia murders — Italy (1997)

In 1997, the southeastern district of Apulia — literally the "heel" of the Italian "boot" — was terrorized by a serial killer who preyed on elderly women, confining his murders to Wednesdays and Thursdays. At the time of the announcement from police, he had already claimed seven victims, including one spinster and six widows. All of those slain lived alone, in ground floor lodgings, and all apparently opened their doors to the killer, "suggesting, the assailant could be a priest or another woman."

Each victim in turn was dispatched with hacking wounds to the throat, inflicted variously with a knife, an ice pick, or a screwdriver. In another strange twist, for what it may be worth, police note that a soccer game was playing on television at the time of each murder.

A vague profile of the killer describes the unknown suspect — male or female — as "a person 35 or 40 years of age, who as a small child may have been maltreated by his grandmother." Thus far, that helpful hint has brought police no closer to a suspect in the case.

"Astrological" murders — California (1969-?)

Between December 1969 and November 1970, police in northern California linked nine unsolved murders to a single perpetrator, still at large. A common bond was seen in the disposal of the bodies, cast off in ravines, and in the killer's hypothetical obsession with astrology. Of nine acknowledged victims, seven died in fair proximity to a seasonal solstice or

said that special chemicals enabled them to lift a suspect's fingerprints from Terry's corpse. Unfortunately, they were not on file with any law enforcement agency in the United States.

Patrick Baltazar, 12, disappeared on February 6. His body was found a week later, marked by ligature strangulation, and the skeletal remains of Jeffrey Mathis were discovered nearby. A 13-year-old, Curtis Walker was strangled on February 19 and found the same day. Joseph Bell, 16, was asphyxiated on March 2. Timothy Hill, on March 11, was recorded as a drowning victim.

On March 30, Atlanta police added their first adult victim to the list of murdered children. He was Larry Rogers, 20, linked with younger victims by the fact that he had been asphyxiated. No cause of death was determined for a second adult victim, 21-year-old Eddie Duncan, but he made the list anyway, when his body was found on March 31. On April 1, ex-convict Michael McIntosh, age 23, was added to the roster on grounds that he, too, had been asphyxiated.

By April 1981, it seemed apparent that the "child murders" case was getting out of hand. Community critics denounced the official victims list as incomplete and arbitrary, citing cases like the January 1981 murder of Faye Yearby to prove their point.

Like "official" victim Angel Lenair, Yearby was bound to a tree by her killer, hands behind her back. She had been stabbed to death, as had four acknowledged victims on the list. Despite those similarities, police rejected Yearby's case on grounds that (a) she was a female — as were Wilson and Lenair — and (b) that she was "too old" at age 22, although the last acknowledged victim had been 23. Author Dave Dettlinger, examining police malfeasance in the case, suggests that 63 potential "pattern" victims were capriciously omitted from the "official" roster, 25 of them *after* a suspect's arrest supposedly ended the killer.

During April 1981, FBI spokesmen declared that several of the crimes were "substantially solved," outraging blacks with suggestions that some of the dead had been slain by their own parents. While that storm was raging, Roy Innis, leader of the Congress of Racial Equality, went public with the story of a female witness who described the murders as the actions of a cult involved with drugs, pornography, and Satanism. Innis led searchers to an apparent ritual site, complete with large inverted crosses, and his witness passed two polygraph examinations, but by that time police had focused their attention on another suspect, narrowing their scrutiny to the exclusion of all other possibilities.

On April 21, Jimmy Payne, a 21-year-old ex-convict, was reported missing in Atlanta. Six days later, when his body was recovered, death was publicly attributed to suffocation, and his name was added to the list of murdered "children." William Barrett, 17, went missing May 11; he was found the next day, another victim of asphyxiation.

Several bodies had, by now, been pulled from local rivers, and police were staking out the waterways by night. In the predawn hours of May 22, a rookie officer stationed under a bridge on the Chattahoochee River reported hearing "a splash" in the water nearby. Above him, a car rumbled past, and officers manning the bridge were alerted. Police and FBI halted the vehicle driven by Wayne Bertram Williams, a black man, and spent two hours grilling him, poking through the car, before they let him go. On May 24, the corpse of Nathaniel Cater, a 27-year-old convicted felon, was fished out of the river downstream, authorities putting two and two together as they focused their probe on Williams.

From the start, he made a most unlikely suspect. The only child of two Atlanta schoolteachers, Williams still lived with his parents at age 23. A college dropout, he cherished ambitions of earning fame and fortune as a music promoter. In younger days, he had constructed a working radio station in the basement of the family home.

On June 21, Williams was arrested and charged with the murder of Nathaniel Cater, despite testimony from four witnesses who reported seeing Cater alive on May 22 and 23, after the infamous "splash." On July 17, Williams was indicted for killing two adults — Cater and Payne — while newspapers trumpeted the capture of Atlanta's "child killer."

At his trial, beginning in December 1981, the prosecution painted Williams as a violent homosexual and bigot, so disgusted with his own race that he hoped to wipe out future generations by killing black children before they could breed. One witness testified that he saw Williams holding hands with Cater on May 21, a few hours before "the splash." Another, 15-years-old, told the court that Williams had paid him two dollars for the privilege of fondling his genitals. Along the way, authorities announced the addition of a final victim, 28-year-old John Porter, to The List.

Defense attorneys tried to balance the scales with testimony from a woman who admitted having "normal sex" with Williams, but the prosecution won a crucial point when the presiding judge admitted testimony on 10 other deaths from the "child murders" list, designed to prove a pattern in the slayings. One of those admitted was the case of Terry Pue, but neither side had anything to say about the fingerprints allegedly recovered from his corpse in January 1981.

The most impressive evidence of guilt was offered by a team of scientific experts, dealing with assorted hairs and fibers found on certain victims. Testimony indicated that some fibers from a brand of carpet found inside the Williams home (and many other homes, as well) had been identified on several bodies. Further, victims Middlebrooks, Wyche, Cater, Terrell, Jones, and Stephens all supposedly bore fibers from the trunk liner of a 1979 Ford automobile owned by the Williams family. The clothes of victim Stephens *also* allegedly yielded fibers from a second car — a 1970 Chevrolet — owned by Wayne's parents. Curiously, jurors where *not* informed of multiple eyewitness testimony naming a different suspect in the Jones case, nor were they advised of a critical gap in the prosecution's fiber evidence.

Specifically, Williams had no access to the vehicles in question at the times when three of the six "fiber" victims were killed. Wayne's father took the Ford in for repairs at 9:00 A.M. on July 30, 1980, nearly five hours *before* Earl Terrell vanished that afternoon. Terrell was long dead before Williams got the car back on August 7, and it was returned to the shop the next morning still refusing to start. A new estimate on repair costs was so expensive that William's father refused to pay, and the family never had access to the car again. Meanwhile, Clifford Jones was kidnapped on August 20 and Charles Stephens on October 9, 1980. The defendant's family did not purchase the 1970 Chevrolet in question until October 21, 12 days *after* Stephens' death.

On February 27, 1982, Williams was convicted on two counts of murder and sentenced to a double term of life imprisonment. Two days later, the Atlanta "child murders" task force officially disbanded, announcing that 23 of the 30 "List" cases were considered solved with his conviction, even though no charges had been filed. The other seven cases, still open, reverted to the normal homicide detail and remain unsolved to this day.

In November 1985, a new team of lawyers uncovered once-classified documents from an investigation of the Ku Klux Klan, conducted during 1980 and '81 by the Georgia Bureau of Investigation. A spy inside the Klan told GBI agents that Klansmen were "killing children" in Atlanta, hoping to provoke a race war. One Klansman in particular, Charles Sanders, allegedly boasted of murdering "List" victim Lubie Geter, following a personal altercation. Geter reportedly struck Sander's car with a go-kart, prompting the Klansman to tell his friend, "I'm gonna kill him. I'm gonna choke the black bastard to death." (Geter was, in fact, strangled, some three months after the incident in question.)

In early 1981, the same informant told GBI agents that "after 20 black-child killings, they, the Klan, were going to start killing black women."

Perhaps coincidentally, police records note the unsolved murders of numerous black women in Atlanta in 1980-82, with most of the victims strangled.

Atlanta murders — Georgia (1980-82)

On May 18, 1982, less than three months after dissolution of the special task force organized to solve a string of grisly "child murders," Atlanta homicide detectives announced that another serial slayer was prowling the city. "Strong similarities" were noted in the recent deaths of three black women, and four other victims were also linked to the series, their murders dating back to June 18, 1980. (One account of the slayings refers to 27 murders, without providing any details.)

According to official statements, the most recent victim had been Lillian Lawrence, age 29, found in a vacant lot on May 15. Like six other women before her, all in their 20s, Lawrence had died from multiple stab wounds to the chest and neck. Two of the most recent victims were nude when discovered, a third partly dressed, and police spokesmen noted the presence of "evidence to suggest sexual activity" in all seven crimes.

Attempting to forestall another panic, Mayor Andrew Young acknowledged "a normal paranoia" in his city following the new reports of a random killer at large. Refusing to discuss the evidence in detail, Young reminded journalists that the manhunt might be thwarted by sensational publicity. From all appearances, the silent treatment fared no better, and the case remains unsolved today, despite a 1988 report from an informant in the Ku Klux Klan, alleging that KKK members murdered the women as part of an ongoing campaign too ignite a "race war" in Atlanta.

"Atteridgeville Mutilator" — South Africa (1956)

South Africa has suffered a veritable plague of serial killers since the fall of apartheid in 1990, but this maniac — still unidentified — got a long jump on the competition, anticipating the national trend by some 35 years. His six victims, all young boys, were slain in the small township of Atteridgeville, near Pretoria, during a five-month period in 1956, found with their tongues and genitals sliced away. To date, no clue to the slayer's identity has been found, and solution of the case is unlikely, to say the least. Curiously, the Mutilator's crimes seem to have opened a floodgate of sorts in Atteridgeville, the settlement spawning at least six other serial stalkers over the next four decades. Their number includes strangler Moses Sithoe (convicted of 38 murders in December 1997; he lived in Atteridgeville and buried his victims in the nearby Skurweberg Mountains), plus such unidentified practitioners as "Axeman," "The Beastman," "**Ironman**," and "Kgabi." So pervasive is the fear, these days, that some older locals suggest the township may be cursed, haunted by some evil spirit that transforms ordinary people into bloodthirsty monsters.

21

"Ax Man of New Orleans" — Louisiana (1918-19)

In the predawn hours of May 23, 1918, New Orleans grocer Joseph Maggio and his wife were murdered in bed. A prowler had chiseled through their back door, used Maggio's ax to strike each victim once across the skull, then slit their throats with a razor to finish the job. Maggio's brothers discovered the bodies and were briefly held as suspects, but police could find no evidence of their involvement in the crime and both were soon released.

A few blocks from the murder scene, detectives found a cryptic message chalked on the sidewalk. It read: "Mrs. Maggio is going to sit up tonight just like Mrs. Toney."

Police could offer no interpretation, so the press stepped in. The *New Orleans States* reported a "veritable epidemic" of unsolved ax murders in 1911, listing the victims as Italian grocers named Cruti, Rosetti (allegedly killed with his wife), and Tony Schiambra (whose spouse was also reportedly slain). Over eight decades, half a dozen authors have accepted the report as factual, relying on the "early" crimes to bolster this or that supposed solution in the case.

Unfortunately, none of them saw fit to look beyond the headlines, or they might have learned the truth and spared themselves embarrassment.

Examination of contemporary documents reveals that no such crimes were noted in newspaper obituaries, coroner's records, or police reports for the year 1911. In fact, no Crutis or Schiambras died in New Orleans that year from *any* cause, while the death of Mary Rosetti — a black woman — was blamed on dysentery. Ironically, there *were* unsolved ax murders in Louisiana during 1911, claiming a total of 16 lives (see next page), but the victims were all black, and none were killed in New Orleans.

On June 28, a baker delivering bread to the grocery of Louis Besumer found a panel cut from the back door. He knocked, and Besumer emerged, blood streaming from a head wound. Inside the apartment, Besumer's "wife" — Anna Lowe, a divorcee — lay critically wounded. She lingered on for seven weeks, delirious, once calling Besumer a German spy and later recanting. On August 5 she died, after naming Besumer as her attacker, prompting his arrest on murder charges. (Nine months later, on May 1, 1919, a jury deliberated all of 10 minutes before finding him innocent.)

Returning late from work that same evening — August 5 — Ed Schneider found his pregnant wife unconscious in their bed, her scalp laid open. She survived to bear a healthy daughter, but her memory of the attack was vague, at best. A hulking shadow by her bed, the ax descending — and oblivion.

On August 10, sisters Pauline and Mary Bruno woke to sounds of struggle in the adjacent room occupied by their uncle, Joseph Romano. They rushed next door to find him dying of a head wound, but they caught a glimpse of his assailant, described in official reports as "dark, tall, heavy-set, wearing a dark suit and a black slouch hat."

The rest of August 1918 was a nightmare for police, with numerous reports of chiseled doors, discarded axes, lurking strangers. Several of the latter were pursued by vengeful mobs, but always managed to escape. At last, with time and the distraction of an armistice in war-torn Europe, the hysteria began to fade.

On March 10, 1919, the scene shifted to Gretna, across the river from New Orleans. A prowler invaded the home of Charles Cortimiglia, helping himself to the grocer's own ax before wounding Cortimiglia and his wife, killing their infant daughter. From her hospital bed, Rose Cortimiglia accused two neighbors, Iorlando Jordano and his son Frank, of committing the crime. Despite firm denials from Charles, both suspects were jailed pending trial.

Meanwhile on March 14, the *Times-Picayune* published a letter signed by "The Axeman." Describing himself as "a fell demon from the hottest hell," the author announced his intention of touring New Orleans on March 19 — St. Joseph's night — and vowed to bypass any home where jazz was playing at the time. "One thing is certain," he declared, "and that is that some of those people who do not jazz it (if there be any) will get the axe!" On the appointed night, already known for raucous celebration, New Orleans was even noisier than usual. The din included numerous performances of "The Mysterious Axeman's Jazz," a song composed for the occasion, and the evening passed without a new attack.

On May 21, the Jordano trial opened in Gretna. Charles Cortimiglia did his best for the defense, but a jury believed his wife, convicting both defendants of murder on May 26. Frank Jordano was sentenced to hang; his elderly father drew a term of life imprisonment.

And still the raids continued. Grocer Steve Boca was wounded at home on August 10, 1919, his door chiseled through, the bloody ax discarded in his kitchen. On September 3, the Ax Man entered Sarah Laumann's bedroom through an open window, wounding her in bed, dropping his weapon on the lawn outside. Eight weeks later, on October 27, grocer Mike Pepitone was murdered at home; his wife glimpsed the killer, but offered detectives no helpful description.

On December 7, 1920, Rose Cortimiglia publicly confessed to perjury in the Jordano trial, explaining that she blamed her neighbors for the slaying out of spite and jealousy. Both prisoners were pardoned and released, unconscious of events that had unfolded five days earlier, in California.

On December 2, Joseph Mumfre, late of New Orleans, was ambushed and shot to death on a Los Angeles street corner. His female assailant, veiled and dressed in black, was identified as the widow of Mike Pepitone. At her murder trial, resulting in a 10-year-prison sentence, she would finger Mumfre as the slayer of her husband — and, by implication, as the Ax Man of New Orleans.

Homicide investigators scoured Mumfre's record and discovered he was serving time in jail, for burglary, during the Ax Man's hiatus from August 1918 to March 1919. Various authors have noted that Mumfre was also locked up between 1911 and 1918, thus implying a connection to the nonexistent "early" murders — but the suspect's motive still remains a mystery.

In 1973, author Jay Robert Nash *(Bloodletters and Badmen)* "solved" the case by calling Mumfre a Mafia hitman, allegedly pursuing a long vendetta against "members of the Pepitone family." The explanation fails when we recall that only one of the 11 victims — and the last, at that — was a Pepitone. Likewise, speculation on a Mafia extortion plot against Italian grocers overlooks the fact that four victims were non-Italians, while several were completely unconnected to the grocery business. At this writing, the Ax Man's case remains a mystery.

Ax murders — Louisiana and Texas (1911-12)

Between January 1911 and April 1912, an unidentified killer (or killers) slaughtered 49 victims in the states of Louisiana and Texas, leaving police baffled. In each case, the dead were mulattos or black members of families with mulatto children. The killers were presumed, by blacks and law enforcement alike, to be dark-skinned Negroes, selecting victims on the basis of their mixed — or "tainted" — blood.

The first attack took place in early January 1911, at Rayne, Louisiana, when a mother and her three children were hacked to death in their beds. The following month, at Crowley, Louisiana — 10 miles from Rayne — three members of the Byers family were dispatched in identical fashion. Two weeks later, the scene shifted to Lafayette, where a family of four was massacred in the small hours of the morning.

Texas endured the killer's first visit in April 1911, when five members of the Cassaway family were axed to death in their home, in San Antonio. As in preceding cases, the victims died in their sleep, with no evidence of robbery or any other "rational" motive.

On November 26, 1911, the action shifted back to Lafayette, Louisiana. Six members of the Norbert Randall family were butchered in their beds, each killed with a single blow behind the right ear. This time, police arrested a black woman, Clementine Bernabet, on suspicion of involvement in the crime. She would be held in custody through spring of 1912, but her incarceration would not halt the carnage. On January 19, 1912, a woman and her three children were hacked to death as they slept in Crowley, Louisiana. Two days later, at Lake Charles, Felix Broussard, his wife and three children were killed in their beds, each with a single blow near the right ear. This time, the killer left a note behind. It read: "When He Maketh the Inquisition for Blood, He forgetteth not the cry of the humble — human five."

Stirred by the quasi-Biblical implications, police made several arrests, including two members of the miniscule "Sacrifice Church." Reverend King Harris, leader of the sect, had addressed a meeting in Lafayette on the night of the Randall massacre, and informants reported links between the Sacrifice

Church and certain voodoo cults in New Orleans. Try as they might, though, police could find no evidence against their several suspects, and all were soon released.

On February 19, 1912, a mulatto woman and her three children were axed in their sleep at Beaumont, Texas. Seven weeks later, on March 27, another mulatto mother, her four children and a male overnight guest were slaughtered in Glidden, Texas.

Police began to note a geographical pattern in the crimes. Since November 1911, the killer(s) had been moving west, striking at stops along the Southern Pacific Railroad line. The next murders, likewise, would occur further westward on that line, in San Antonio.

Meanwhile, in early April 1912, Clementine Bernabet surprised authorities with a confession to the early crimes. While she admitted sitting in on meetings of the Sacrifice Church, Bernabet insisted that the slayings were related to the voodoo charm — or *candja* — purchased from a local witch doctor. The charm reportedly insured Bernabet and her friends that "we could do as we pleased and we would never be detected." For no apparent reason, they had chosen to test the magic by committing a random series of ax murders. Police were ultimately dubious, and Bernabet was never sent to trial.

On the night of April 11-12, five members of the William Burton family were hacked to death in their beds, in San Antonio. Two nights later, in Hempstead, Texas, the ax-wielding nightstalker claimed three more mulatto victims, thereafter lapsing into a four-month hiatus.

The lull was broken in San Antonio, at 4:00 a.m. on August 6, 1912, when the wife of mulatto James Dashiell awoke to the pain of an ax shearing through her arm. The killer had missed his mark for the first time, and he took to his heels as anguished screams roused the sleeping family. His shaken victim glimpsed only one prowler, and she could offer no coherent description to police.

The bungled raid in San Antonio wrote *finis* to the murder spree, and left police without a single solid piece of evidence. Defectors from the Sacrifice Church referred authorities to the text from the *New Testament* — *Matthew* 3:10 — "And now also the axe is laid unto the root of the trees: therefore every tree which bringeth not forth good fruit is hewn down, and cast into the fire" — but detectives never managed to identify a valid suspect in the case.

Ax murders — New York (1985)

On May 25, 1985, Janet Scott, age 85, was found dead in her New York City hotel room. An autopsy determined that death was caused by repeated blows to the head with a heavy, sharp instrument similar to an ax or hatchet. Following the murder, splintered pieces of the victim's skull were removed and placed near the body, in a pattern bearing some apparent significance to the killer.

Five days later, friends of 58-year-old Ruth Potdevin became concerned when she failed to arrive at a business luncheon that had convened in another downtown hotel. One member of the party was sent to check her room and found the door ajar. Inside, Potdevin lay dead on the floor, her skull crushed by more than 40 blows with an ax-like instrument. Once more, selected fragments of the skull and scalp had been arranged to form a cryptic pattern on the floor.

The day after Potdevin's murder, two blacks were arrested for trying to purchase a radio with one of her stolen credit cards, but police were unable to link them with the actual murder. On June 10, 1985, authorities announced that there were sufficient similarities between the two recent homicides to treat them as the work of a single killer — and there the matter rests. Thus far, there have apparently been no new murders in the series, and the case remains unsolved.

"Babysitter" — Michigan (1976-77)

The terror came to Oakland County, Michigan, in 1976. Authorities would later disagree on body counts and motives, even the description of their suspect, but there was no argument about the impact that a string of grisly murders had upon the wealthy bedroom communities, northwest of Detroit. Someone was killing children, claiming one victim after another, seemingly with impunity, while police watched helplessly from the sidelines.

The first to die was Cynthia Cadieux, 16, abducted from Roseville on January 15, 1976. She was found naked and dead the next morning, lying on a rural road in Bloomfield Township. Raped and bludgeoned with a blunt instrument, she had been dragged some distance over snow-covered pavement, her clothing piled 15 feet from the body.

Four days later, in Birmingham, 14-year-old Sheila Shrock was raped and shot to death inside her home. Police made the discovery while checking out a prowler call. Two blocks away, John McAuliffie had been terrorized, bound, and robbed of five dollars by a gunman who invaded his house. Police were left with a description of the assailant, but they had no other leads.

On February 13, 12-year-old Mark Stebbins left the American Legion hall in Ferndale, heading homeward shortly after noon. He never got there, and his lifeless body would be found in Southfield six days later, laying in the snowy parking lot behind an office building. Dead at least 36 hours when found, Stebbins had been sexually assaulted, then smothered, his body cleaned with meticulous care before he was laid out for discovery.

The pattern seemed to break with 13-year-old Jane Allan, abducted while hitchhiking in Royal Oak on August 8, 1976. Her body was found three days later at Miamisburg, Ohio, with the cause of death listed as carbon monoxide poisoning. Thus far, police saw no link between the four murders, nor could they find a connection with the unsolved September 1972 strangulation of teenager Donna Serra, in Ray Township. Unique methods of murder and disposal, along with the rape of both sexes, suggested different killers — at least two, and perhaps as many as four.

The pattern was established in December, with 12-year-old Jill Robinson's disappearance from Royal Oak, three days before Christmas. Her body was discovered December 26, near Troy in southern Oakland County, laid out neatly in a roadside snow bank. The cause of death had been a single close-range shotgun blast — another deviation — but the victim's body had been scrubbed before she died. The coroner could find no evidence of sexual assault.

On January 2, 1977, 10-year-old Kristine Mihelich left her Berkley home to buy a magazine and vanished on a three-block walk. Her body was discovered January 21, in Franklin Village, near the spot where Cynthia Cadieux had been discarded one year earlier. Unlike her predecessor, Kristine had not been raped; instead, she had been suffocated, her body washed and laid out in a funeral position, as with victims Robinson and Stebbins.

Homicide detectives were convinced of a connection in at least three cases now, and they did not have long to wait for number four. On March 16, 11-year-old Timothy King disappeared in Birmingham, his case igniting a general panic throughout Oakland County. Witnesses recalled seeing Tim with a shaggy-haired man who drove a blue Gremlin compact, but no one had noted the car's license number. Appearing on local television, Timothy's mother begged for the safe return of her child, promising that his favorite chicken dinner would be waiting for him at home.

The search ended on March 23, with discovery of the boy's corpse in a roadside ditch, near Livonia. Another victim of suffocation, Timothy had been scrubbed and manicured after death, with his clothing cleaned and pressed. Medical examiners reported evidence of sexual assault, but they "detected no proof that the killer was a male." Examination of the stomach contents showed that Timothy had been allowed one final chicken dinner prior to death, presumably in a ghoulish response to his mother's TV broadcast.

The media began to call their man the "Babysitter," after the apparent care he lavished on his victims while he held them captive. Authorities could not agree upon the killer's motives, some suggesting that he scrubbed the bodies to remove incriminating evidence, while others read the act as a ritual exorcism of guilt. The molestation of male victims pointed to a homosexual killer, but why, then, were female victims also chosen? The shotgun death of Jill Robinson was another riddle. One source hypothesized that Jill had survived attempted suffocation, suddenly reviving on the roadside; another theory noted that she had begun to menstruate, suggesting that the killer had altered his pattern to cope with the only "adult" victim.

On March 27, Dr. Bruce Danto, a Detroit psychiatrist, published an open letter to the Babysitter, theorizing on his motives, pleading with the man to call for help or turn himself in to police. Among the predictable rash of crank calls, one stood out. The male caller told Danto simply, "The article was wrong. You better hope it doesn't snow any more."

In short order, Danto began receiving letters and calls from a man who gave his name as "Allen," describing himself as the murderer's roommate. According to the caller, he and his friend had soldiered together in Vietnam, the Babysitter returning home with a deep bitterness toward affluent America. Suburban children were selected as the victims, he explained, in a twisted effort to "bring the war home" and educate wealthy slackers to the suffering of combat veterans. On one occasion, "Allen" made a date to meet with Danto, but he never showed.

In Oakland County, spring and summer passed without another "pattern" homicide, parents growing apprehensive as autumn turned to winter and the snow began to fall. Aside from cleanliness, fresh snow appeared to be the Babysitter's chief obsession. Safety programs instituted the previous winter were revived, police patrols beefed up in grim anticipation of another crime that never came. To date, there have been no more calls or letters from "Allen," no more homicides attributed to the Babysitter.

Battle Creek murders — Michigan (1982-83)

Between August 1982 and March 1983, residents of Battle Creek, Michigan, were stunned by the local murders of three young women. Authorities suggested possible Satanic motives in the case, and while no link with devil-worship was ever proved, the mere suggestion was enough to spread a pall of fear in Battle Creek.

The first to die was 20-year-old Margaret Hume, an ex-cheerleader and National Honor Society member, found strangled in the closet of her own apartment on August 18, 1982. She had been living on her own for just three months before she died, her body hidden by a pile of clothing and bedding.

Patricia Rosansky, age 17, was walking to school on February 3, 1983, when she disappeared within two blocks of campus. She was found outside town on April 6, her skull crushed, body concealed by leaves and branches in a shallow ravine. "Street talk" linked her murder to a local Satanic cult, and while no charges have been filed, police admit their leading suspect is a self-styled Satanist who boasts of leading black masses around Kalamazoo.

On March 13, 17-year-old Karry Evans disappeared from rural Bellevue, 13 miles from Battle Creek. Last seen walking near her grandparents' home, she was found by mushroom hunters on May 10, strangled to death, her body concealed by brush in a swampy area south of town. Once again, there were rumors of demonic involvement, with Evans describing her own occult beliefs in letters to friends, allegedly sporting a jacket with the Satanic emblem "666."

To date, no suspects have been named or prosecuted for the crimes in Battle Creek. With passing time, it seems unlikely that the case will now be solved, but homicide detectives still invite new leads, in hopes that someone, somewhere, may provide a crucial piece of evidence to break the stalemate.

Bay Area child murders — California (1983-91)

No murder case is more disturbing to authorities than one in which they are convinced they know the killer, but sufficient evidence is lacking to support a formal charge. Imagine such a case with multiple victims, all young girls, the prime suspect flaunting himself to the media, and you begin to grasp the brooding anger that has haunted police in northern California for the past 15 years.

The nightmare began on November 19, 1983, when 5-year-old Angela Bugay vanished within 50 feet of her Antioch home. Her corpse was found seven days later, autopsy results disclosing that the girl was sexually assaulted, then suffocated by her kidnapper. The investigation went nowhere, and it was hopelessly stalled by June 3, 1988, when 7-year-old Amber Swartz disappeared from a quiet residential street in Pinole, a few miles to the west.

Amber had been missing for three days, when a total stranger showed up on her mother's doorstep, introduced himself as Tim Binder, and explained that he had been out searching for the missing girl. Clearly distraught, tears brimming in his eyes, he told Kim Swartz, "I tried to save her. I couldn't. I looked everywhere. I did everything I could to save Amber." Before he left, the stranger solemnly proclaimed, "You realize that we're looking for a dead body."

The visit was strange and disturbing enough to concern the police. A background check identified the visitor as Timothy James Binder, born February 26, 1948, the son of a career military officer and a former army nurse. A Hoosier native, Binder had married his high-school sweetheart in 1968, but they divorced 11 years later. Meanwhile, he had settled in Oakland and gone to work for the Social Security Administration, as a claims adjuster, in 1975. Binder was promoted in 1979, then abruptly dismissed in 1985. The reason: His superiors had learned that he was using government computers to identify young girls in Colorado, recording their addresses and birth dates, sending 50 dollars to each — nearly $2,000 in all — on her birthday. In his own defense, Binder claimed he got the notion from a 1950s TV show, "The Millionaire," about a wealthy eccentric who bestows financial rewards on deserving strangers, but his boss didn't buy it, and Binder was out.

Detectives spoke to Binder shortly after his appearance at the Swartz home, in Pinole, and they brought along a bloodhound that reacted strongly — so they later said — to the scent of Amber Swartz in Binder's van. A search of the vehicle turned up photos of several young girls taped to the dashboard, sun visors, and windshield — but nothing in the way of solid evidence to link Binder with the latest disappearance. Interviewed by local detectives and FBI agents, Binder professed a love for children, manifested in compulsive urges to search for kidnap victims. He also maintained a file of news clippings on the Bugay case, and had mailed a letter to Angela's mother on June 2 — one day before Amber Swartz was abducted. In passing, Binder predicted to lawmen that the next child kidnapped in the district would be 9 or 10 years old.

A month after his first uninvited visit, Binder telephoned the Swartz home to report his "progress" — none — and to admit that he was now a suspect in the case.

"But of course, they're never going to find anything," he told Kim Swartz, "because there's nothing to find."

It was the start of a bizarre, long-running correspondence between Binder and Kim Swartz, his obsessive behavior swiftly convincing Amber's mother that he was, indeed, responsible for the girl's disappearance.

Police, meanwhile, had hit another macabre detour in the case, when — on June 15, 1988 — their bloodhounds tracked Amber's scent to the gravesite of Angela Bugay. They already knew that Tim Binder visited the cemetery often, sometimes reclining on Angela's grave to drink a beer, other times leaving coins when he left. As for the scent traces of Amber Swartz in Binder's van, and now at the grave he so frequently visited, such evidence was inadmissible in court. So, too, were the results of three polygraph tests administered to Binder by the FBI, in June. Two of the test results were "inconclusive," while the third "clearly indicated deception" in Binder's denial of guilt.

On November 14, 1988, Binder wrote a cryptic letter to Kim Swartz. It read: "I have learned many valuable lessons and made some decisions in the past few months. One of the lessons is that only I can decide what is the proper course of action for me to take, and one of the decisions is that I must not let fear of possible consequences ever deter me from actions conceived in love and compassion and a desire to help." Uncertain what to make of the note, Mrs. Swartz turned it over to police.

Five days later, on November 19, Tim Binder failed a firefighter's agility test in Hayward, California, south of Oakland. That same day, 9-year-old Hayward resident Michaela Joy Garecht vanished on an errand to the grocery store. Bright and early the next morning, Binder launched a two-week private search, which failed to turn up any traces of the missing child. Police and federal agents, meanwhile, thought it more than coincidental that Michaela Garecht was 9-years-old — the very age predicted by their leading suspect for the next kidnap victim. Questioned by detectives concerning his search for Michaela, Binder described a "mental picture" of her kidnapping, but there was still no evidence to link him with the crime.

On January 6, 1989, Tim Binder was briefly detained and questioned by police in San Pablo, California, after they found him sitting in his van, illegally parked on the sidewalk, talking to a group of children. Inside the van, officers found an open beer bottle and the names of missing Bay area girls, written in crayon. A pat-search turned up a large piece of stone in Binder's pocket, Tim explaining, "It's a broken angel's wing from a young girl's marble headstone. I didn't know her, but I would have liked to." Despite his claim that he was "just making friends," Binder was arrested on a misdemeanor charge of "annoying and disturbing children," after two 12-year-old girls described his persistent efforts to offer them a ride. At his booking, a note was found in Binder's wallet, reading —

> I love you Amber. You are my first, and I tried so hard for you. Tried + cried and still ache in my heart. They will always try to pull me back, but I never will. They don't know about us. They never heard of us.

Binder spent the night in jail, and while the charges were later dismissed without trial, Bay Area authorities resolved to keep an even closer watch on him. His specific whereabouts were unknown for January 20, 1989, when 13-year-old Ilene Misheloff vanished from Dublin, midway between Hayward and Antioch, but he was soon on the hunt, launching another unsolicited one-man search for the third missing child in eight months. On February 11, Binder later claimed, he was accosted by FBI agents while "searching" a half-mile from Ilene's house, and "They scared me off," prompting him to withdraw from the case.

On May 23, 1991, young Sheila Cosgrove received a peculiar letter at her home in Fairfield, north of Antioch. The note, signed "TJB," was written backwards, so that it had to be read in a mirror, and the envelope contained two coins: a silver dollar and an Indian-head penny. The envelope was postmarked from Oakland, and a second backwards letter followed a few days later, signed, "Your friend, Tim."

While the first note had simply related the history of the 1921 silver dollar, number two closed on a more intimate tone: "I dare not send you a hug and a kiss, so instead I send you one-third of a hug, and two-millionth of a kiss, and thirteen dodecillian dreams." A third letter included Tim Binder's return address and police dropped by to have a chat with him, concerning his interest in underage girls. That visit prompted yet another mailing to Sheila, Binder advising the girl that "I am not a threat to you and never will be." He signed off, "Love to you all, Tim."

Two days after Christmas 1991, 14-year-old Amanda ("Nikki") Campbell vanished within a few paces of her Fairfield home. By this time, no one was terribly surprised when Tim Binder telephoned the hotline, on December 30, and offered to help find the missing girl. On a hunch, detectives took their bloodhounds back to Oakmont Cemetery, on New Years Day, and the dogs tracked Nikki's scent directly to the grave of Angela Bugay. Six days later, in a second test, the bloodhounds "indicated strongly" that Nikki's scent was also found inside Tim Binder's van.

For his part, Binder called the test harassment, explaining to police, "I was picking up cans out there while I was searching for her. That's probably how her scent could have gotten in my car."

He also penned another note to Sheila Cosgrove, expressing "shock and sadness" over learning that the latest missing girl had not lived far from Sheila's home.

By this time, Binder was also mailing a steady stream of letters to Fairfield Detective Harold Sagan, an investigator on the Campbell kidnapping who had researched Tim's background the previous spring, after Binder started sending his unwelcome notes to Sheila Cosgrove.

In one typical letter to Sagan, discussing the area's several missing girls, Binder wrote, "I will always love them. Will you?"

By March 1992, he was literally mailing chess moves to Sagan, i.e. "pawn to king four," "Bishop to rook." The weird behavior finally boomeranged nine months later, when detectives secured a warrant to search Binder's home on December 9. No incriminating evidence was found, but the press had Binder's story now, complete with all the tales of weird behavior, and he was publicly identified as a suspect in Nikki Campbell's disappearance, his name inevitably linked to the four other dead or missing girls.

Binder responded to the adverse exposure with a publicity campaign of his own, granting press interviews and volunteering for a spot on Jane Whitney's TV talk shown in January 1993. Six months later, on June 9, Binder filed a $25 million harassment claim against Detective Sagan and the city of Fairfield. The press conference included a statement from Binder, denying any part in the Campbell abduction, claiming he was "forty miles away from Fairfield" on December 27. The damage claim was formally rejected in August, and Binder's attorney proceeded with civil litigation. A federal court dismissed the lawsuit in May 1995, remanding it to state court for a hearing.

The case of Northern California's dead and missing girls, meanwhile, had taken yet another bizarre turn. On February 14, 1995, spokesmen for the FBI's San Francisco field office informed Detective Sagan that Binder "has been eliminated as a suspect" in the death of Angela Bugay. The G-men refused to say more, since the Antioch case was at "a very sensitive stage, and any information is closely guarded," but another 14 months would pass before the arrest of murder suspect Larry Graham, on April 24, 1996.

The news left Sagan and other investigators confused. If Binder had no part in the Bugay homicide, what was his obsessive interest in the child, complete with ongoing visits to her grave? No charges were filed against Larry Graham in the other four cases, and Tim Binder remains the only named suspect in the disappearances of Amber Swartz, Michaela Garecht, Ilene Misheloff, and Nikki Campbell. He also continued his uninvited correspondence with young girls, once posing as a female high school student, when he wrote to a 13-year-old girl in Walnut Creek.

In March 1996, detectives applied a voice stress analyzer — a kind of long-distance "lie detector," inadmissible in court — to Binder's recorded statement from June 1993, concluding his denials of involvement in the Campbell kidnapping were false. Police speculate, without producing any evidence to back it up, that the four missing girls may have been secretly buried in open graves, either in Oakmont Cemetery, or one of the other local graveyards where Binder often volunteered his services as a maintenance man.

Such speculation notwithstanding, the city of Fairfield settled Binder's lawsuit out of court, with a $90,000 damage payment on May 2, 1997. Binder remains at liberty, no charges have been filed against him, and no trace has been found of the four missing girls. Their case remains officially unsolved.

"Bible John" — Scotland (1968-69)

On the morning of Friday, February 23, 1968, a resident of Glasgow, Scotland, found a lifeless, naked woman sprawled in back of his apartment building. Officers were on the scene in minutes, noting that the woman lay spread eagle on her back, with no sign of her clothing at the scene. The victim, raped and strangled, was identified as 25-year-old Patricia Docker, employed as an auxiliary nurse at Glasgow hospital. Last seen by her parents on Thursday night, when she left home to go dancing, Docker had been dressed in a light orange dress and gray coat, with a brown purse and matching shoes. No trace of the missing bag or garments was ever found.

Eighteen months elapsed before the killer struck again, on August 16, 1969. That Saturday night, 32-year-old Mima MacDonald failed to return from an outing at the Barrowland Ballroom, her ravaged, semi-nude body was discovered on Monday morning in a vacant apartment on Mackeith Street a few blocks from her home. She had been strangled with her own nylon stockings, left knotted around her neck. Police noted that both victims were petite, both had spent their final living hours at a dance hall, and that both were menstruating when they were murdered. The last point, if not mere coincidence, suggested the possibility of some private sexual obsession on the killer's part, but it brought authorities no closer to their goal of an arrest.

Customers from the Barrowland Ballroom helped piece together Mima MacDonald's last hours of life. She had left around midnight, in the company of a tall, slender man, a redhead with his hair cut short, wearing a stylish suit that may have been hand-sewn. Observers pegged his age somewhere between 25 and 35 years, but no one seemed to know his name. The couple was last seen walking in the general direction of Mackeith Street, less than a mile from the dance hall. A sketch of the suspect was prepared and published, but it led detectives nowhere.

Eleven weeks after the MacDonald murder, on the night of October 30, 29-year-old Helen Puttock and her sister Jeannie dropped by the Barrowland Ballroom. Both wound up dancing with men who gave their names as "John," although neither was ever identified further. Helen's John was 5-foot-10, a redhead in his early 30s, whose courtesy and custom-tailored suit convinced Jeannie that he "wasn't the Barrowland type" — a reference to the rough working-class types who patronized the densely packed ballroom. Still, despite "John's" seeming courtesy, he underwent a rapid mood shift at one point, causing an angry scene with the manager over some pocket change lost to a defective cigarette machine.

When it was time to leave, red-haired "John" shared a taxi with the sisters, Jeannie afterward recalling his comments on the subject of religion. The man described himself as a teetotaler and avid bible student who knew the Good Book by heart, priding himself on his ability to quote verses from memory. The taxi dropped Jeannie off first, and she waved good-bye to her sister, unaware that it would be the last time she ever saw Helen alive.

Around 7:00 a.m. on October 31, a woman walking her dog found Helen Puttock's strangled body, clothing torn and disarranged, not far from her Glasgow apartment. As with Mima MacDonald, the murder weapon was one of Helen's own stockings, left coiled around her neck. And like the strangler's two previous victims, Puttock had been menstruating when she died.

Police were galvanized by the latest murder, questioning hundreds of men who resembled the elusive killer journalists had now dubbed "Bible John." One innocent local, Norman MacDonald — no relation to Mima — was hauled in so often that detectives finally issued him a special pass, to avert further harassment. In addition to grilling lookalikes, investigators also visited 240 Glasgow tailors, seeking one who might recognize a particular customer with a taste for hand-stitched suits... but all in vain.

In 1970, bereft of suspects, the police consulted a forensic psychiatrist, Dr. Robert Brittain, to obtain a "profile" of their quarry. Brittain guessed that Bible John was less than 35 years old, an introspective man who shied away from social contacts, sexually dysfunctional, who suffered an ambivalent love/hate relationship with his mother. In fact, Brittain suggested, he might be a latent homosexual, perhaps a closet transvestite. Another hobby, verging on obsession, would involve a preoccupation with weapons (though none had been used in his crimes).

It would appear that Bible John "retired" after the Puttock homicide, in 1969, although one published report mentions another spate of unsolved Scottish murders in 1977-78, briefly prompting rumors that the strangler had returned to active duty. No more details were forthcoming on the later crimes, and Glasgow police still peg the stalker's body count at three victims. Forensic science took a stab at the case in 1996, with exhumation of an unnamed suspect's corpse in Lanarkshire, for DNA comparison with the semen stain found on Helen Puttock's clothing, but the test results were "inconclusive," and the case remains officially unsolved.

Bingham poisonings — England (1911)

Historically, Bingham family members have been the official custodians of Lancaster castle in England. William Hodges Bingham, patriarch of the clan, served as chief caretaker for three decades prior to his death, in January 1911, thereafter succeeded by his son, James. Soon after his appointment, James brought his sister Margaret to work as a housekeeper in the castle, but her stay was short-lived, ending with her untimely death a few weeks later.

Margaret was replaced, in turn, by half-sister Edith Agnes Bingham, a shrewish backbiter who quickly rubbed James the wrong way. They quarreled incessantly, and James made plans to ease her out of her position. A replacement had been scheduled to begin work on August 14, 1911, but plans abruptly changed on August 12, when James collapsed and died.

Police discovered that his final meal had been steak, prepared by Edith, and an autopsy revealed that James had died from arsenic poisoning. When Margaret and William Bingham were exhumed, more arsenic was found, and Edith faced a charge of triple murder, based on the theory that she killed her relatives to gain a small inheritance. Her barrister reminded jurors that there was no evidence of Edith possessing arsenic at any time, and she was acquitted after 20 minutes of deliberation, leaving the file perpetually open.

"Black Widow" murders — Ohio (19??-21)

Details are damnably sketchy on this unique case, in which authorities apparently "lost" the suspect after her arrest, but before she had been publicly identified. On May 1, 1922, according to the media reports, police in Cleveland jailed a local woman on suspicion of poisoning her husband for the sum of $11,000 in life insurance. Announcing her arrest the next day, prosecutor Edward Stanton told reporters that the suspect had been married five times, divorcing her first two husbands, after which the next three died in mysterious circumstances. Two children from her first marriage had also died years earlier, reportedly from "accidental" consumption of poison tablets kept around the house.

The suspect sat in jail, her name withheld from journalists, while authorities exhumed the corpse of husband number five, deceased in May of 1921. Acquaintances recalled the woman saying of her mate, "I would like to get rid of him. I would like to give him poison."

Several weeks before he died, she told a creditor, "I've got $5,000 coming within a couple of weeks." It came as no surprise, therefore, when arsenic was found in the remains on May 5, 1922, and prosecutors spoke of digging up the other victims, one of them interred at Pittsburgh.

And there, incredibly, the story ends. Although the case had been reported in the Cleveland press and in the *New York Times*, it disappears without a trace beyond May 7, 1922, the suspect still unnamed. A search of the official files, conducted by police in Cleveland during April 1988, revealed no documents relating to the prisoner, her victims, or the full-scale homicide investigation that made headlines at the time. Likewise, there is no record of a trial. At this late date, it is impossible to gather any further information, and the case remains as it began, in mystery.

"Black businessman" murders — Illinois (1971-72)

Initially billed in media reports as the murder of six black "businessmen," Chicago's string of unsolved homicides in 1971 and '72 had several things in common: all the victims were black males; each was shot in the back of the head, execution-style; and all were discarded, like so much refuse, in the muddy South Branch of the Chicago River.

Lee Wilson was the first to die, in September 1971. Employed as a laborer in a meat packing plant, Wilson worked a shift from 4:00 p.m. to midnight. Dropping a co-worker off around 1:00 a.m. on September 2, he started for home but never arrived. Wilson's car was recovered later that day; his body — hands bound, a bullet in his brain — was fished from the river on September 6. Robbery was suggested as a motive, though Wilson carried no more than three dollars on the night of his death.

William Thomas, a baggage handler at O'Hare Airport, habitually traveled with two or three hundred dollars in his pocket, in case of "emergencies." On the night of November 4, 1971, he called home and told his wife not to hold dinner because he would be working late. Around 9:30 p.m., he picked up an employee's airline pass to Florida... and disappeared. The pass was in his car when it was found abandoned three days later. Thomas, bound and shot like Lee Wilson before him, was pulled from the Chicago River on December 12.

Meanwhile, the elusive slayer had selected victim number three. A taxi driver with his own cab, 47-year-old Albert Shorter was off duty and cruising the bars when he vanished on November 17. The victim's Cadillac was found the next day; his lifeless body was recovered from the river on November 21.

Vernell Lollar, although unemployed, was flush with $900 from an insurance settlement when he vanished on November 26. His body, sans cash, was retrieved from the Chicago River on December 13.

Lieutenant Scott (his name, not a military rank) was the first victim to qualify as an actual businessman. A partner in a local snack shop, he withdrew $2,000 from a pension fund on the afternoon of December 13, 1971, and vanished the same evening. His car was found the next day, Scott's body hauled ashore on New Year's Eve.

The final victim in the murder series, Richard Stean, was 28 years old, a partner in a television sales and service business. He left home around midnight on January 2, 1972, carrying $2,000 earmarked for a building contractor he was scheduled to meet the next morning. Stean missed his appointment, and his car was recovered on January 6, after witnesses saw its four passengers enter the infamous Cabrini Green housing project. On February 5, Stean's body was found in the river, but FBI agents were already working the case, tracking anonymous callers who demanded an $11,000 ransom payment from Stean's father. The drop was made on schedule, but no one ever came to get the cash.

A special task force was created in a bid to crack the case, but officers were getting nowhere fast. With half a dozen victims on their hands, no suspects, and a dearth of clues, police could only say, "The trail is cold." So it remains, nearly two decades after the last acknowledged murder in the series.

Bothell murders — Washington (1995-97)

Apparently unrelated to the elusive "Green River Killer," the discovery of multiple skeletons near Bothell, Washington, has King County authorities speculating on the presence of another phantom slayer in their midst. Captain Bob Woolvert, of the Bothell Police Department, told reporters on February 12, 1998, that there was "a strong indication" of at least two corpses buried at the site, adjacent to the town's North Creek business park. While declining to give details on the state of the remains, initial reports indicate that one of the fragmentary skeletons, including a skull, belonged to someone below the age of 20, dead for less than three years.

Seventy investigators, including police detectives, lab technicians from the King County Medical Examiner's Office, and volunteer search-and-rescue workers, labored through a steady downpour to search for more remains of the unidentified victims. Police Chief Mark Ericks of Bothell told the press, "This is as bad as it could get. The rain and mud is horrible, and it's making our job harder and harder. We could use 30 more people to help." Investigators from both King and Snohomish Counties were represented in the dig, concerned that the skeletons might represent new victims for one or another of the area's several unidentified serial killers.

According to media reports, the first set of bones was found by a transient on Tuesday, February 10, lying atop straw that was scattered over a recently-graded construction site. Authorities were notified, and commenced to dig at the scene, suggesting to reporters that the first bones found had been unearthed and scattered by animals. At this writing, the two known victims remain unidentified, no further remains have been found, and cause of death remains undetermined… although clearly, neither one of the corpses buried itself. In an area known for its human predators, authorities suspect there may be worse in store before the excavation is completed.

British child murders — England (1978-84)

On April 21, 1986, detectives of Scotland Yard held a conference to examine evidence and discuss possible connections in the deaths and disappearances of 16 British youngsters in the past eight years. The victims ranged in age from five to 16 years, with officers reporting that at least seven cases appeared to be linked though the proximity of fairs and circuses. In several other cases, links were theorized between the homicides and streams or lakes habitually used by anglers.

Three of the murders — those of 11-year-old Susan Maxwell, 5-year-old Caroline Hogg, and 10-year-old Sarah Harper — were ultimately solved with the conviction of a predatory pedophile. That defendant was cleared in the 13 remaining cases, however, with victims identified as: Genette Tate, 13, missing from Aylesbeare, in Devon, on August 19, 1978; Sean McGaun, 15, murdered on April 7, 1979; 15-year-old Marion Crofts, 14, murdered at Fleet, in Hampshire, on June 9, 1981; 8-year-old Vishal Mehrota, slain in Putney, West London, on July 29, 1981; Jason Swift, 14, murdered at Hackney, East London, on July 11, 1983; 9-year-old Imnan Voha, killed the same afternoon at Preston, in Lancashire; Collette Aram, 16, murdered at Keyworth, in Nottinghamshire, on October 30, 1983; 15-year-old Lynda Mann, killed at Narborogh, Leicestershire, on November 21, 1983; Chris Laverack, age 9, murdered in Hull on March 9, 1984; Mark Teldesley, 7, vanished from Workingham, Berkshire, on June 1, 1984; and 6-year-old Barry Lewis, murdered in Walworth, South London, on September 15, 1984.

To date, despite the grilling of numerous suspects and pursuit of countless "leads," the homicides and disappearances remain unsolved, police unable to state with certainty how many may have been the work of one elusive predator.

Brooklyn murders — New York (1989)

On July 22, 1989, spokesmen for the New York City Police Department published a sketch of an unidentified black male, suspected in a series of daylight robberies through Brooklyn's Parkville neighborhood. The victims were all elderly citizens, apparently followed home by a lurking predator who then forced his way inside their apartments, beating and terrorizing the victims before he looted their homes. At least two female victims had been killed, on June 9 and July 14, before police issued their sketch and announcement, with the most recent robbery in the series reported on July 17. Judging by the stony silence since that time, it would appear that New York's finest never caught the man responsible.

"BTK Strangler" — Kansas (1974-77)

Residents of Wichita, Kansas were ill-prepared to cope with monsters in the early days of 1974. Their lives, by and large, were conservative, well-ordered, and purposeful. They had no previous experience to brace them for the coming terror, and it took them absolutely by surprise.

On January 15, four members of the Otero family were found dead in their comfortable home, trussed up like Thanksgiving turkeys and strangled with lengths of cord cut from old Venetian blinds. Joseph Otero, 38, lay face-down on the floor at the foot of his bed, wrists and ankles bound with samples of the same cord that was wrapped around his neck. Close by,

Julie Otero lay on the bed she had once shared with her husband, bound in similar fashion and already cooling in death. Joseph II, age 9, was found in his bedroom, duplicating his father's position at the foot of his bed, a plastic bag covering his head. Downstairs, 11-year-old Josephine hung by her neck from a pipe in the basement, dressed only in a sweatshirt and socks.

Aside from the killer's ritualistic M.O., police knew the attack had been planned in advance. Someone had cut the home's telephone lines outside, while bringing an ample supply of cord to bind and strangle four victims. Neighbors filed reports of a "suspicious looking" stranger in the area, but published sketches of the suspect led police precisely nowhere.

Ten months later, in October, a local newspaper editor received an anonymous call from the killer, directing him to a particular book in the Wichita Public Library. Inside the book, he found a letter filled with numerous misspellings, claiming credit for the massacre and promising more victims to come. Signing himself the "BTK Strangler," the author provided his own translation in a postscript. He wrote: "The code words for me will be... Bind them, Torture them, Kill them."

Police requested that the letter be withheld, against the possibility of false confessions in the case, but no one came forward. No evidence materialized. Twenty-nine months would pass before the killer showed his hand again.

On March 17, 1977, 26-year-old Shirley Vian was murdered in her Wichita home, stripped, bound and strangled on her bed, left with a plastic bag over her head, the traditional cord wrapped tight around her neck. Vian's three children, locked in a closet by the armed intruder who invaded their home, managed to free themselves and call police. Again, the crime was clearly premeditated: the killer had stopped one of Vian's sons on the street that same morning, displaying photographs of an unknown woman and child, allegedly seeking directions to their home.

On December 9, 1977, Nancy Jo Fox, 25, was found dead in the bedroom of her Wichita apartment, a nylon stocking twisted around her neck. Unlike previous victims, she was fully clothed. An anonymous caller directed officers to the scene, and police traced the call to a downtown phone booth, where witnesses vaguely recalled "someone" — perhaps a blond 6-footer — using the booth moments earlier.

The killer mailed a poem to the local press on January 31, but it was routed to the advertising section by mistake and overlooked for days. Disgruntled at the absence of publicity, he shifted targets, firing off a letter to a local television station on February 10. "How many do I have to kill," he asked, "before I get my name in the paper or some national attention?"

In his latest note, the strangler claimed a total of seven victims, naming Vian and Fox as the latest. Number seven remained anonymous, with a taunting punch line: "You guess the motive and the victims."

Unable to document the killer's claim, authorities still took him at his word, announcing theoretical acceptance of the body count.

Alternately blaming his crimes on "a demon" and a mysterious "factor X," the strangler compared his work to that of Jack the Ripper, New York's "Son of Sam," and the L.A. "Hillside Strangler" (then still at large). Psychiatrists who analyzed the letters felt the killer saw himself as part of some nebulous "grand scheme," but they were unable to pinpoint his motive or predict his next move.

In fact, there was none. With more than two decades having passed since his last whining plea for attention, the BTK Strangler has claimed no more victims in Wichita, penned no more notes or poems to the press. He has vanished, as if from the face of the earth, leaving questions and riddles behind.

"Canton Ripper": See "Guangzhou Ripper"

Castration murders — United States (1981-86)

Around 7:00 p.m. on June 14, 1982, sheriff's deputies in Wasatch County, Utah, were summoned to the banks of Daniels Creek, where a fly fisherman had reported the grisly discovery. Upon arrival, they found a man's nude body, lying on its back, knees raised, the genitals hacked off and missing from the scene. Autopsy results disclosed that the castration had occurred postmortem, after the victim was shot once in the back of the head with a .38 caliber pistol. In the absence of ID, detectives circulated flyers bearing the description of the dead man's tattoos, but 16 months elapsed before they scored a hit. On October 11, 1983, the victim was identified by fingerprints as Marty Shook, age 21, from Truckee, California. He had last been seen alive two days before his corpse was found in Utah, when he left his mother's home on a hitchhiking trip to Colorado.

Another four years and seven months passed before Utah authorities submitted details of their unsolved murder to the FBI's Violent Criminal Apprehension Program (VICAP), in May 1988, for analysis and comparison to other crimes reported from around the country. A year after *that,* in May 1989, the feds reported back on a strikingly similar case from Pennsylvania. There, six miles north of Williamsport, another young man had been found, nude and emasculated, shot once in the back of the head on August 19, 1981. The victim was identified from fingerprints on September 27 as 30-year-old Wayne Rifendifer, a North Carolina native with a record of arrests for larceny. Ballistics tests now proved that Shook and Rifendifer had been shot with the same gun.

Authorities also suspect the same killer at work in the November 1986 murder of 26-year-old Jack Andrews, an Oklahoma native with a criminal past, found nude and wrapped in a blanket at a highway rest stop near Litchfield, Connecticut. In addition to the standard missing genitals, Andrew's nipples were cut off, and both legs had been severed at mid-thigh. None of the missing parts were ever found, and cause of death was not determined in the Litchfield case. Andrews, at least, had not been shot.

To date, no progress has been publicly reported in these cases, and while homicide detectives theorize about a transient killer — possibly a long-haul truck driver — who preys on hitchhikers, they are no closer to a suspect now, than back in 1981. Barring spontaneous confession by the killer(s), there is no real prospect for solution of the case.

Chatham/Avalon Park murders — Illinois (1992)

In the summer of 1992, Chicago's mostly black Chatham and Avalon Park neighborhoods were terrorized by a gunman who killed at least four victims and robbed an estimated 20 more. The killer's targets of preference were elderly residents, generally accosted in their own yards or driveways, upon returning home from some errand. According to eyewitness statements, the shooter was a light-skinned African American, apparently in his twenties, 5-feet-11-inches tall, weighing between 150 and 170 pounds. He frequently wore sunglasses, and had a fondness for all-black clothing, offset on occasion with a loud purple shirt.

By Labor Day 1992, residents of the target neighborhoods were complaining to the press about supposed police inaction on the case. Authorities predictably responded with denials, stating that they had expended their best efforts to solve the case, and would continue doing so. Ironically, press coverage of the controversy named only one of the killer's four victims to date: Thomas Hodges, gunned down in his own garage on July 22, 1992, is believed to be the second of four persons killed in the series. The rest remain anonymous to most Chicagoans and to the world at large, but their loss was keenly felt in this section of the Windy City, occupied primarily by blacks who have achieved a modest measure of success.

In fact, some said, it was the very middle-class look and feel of Chatham and Avalon Park that may have drawn the phantom gunman in the first place.

As resident Nathaniel Gordon told the *Chicago Tribune,* "Right now, it's kind of like bad times. People don't have money, and they come through Chatham because people look like they have money, and there are a lot of old people. And it is attractive to criminals because it is so quiet, and they can do their thing in isolation."

Thus far, despite the self-described best efforts of Chicago Police, there have been no reports of any suspect or solution in the case. Perhaps the sudden fanfare of publicity drove Chatham's stalker to go looking for another hunting ground; or, then again, he may have been arrested and incarcerated on some unrelated charge. Six years and counting since the last known murder in the series, it is doubtful that authorities will ever know the truth.

Chicago child murders — Illinois (1956-57)

Within an eight-month period, in 1956-57, three Chicago teenage girls were slaughtered in a grisly string of homicides that have remained unsolved for more than 40 years. No positive connection in the case was deduced, but they have entered modern folklore as a series, and are so considered here. The evidence required to prove —or disprove — a connection, like the killer, has remained elusive.

On December 28, 1956, 15-year-old Barbara Grimes and her sister Patricia, 13, failed to come home from a neighborhood theater. Reminded of an October 1955 triple murder involving three young boys (solved 40 years later, by chance), Chicago panicked. Elvis Presley, star of the last movies seen by the sisters, made a public appeal for the girls to go home and be "good Presley fans." Columnist Ann Landers received an anonymous letter written by a girl who had seen the Grimes sisters forced into a car by a young man. A partial license number of the car led nowhere, and the author of the note was not identified.

On January 22, 1957, a motorist in Du Page County spotted the victims in a roadside ditch, their naked, frozen bodies laid out side by side. Both sisters had been raped and beaten, but the coroner reported that their deaths resulted from exposure to the freezing weather. Homicide detectives stubbornly refused to comment on reports that Barbara and Patricia had been mutilated, with the lips of one girl sliced away.

On August 15, 1957, 15-year-old Judith Anderson went missing on the one-mile walk between a friend's house and her home. There was no doubt of mutilation a week later, when her dismembered remains surfaced in two 55-gallon oil drums, floating on Montrose Harbor. One barrel contained the girl's severed head, with four .32-caliber slugs in the brain. Police discovered that the victim had been threatened by a man, or boy, who telephoned her on the job, at a local modeling agency, but there the trail went cold.

A short time later, homicide detectives picked up Barry Cook, a youth suspected in the strangulation death of Margaret Gallagher, a middle-aged victim, on Foster Beach. The evidence was marginal, at best, and Cook was cleared of murder charges at his trial. He subsequently went to prison for 11 years on conviction of aggravated assault and attempted rape, in an unrelated case, but despite public speculation, no evidence exists to link him with the teenage murders.

Years after the fact, "psychic" Peter Hurkos fondled snapshots of the victims in Chicago, searing for "vibrations" from their killer, but he came no closer to an ultimate solution than police who had pursued the case from the beginning. Any comfort derived from the passage of time resides in speculation that the killer may, by now, have joined his victims in the grave.

Columbus murders — Ohio (1965-66)

On May 23, 1966, Loren Bollinger, a 40-year-old rocket scientist at Ohio State University in Columbus, was ambushed and shot to death outside his downtown office. Five bullets were extracted from his corpse, including one that pierced his brain. Ballistics tests linked the .25-caliber weapon to the murders of two gas station attendants, in or near Columbus, over the past eight months. Appealing for public help in their search for the gunman, police also connected the weapon to a case from September 1965, in which another service station employee was robbed, then shot and left for dead by his male assailant. In spite of a description from the sole surviving victim, homicide investigators are no closer to solution of the case at present than they were in 1966.

Connecticut murders — (1969)

On July 1, 1969, Connecticut police announced that they were seeking links between the recent deaths of two young girls. Mary Mount had been abducted from New Canaan, in Fairfield County, on May 27, while 14-year-old Dawn Cave was reported missing from Bethany, three days later and 35 miles to the northeast. Mount's body was found on June 17, Cave's remains discovered two weeks later, in a meadow northwest of New Haven. Autopsies revealed that both girls had been killed shortly after they were kidnapped, each dispatched by heavy blows from a blunt instrument.

New York City police entered the case on July 9, when 9-year-old Wanda Waldonado was raped and strangled in Brooklyn. Witnesses recalled a white car near the scene of the crime, sparking memories in Connecticut, where another white vehicle — with New York license plates — had been reported from Bethany and New Canaan, its driver attempting to lure children away from their homes. The tantalizing "lead" took homicide investigators nowhere in their search for suspects, however. After 22 years, the murders in Connecticut — and the "connected" crimes in Brooklyn — still remain unsolved, the killer(s) unidentified.

"Couples" murders — Ohio (1979-82)

In three years' time, between August 1979 and October 1982, eight victims were dispatched in grisly style by a killer (or killers) who preyed on young Ohio couples, randomly selecting victims in a triangle of death that stretched from Akron and Toledo in the north, to Logan in the south. No motive has been ascertained in any of the slayings, and the killer remains unidentified.

The first to die were Richard Beard, 19, and Mary Leonard, 17, gone missing from an Akron drive-in theater on August 24, 1979. Their fate remained a mystery until May 29, 1985, when a backhoe operator in Northamptom Township unearthed a skull and other skeletal remains. A second skull and more bones were discovered on May 30, a single bullet hole suggesting the cause of death. The victims were identified from dental records on May 30, but no clue to the identity of their killer was forthcoming.

In the meantime, other unsolved slayings kept detectives occupied. A young Toledo couple had been beaten to death in May 1981, their bodies locked in the trunk of the dead boy's car. The crime was repeated on August 3, with victims Daryl Cole and Stacy Balonek, both 21. This time, two bloody baseball bats were found beside the corpses, in the trunk of Daryl's car, abandoned two blocks from the Balonek home in suburban Maumee. The evidence suggested at least two killers, but again police were left without the necessary evidence to name a suspect. Detectives called it "a coincidence" that three of the four Toledo victims had worked for the same supermarket chain.

On October 4, 1982, the action shifted to Logan, 110 miles south of Akron, with the disappearance of 19-year-old Todd Schultz and his date, 18-year-old Annette Johnson. Searchers found their mutilated torsos in the Hocking River 10 days later; missing arms and legs were found October 16, buried in a nearby cornfield. As in Akron and Toledo, there was nothing to suggest the killer's motive or identity.

Authorities stop short of looking on the "couples" murders as a series, but the similarity in choice of victims and the show of brutal violence cannot be ignored. The occupational connection in Toledo indicates a link between two sets of homicides, at least, but nothing more can be advanced with certainty about the ghoulish string of crimes that terrorized the Buckeye State for three long years.

Croydon murders — England (1928-29)

The unsolved poisoning of three victims in South Croydon, England, during 1928 and '29, involved two interrelated families, the Sydneys and the Duffs. No motive was ascertained for the crimes, and at this writing no suspect has been identified.

First in the series of victims was Edmund Creighton Duff, 59, the son-in-law of elderly Violet Sydney. Returning to his Croydon home on April 26, 1928, at the conclusion of the fishing holiday, Duff complained of nausea and leg cramps after eating supper. His condition worsened overnight, and he was pronounced dead on April 27. An autopsy yielded negative results, and his death was attributed to unknown "natural causes."

Ten months later, on February 14, 1929, Vera Sydney — Violet's 40-year-old daughter — remarked on feeling "seedy" after lunch. The cook, her mother, and the family cat all suffered after sharing the meal, but they recovered, whereas Vera steadily declined. She died on February 16, after hours of cramps and vomiting, which her physician blamed on "gastric influenza."

Violet Sydney was the last to go, falling ill after lunch on March 5. Already under medical care in her bereavement, she died hours later. On her deathbed, she blamed the "gritty" tonic prescribed by her doctor. An analysis of the medicine showed nothing out of place, and the cause of Violet's death remained a mystery.

Surviving relatives demanded an investigation, and the female victims were exhumed on March 22, 1929, autopsies revealing traces of arsenic in both bodies. Edmund Duff was exhumed (over his widow's protest) on May 15, and this time arsenic was found, the discrepancy from his first autopsy "explained" by a suggestion that physicians may have analyzed organs from the wrong corpse in 1928. Inquests on Duff and Vera Sydney attributed their deaths to murder by persons unknown; in the case of Violet Sydney, there was insufficient evidence to tell if she was murdered or committed suicide. In either case, the mystery remains unsolved today.

Cumminsville murders — Ohio (1904-10)

A suburb of Cincinnati, Cumminsville is normally a peaceful place, but in the six-year period from 1904 to 1910 it earned the grisly reputation of a "murder zone," where women walked in fear and dreaded riding streetcars after nightfall. A ferocious "mad killer" was on the loose, claiming five victims within a mile of the point where Spring Grove Avenue meets Winton Road, eluding the police and neighborhood patrols to leave a nagging legacy of doubt and mystery behind.

Mary McDonald, 31, had "been around" before she met her killer in the predawn hours of May 4, 1904. An ill-fated affair with her late sister's husband had left her to find solace in whiskey, but things were looking up that spring, with her engagement to be married. Shortly after 1:30 a.m., she left a local tavern in the company of her fiancé, and he saw her safely aboard an "owl car," homeward bound. Near daybreak, the switchman on a train near Ludlow Avenue spied Mary's body by the tracks and help was summoned. She was still alive but incoherent, with a fractured skull and one leg severed. She died hours later from her injuries. Police initially dismissed her death as accidental, later shifting to the view that she was beaten and pushed in front of a train in a deliberate act of murder.

Louise Mueller, 21, was the next to die, leaving home for a stroll on October 1, 1904. She never returned, and her body was found the next morning, the skull battered to pulp, in a gully beside some disused railroad tracks. Her killer had scooped a shallow grave from the soft earth nearby, but the corpse lay above ground, as if some passerby had disturbed the hasty burial.

At 9:00 p.m. on November 2, 18-year-old Alma Steinigewig left her job as an operator at the local telephone exchange, vanishing before she reached her home. The next morning, a streetcar conductor spotted her corpse in a nearby vacant lot, her skull crushed by savage blows. The victim's clothes were muddy, indicating she was dragged across the lot, and officers discovered footprints near the body that would ultimately lead them nowhere. Clutched in Alma's hand, they found a streetcar transfer punched at 9:40 p.m. on the day of her death.

An ugly pattern had begun to form, and homicide investigators hauled in suspects by the dozens, forced to free them all for lack of evidence. One who eluded them, a stocky man remembered for his heavy beard, had turned up at the Mueller crime scene, wringing his hands and crying out, "It was an accident!" Other witnesses placed him, or his twin, at the scene of Alma Steinigewig's death, but he was never identified, his link — if any — with the case remaining open to conjecture.

Six years passed before the killer struck again, claiming 43-year-old Anna Lloyd on December 31, 1909. Employed as a secretary at a local lumberyard, the victim worked until 5:30 p.m. that New Year's Eve, her body found hours later, a short distance from the office. She had been gagged with a cheap black muffler, her skull crushed, throat slashed, leaving signs of a fierce struggle behind. A single strand of black hair was clutched in her fist, but primitive forensics tests of the day rendered it useless as evidence. Police initially called the slaying a contract murder, but no suspect or motive was ever identified.

The stalker claimed his final victim on October 25, 1910, when 26-year-old Mary Hackney was found in her cottage on

Dane Street, her skull fractured and throat slashed. Suspicion focused briefly on her husband, but police discovered Mary was alive when he reported to his job that day. A spate of letters, signed with the initials "S.D.M.," was mailed by someone claiming knowledge of the crimes, but homicide investigators finally dismissed them as a hoax.

The fading memories of murder were revived in December 1913, by investigators of the Burns Detective Agency, assigned to check out unsolved acts of violence in a recent streetcar strike. Those private eyes told Cincinnati's mayor they had discovered an "indefinite" solution in the case of Anna Lloyd, pointing the finger of suspicion at a one-time streetcar conductor, then confined to a sanitarium as hopelessly insane. A search of his old lodgings had turned up a threatening letter, addressed to persons "who saw him in the act of December 31," and authorities leaped to a theoretical connection with the three-year-old murder. Ultimately fruitless, the investigation petered out a few days later, and the crimes in Cumminsville remain unsolved.

Days Inn murders — Indiana (1989)

A transient gunman with a fondness for the Days Inn motel chain was apparently responsible for the murder of two clerks in separate towns, on March 3, 1989. Killed that day were 24-year-old Mary Gill, at the Days Inn in Merrillville, and 34-year-old Jeanne Gilbert, at the chain's motel in Remington. Robbery was suspected as a motive in both cases. It was early March 1991 before Police Chief Jerry McCory, in Merrillville, announced a description of the suspect: a white male in his late 30s or early 40s, 6-feet tall, about 180 pounds, with graying "salt-and-pepper" hair. The description was vague enough to fit millions of suspects across the United States, and no further leads have been announced to date. The case remains unsolved, the gunman still at large.

"Death Angels" — California (1969-??)

A fanatical offshoot of the Nation of Islam (Black Muslims), the "Death Angels" cult was apparently founded in California around late 1969 or early 1970. Members adhere to the Black Muslim philosophy — i.e., that whites are "beasts" and "grafted devils" spawned from ancient genetic experiments — but members of the cult carried their beliefs into action, purposefully striving to exterminate Caucasians. On joining the Death Angels, recruits were photographed, afterward earning their "wings" — drawn on the snapshot with a ballpoint pen — by killing a specified number of whites. Based on a point system geared to emotional difficulty, candidates were required to kill four white children, five women, or nine men. Murders were verified through media reports, eyewitness accounts by fellow cultists, and/or Polaroid snapshots. (As reported by author Clark Howard, in *Zebra*, one Death Angel candidate flew to Chicago — "New Mecca" in Black Muslim parlance — with a collection of photographs, seeking promotion to the nonexistent rank of lieutenant in the cult. His unexpected visit puzzled members of the headquarters staff and might have been disastrous, had he not been intercepted by the leader of the secret group, who "counseled" him and sent him home.)

By October 1973, the killer cult had at least 15 accredited members, their winged photographs displayed on an easel at covert gatherings. Together, those 15 were theoretically responsible for killing 135 men, 75 women, 60 children, or some combination of victims sufficient to earn their "wings." The California State Attorney General's office had compiled a list of 45 similar murders, committed at random with cleavers, machetes, or close-range gunshots, all involving white victims and black assailants, with known suspects invariably linked to Muslim religion. Thus far, attacks had been recorded in San Francisco, Oakland, Berkeley, Long Beach, Signal Hill, Santa Barbara, Palo Alto, Pacifica, Los Angeles, and San Diego, plus rural areas in the counties of Alameda, Contra Costa, Los Angeles, San Mateo, Santa Clara, and Ventura.

By January 28, 1974, when California law enforcement officers convened a secret conference on the problem, sixty-four persons were known to have died in ritualistic racist attacks, and three more deaths were recorded by late March. A rare survivor, Thomas Bates, was thumbing rides near the Bay Bridge at Emeryville, south of Oakland, when two black men pulled up in an old model Cadillac. Rolling down his window, the passenger grinned at Bates, said, "Hello, devil," and then opened fire with a pistol at point-blank range, wounding Bates in the hip, stomach and arm. Bleeding profusely, Bates managed to reach a nearby motel, where employees phoned for police and an ambulance.

By early 1974, San Francisco was paralyzed with fear at the sudden rash of "Zebra" murders, committed on random white targets by black assailants, claiming 15 dead and eight wounded over a six-month period. Four Death Angel candidates were sentenced to life imprisonment in that case, but the cult's present status remains uncertain, the question of continuing murders side-stepped by law enforcement spokesmen and Black Muslim leaders alike.

Decapitation murders — Texas (1979)

Residents of Houston, Texas, are accustomed to reports of violent death, but nothing in their past experience prepared them for the string of crimes that dominated headlines in the latter part of 1979. Between the last week of July and first week of October, four lives were extinguished by a killer who seemed bent on claiming human heads as trophies of the hunt. Despite sensational publicity surrounding the attacks, the case remains unsolved today.

The first attack took place in southwest Houston, with a female victim cornered and beheaded in her own apartment, on July 27. Investigators had not found her missing head by August 10, when yet another victim was discovered, spared complete decapitation when her killer was disturbed and frightened off.

Five blocks away, the residents around Freed Park were roused from sleep by screams and gunshots in the late-night hours of October 3. Police responded to the call but found no evidence of any crime in progress. Daylight on October 4 would lead them to the body of 16-year-old Jean Huffman, shot to death and dumped beside a picnic table with her jeans unzipped. Nearby, her boyfriend's car was found abandoned on a used-car lot, the headless body of its owner — 18-year-old Robert Spangenberger — locked inside the trunk.

To date, no trace of either missing head has been discovered, and police in Houston hesitate to link the several homicides, despite the geographic and forensic similarities. The killer's motive and identity remain unknown.

Denver murders — Colorado (1911-12)

A puzzling case from Colorado made the headlines during August 1912, when music teacher Signe Carlszen was reported slain in Denver. On the night of August 9, she left a student's home at nine o'clock, prepared to hike across a lonely, open field to reach the streetcar that would take her home. When she had not arrived by 2:00 A.M., her father launched a search, but seven hours passed before a farmer found her body in the field.

According to reports, the victim was discovered with a scarf wound tight around her neck, skull fractured by at least six heavy blows. Some of the head wounds measured three inches across, and local papers reported that "The blows caused her eyes to bulge from their sockets." One article additionally claimed that Carlszen's body had been mutilated with a knife.

Confusion still surrounds the other victims in this case, with Signe Carlszen seemingly the last to die. On August 11, the *New York Times* reported that police were checking out "a half-dozen similar crimes" in Denver and its suburbs, spanning the past six months. Local reports, meanwhile, linked Carlszen's death to a triple murder reported from Colorado Springs on September 17, 1911. Victims in that case were named as Mr. and Mrs. H.F. Wayne, together with a female houseguest, Mrs. A.J. Burnham. Homicide investigators labored long and hard to solve the case, but all in vain. Their search was fruitless, and the crimes remain unsolved.

"El Depredador Psicópata" — Mexico (1995-97)

Investigators from Mexico's Federal Judicial Police — the *federales* — have spent the past three years hunting a serial killer blamed for the murders of at least 16 girls and young women in the neighborhood of Ciudad Juarez. Most of the victims claimed by *El Depredador Psicópato* — literally, the "Psychopathic Depredator" — have fallen between the ages of 14 and 18 years. The majority were strangled, but evidence of sexual assault is inconsistent, with some of the victims raped while alive, others assaulted postmortem, and still others suffering no rape at all.

The murder spree began around Ciudad Juarez (across the border from El Paso, Texas) in August 1995, and police initially considered it "solved" with the arrest of an Egyptian national, one Abel Latif Sharif, who allegedly confessed to the first five slayings. Unfortunately for investigators — and the for future victims — the homicides accelerated after Sharif's "confession" (possibly coerced by over-zealous *federales),* until 16 dead were listed by the end of 1997. With one suspect in custody, police initially blamed the subsequent murders on a fiendish copycat, then altered their theory to cast Abel Sharif as one member of a predatory "wolf pack" stalking the city. Sharif, for his part, has recanted his confession and now blames the murders on a gang of *coyotes* — professional smugglers of illegal aliens — who sometimes murder their clients after receiving payment in advance. Whatever the truth, at least 11 brutal murders are unsolved to date, at least one "psychopathic depredator" still at large.

Detroit murders — Michigan (1980)

Detroit has seen its share of violence, from the bootleg wars of Prohibition to the catastrophic riots of the latter 1960s, fueled by street gangs, racist groups and drug rings. But by any estimation, 1980 was a "special" year. From January through December, 18 women were dispatched in brutal fashion, 12 of them strangled, all but one discarded outdoors, with little or no effort made to conceal their remains. Their murders spanned Detroit, without apparent pattern, but when plotted on a map they formed a narrow corridor of death, running northwest from the Detroit River at Belle Isle to Eight Mile Road, then westward to the city limits. Despite the arrest of two separate suspects — and the ultimate conviction of one — at least 13 of the slayings remain unsolved today.

Lois Johnson, a 31-year-old alcoholic barmaid, was the first to die, on January 12. Her frozen body was discovered by a trucker, in the early morning hours, torn by a total of 26 stab wounds in the neck, chest and abdomen. An autopsy proved she was falling-down drunk when she died.

A month later, on February 16, 26-year-old Patricia Real became victim number two. A known prostitute and heroin addict, she had been shot to death on the street, her death scarcely causing a ripple in greater Detroit. Helen Conniff was a different story. At age 23, she was a devout "born-again" Christian and a student at Oakland University, determined to succeed on her own terms. On the night of March 10, she left her class early to visit her boyfriend but never arrived. When the man's roommate arrived home at 10:30 p.m., he spotted Conniff's body hanging from a nearby fence, strangled with a dog leash.

Twenty-year-old Cecilia Jacobs was next, found strangled in a Detroit alley, fully clothed, with no apparent effort made at sexual assault. The same lack of motive was evident on March 31, when 26-year-old Denise Dunmore was strangled in the parking lot of her apartment complex with no sign of rape, her expensive jewelry undisturbed. Arlette McQueen, 21, had been working the night shift at an Oak Park supermarket over four months, but April 9 marked the first night she had taken the bus home. Her strangled body was found the next morning, dumped between houses a block from her destination.

A known prostitute, Jeanette Woods was twice hospitalized for beatings in the months before she met her killer. Nothing kept her from the streets, but she would sometimes take a break from "business," and on April 18 she was scheduled to meet her boyfriend around 9 o'clock. She failed to keep the rendezvous, and it was 1:30 a.m. before a pedestrian found her body — battered, raped and strangled, her throat slashed in an ugly *coup de grace.*

Two weeks later, 20-year-old Etta Frazier was discovered in an old garage behind a burned-out house. Nude, bound hand and foot, she had been beaten about the face, tortured with lit cigarettes, and sexually abused before she was finally strangled to death. While not a prostitute, the victim had a record of arrests for disorderly conduct and neglecting her young son.

Rosemary Frazier was no relation to Etta, but the 28-year-old's death bore striking similarities to that of her immediate predecessor. An epileptic and long-time mental patient, Frazier was found nude, battered and strangled on a grassy slope near the Rosedale Park Community House. In the wake of her death, relatives staunchly denied police reports characterizing Rosemary as a streetwalker.

On May 31, Linda Monteiro was murdered four blocks from the Conniff crime scene, in almost identical style, strangled in her own driveway as she returned home from a nightclub. Two weeks later, Diane Burks made the list, found with hands tied behind her back, nude but for panties and slacks that had been lowered to her knees. The 22-year-old prostitute and drug addict had been strangled to death with an intertwined chain and telephone wire.

Cassandra Johnson was the victim for July, described by police as a 17-year-old prostitute. Her bludgeoned body was discovered shortly before noon on July 2. Another working girl, 23-year-old Delores Willis, was last seen with a "trick" on the night of August 26, found strangled the next morning, her scalp laid open to the bone.

On September 29, 19-year-old Paulette Woodward phoned her mother from business school, around five o'clock, to say she was on her way home. Anxious relatives were still waiting the next morning, when police reported the discovery of Paulette's body. Beaten and strangled to death, she had not been sexually assaulted by her killer.

Betty Rembert, age 26, was found beneath a hedge on October 8, her legs protruding toward the sidewalk. Cause of death would be a toss-up, with a stab wound in the victim's neck and crushing injuries inflicted to her skull. Two months later, on December 17, 30-year-old prostitute Diane Carter rounded off the list. Last seen around 3:00 A.M., she was found eight hours later, lying in some bushes on a vacant lot, a single bullet wound in the base of her skull.

By that time, police had two suspects in custody, charged with a total of five homicides. David Payton, age 23, was locally famous for high-school athletics, employed since graduation from college as a girl's basketball coach. Arrested on November 17, he was grilled by police for 84 hours prior to arraignment, ultimately signing confessions to four of the slayings. According to Payton's statements, he had murdered Jeanette Woods, Rosemary Frazier, Diane Burks, and Betty Rembert in arguments over the price of oral sex, beating, strangling, or slashing each in turn as they rejected his paltry offers.

It appeared to be a solid case, but problems soon developed. On December 15, detectives bagged another suspect, Donald Murphy, charged with murdering two Detroit prostitutes in October and November. Confessing those crimes, Murphy *also* copped to the slayings of Woods, Burks and Rembert, providing enough details that several investigators found themselves "absolutely convinced" of his guilt.

Despite the flagrant contradicting evidence, prosecutors continued in both cases, Payton charged in four murders, Murphy facing trial on the original two. On March 20, 1981, a judge dismissed the murder charges in Payton's case, finding that a previous magistrate had "abused judicial discretion" by admitting Payton's confessions as evidence. (Payton still faced rape and armed robbery charges in unrelated cases.) Prosecutors vowed to appeal the decision, but some authorities seemed quietly relieved. A source close to the investigation told reporters that police were "convinced Payton was the wrong guy after Murphy came along," using the recent dismissal as a means of "saving face." Advised of the reports, prosecutor William Cahalan replied, "That's interesting. All I can say is that we have the right man [Payton] charged with the right crimes."

However that may be, Dave Payton never went to trial for any of the murders in Detroit, while Donald Murphy was convicted only of the two originally charged. Assuming Murphy's guilt in other crimes that he confessed, we still find ourselves with 13 victims unaccounted for, their killer(s) still at large.

Dismemberment murders — Oklahoma (1976-95)

Authorities in the Sooner State officially stop short of blaming a single killer for the murder and dismemberment of four women in downtown Oklahoma City, despite striking similarities in each case. The first "Jane Doe" victim — or what remained of her — was found near the state capitol building, in 1976. Three more followed, all retrieved from the Stiles Circle-Lincoln Terrace neighborhood, around Oklahoma City's Medical Center. The fourth victim was found in 1985, during construction of the Centennial Expressway, but none of the women have yet been identified. A possible fifth victim, described as Hispanic or Native American, was unearthed — minus head, hands, and feet — from a shallow grave fifty miles west of Oklahoma City, along an abandoned stretch of highway, on April 22, 1995. Investigators cite "similarities in the method of dismemberment" as a possible link to the other four murders, all of which remain unsolved today.

"Doodler" — California (1974-75)

Ten years before the discovery of AIDs, the gay community in San Francisco was confronted with another lethal menace, wrought in human form. Between January 1974 and September 1975, the faceless stalker was responsible for 17 attacks with 14 deaths that stymied homicide investigators in the city by the bay.

Initially, considering discrepancies in choice of victims, the police believed they had *three* vicious killers on the prowl. Five of the victims were Tenderloin drag queens, mutilated by a slasher who apparently despised transvestites. Six others were selected from the sadomasochistic world of "leather bars" — dives with names like Ramrod, Fe-Be's, Folsom Prison — and dispatched with hacking knife wounds. (One, attorney George Gilbert, was slaughtered at his home in San Francisco's most posh high-rise.) The last six were middle-class businessmen, stabbed by an assailant who picked them up in Castro Village bars, wooing his victims with cartoon portraits and pausing for sex before wielding his blade.

Three of the latter victims survived their ordeal, providing police with descriptions of the killer, although they would later refuse to testify in court. The slasher's taste for comic art provided newsmen with a handle on the case, and so "The Doodler" was born.

In time, as leads were run down and eliminated, homicide investigators realized that they were searching for a single killer in their string of unsolved homicides. In 1976, suspicion focused on a particular suspect, described by police as a mental patient with a history of treatment for sex-related problems. Questioned repeatedly, the suspect spoke freely with police, but always stopped short of a confession. Meanwhile, the surviving victims stubbornly refused to make a positive I.D., positive I.D., afraid of ruining their lives by "coming out" with an admission of homosexuality.

On July 8, 1977, frustrated authorities announced that an unnamed suspect had been linked to 14 deaths and three assaults in San Francisco during 1974 and '75. Indictment was impossible, they said, without cooperation from survivors of the "Doodler's" attacks. At this writing, the case remains a stalemate, officially unsolved, with the suspect subject to continuing surveillance.

Drive-by murders — California (1993)

Gunfire in the streets is not uncommon in Los Angeles, where turf wars between drug-dealing street gangs added the phrase "drive-by shooting" to America's criminal lexicon in the 1980s. Hundreds of gang members and innocent bystanders, most of them black or Hispanic, have been killed or wounded in such shootings over the past two decades, but there was something radically different about the drive-by murders that terrorized L.A.'s Harbor City district in the early months of 1993.

The gunman in those crimes was white, with red hair, driving a red-and-white Jeep Wrangler as he prowled the streets of Harbor City after dark. He seemed fixated on a certain area, all four of his attacks falling within a two-block radius, and his technique never varied. In each case, the unknown shooter appeared to single out a black or Latino pedestrian, as if to ask for help.

"He beckons to them," said Police Lieutenant Sergio Robleto, "and as soon as they come up to the car, he shoots them for no apparent reason. He doesn't miss."

Howard Campbell, age 32, was the first victim, shot dead on January 31, 1993. Two weeks later, 35-year-old Michael Meador was killed at the very same spot. Joseph Maxwell, 26, answered the gunman's call on April 15 and was killed for his trouble, two blocks away from the first murder scene. On May 22, a 38-year-old black man (unnamed in the press), was shot three times, one block away, but managed to survive his wounds.

Aside from similar descriptions of the gunman and his vehicle, authorities note that three of the shootings occurred between 8:00 and 9:30 p.m., while the fourth took place at dawn. Los Angeles authorities, already plagued by serial killers, were reluctant to claim yet another at large, but Lieutenant Robleto acknowledged the grim possibility. "There are murders in the same location all over the city," he told reporters, "but when you have a third one, it starts to look really bad. It certainly looks like the same person."

And yet, despite increased patrols, vigilant neighbors, and a distinctive vehicle, the gunman seems to have vanished. At this writing, no new murders in the series have been publicized, nor have authorities identified a suspect in the case.

Flat-tire murders — Florida (1975)

On August 29, 1975, Dade County's assistant medical examiner announced his belief that one man was responsible for five recent murders of women in southern Florida. Homicide detectives were convinced of a connection in the July slayings of Ronnie Gorlin, 27, and Elyse Napp, 21, while the medical examiner's report named three other victims. Barbara Stephens, 23, had been abducted from a South Dade shopping mall and stabbed to death in February 1975, while a pair of 14-year-old high-school classmates, Barbara Schreiber and Belinda Zeterower, had been killed at Hollywood in June.

At that point, Sergeant Erwin Carlstedt of Sonoma County, California chimed in with his theory of a single killer, moving coast-to-coast with more than 30 homicides behind him — probably a reference to Ted Bundy, before he was publicly identified as a suspect in murders spanning the continent. Florida investigators had no comment on the theory, concentrating on their search for an elusive killer who deflates his victims' tires in parking lots, then charms them with an offer of assistance. None of the "flat-tire" victims were included in Bundy's 1989 confession to twenty-odd murders, and the case remains unsolved at this writing.

Fort Lauderdale murders — Florida (1981)

On February 17, 1981, the body of a young, unidentified black woman was found on the outskirts of Fort Lauderdale's ghetto. The medical examiner's report described her death as a homicide committed by "unspecified means." On June 1 of that year, the skeletal remains of a second black girl, roughly 13 years old, was discovered in the same vacant field; once again, authorities had no I.D. and no cause of death for the victim.

Victim number three *was* identified — as Eloise Coleman, age 30, a neighborhood resident. Her corpse was found on June 10, 1981, again in the same field, 100 yards from the site of the original murder. Cause of death was described as blunt trauma to the victim's skull, produced by a powerful blow. Coleman was last seen alive — except by her killer — when she left the family home on Sunday evening, June 7.

At this writing, police remain baffled by the slayings of three black females in Fort Lauderdale. Unwilling to call the crimes "a series," homicide investigators have acknowledged the remarkable similarities and apparent geographical connections. The killer (or killers) remain unidentified.

Fort Wayne child murders — Indiana (1988-90)

Local authorities cite FBI psychological profiles as their basis for declaring that two "identical" rape-slayings of young girls, committed twenty-six months apart, "are actually separate cases and will be pursued individually."

Some Fort Wayne residents regard that decision as a critical mistake, and while neither side can prove its case in the absence of a suspect, the fact remains that both murders — plus 10 other attempted abductions of children in the same neighborhood — remain unsolved today.

The first victim, 8-year-old April Marie Tinsley, was abducted near her Fort Wayne home on April 1, 1988 by the driver of a blue pickup truck. Found three days later in a DeKalb County ditch, she had been raped and murdered, then redressed before her body was dumped. Autopsy results attributed her death to suffocation, sometime on April 2 or 3.

Police had no leads in that case two years later, when 7-year-old Sarah Jean Bowker was snatched off a Fort Wayne residential street on June 13, 1990, her body found the next day in a shallow creek not far from home. Like April Tinsley, Sarah Jean had been sexually assaulted, then smothered to death, and authorities described the crimes as "identical"... at least, until the FBI's Investigative Support Unit (formerly Behavioral Science) became involved. The resultant profiles, as described by Fort Wayne lawmen in their statements to the press, "strongly indicate that the killings, though similar, are not related."

And still, there was no suspect to be found, although *someone* clearly harbored an unhealthy interest in the children of

Fort Wayne. Following Sarah Bowker's death, 10 more abduction attempts were reported to authorities, the latest on March 25, 1991, when a 12-year-old girl narrowly escaped the stranger who tried to force her into his car. Lieutenant Ed Tutwiler, with the Allen County Sheriff's Department, acknowledged "a certain amount of paranoia running in this," and planned a meeting with nervous parents, "to try to quell some of the rumors that are running wild out there."

The murders of two children were no rumors, though, and the formation of a task force meant to solve the case — ironically announced on the same day as the last attempted kidnapping — has thus far shed no new light on the case.

Fort Worth murders — Texas (1984-85)

Between September 1984 and January 1985, a string of brutal homicides and disappearances spread fear among the female residents of Tarrant County, Texas. Four young women and a teenage girl would lose their lives before the crime spree ended, as mysteriously as it had begun. Police have yet to name a suspect in the case, which still remains unsolved.

On the night of September 30, 1984, firefighters were called out to an apartment occupied by Cindy Davis, on the city's southwest side. They extinguished a small fire, traced to a cigarette dropped on the bed, but there was no sign of the 23-year-old aspiring model. Neighbors reported the sound of loud voices, raised in anger, and a car squealing away from the scene shortly before the blaze erupted.

Three weeks later, on October 22, 23-year-old Cindy Heller stopped to help stranded motorist Kazumi Gillespie on the southwest side of Fort Worth. Though strangers, the women spent two hours together in a tavern, while Gillespie tried in vain to phone a friend. When they split up at last, Gillespie remained at the bar. Heller agreed to drive by the friend's apartment and leave a note on his door. It was there when he came home at midnight, but Heller had vanished. Her car was found nearby the next morning, the interior gutted by fire, dry blood smeared on one door handle. No trace could be found of the two-time entrant in local beauty contests.

Police noted striking similarities in the apparent abductions — victims of identical age and given names, missing in circumstances that included suspicious fires — but they were not prepared to link the cases yet. Shortly before midnight on December 10, Angela Ewart left her fiancé's home in the Wedgewood section of southwest Fort Worth, stopping for gas at a station nearby. From there, the 21-year-old model and one-time beauty contestant vanished into limbo, her car discovered the next morning, doors locked, with a broken knife lying nearby. A flat tire, reported to police by passing motorists, had been switched with a spare by the time patrolmen arrived on the scene.

On December 30, 1984, 15-year-old Sarah Kashka left her home in Denton for a party in Fort Worth, arriving to find the festivities canceled. Sarah's date dropped her off at a Wedgewood apartment, not far from the station where Angela Ewart was last seen alive, but her bad luck was holding. The friends she intended to visit were out for the evening, and Sarah had vanished before they came home. Two days later, her body was found in a marshy area near Mountain Creek, in southwest Dallas, torn by stab wounds that had caused her death. Police initially divorced her murder from the disappearances, citing "a difference we really can't talk about," but they later hedged their bets. As Detective Ben Dumas told reporters, "we can't establish any thread, because we only have one girl found."

That changed on January 5, when children playing on the campus of Texas Christian University stumbled over Cindy Heller's decomposing corpse. She had been tortured, strangled, and beheaded, with her skull recovered from a nearby lake on January 9. That same day, 20-year-old Lisa Griffin was found, shot to death execution-style, in southwestern Fort Worth. Sheriff's deputies charged a former mental patient with that murder, but he was released when his fingerprints failed to match others lifted from Griffin's abandoned car.

A final, grisly twist was added to the case on January 23, 1985, when construction workers uncovered human bones beside some railroad tracks, 10 miles south of the Wedgewood "murder zone." Forensic tests identified the skeletal remains as those of Cindy Davis, missing since September, but that evidence would bring authorities no closer to a suspect in the case.

"Four P movement" — United States (1967-??)

In 1969, while gathering material for a book on the Charles Manson case, journalist Ed Sanders encountered reports of a sinister Satanic cult alleged to practice human sacrifice in several parts of California, luring youthful members from college campuses throughout the western half of the United States. A spin-off from the Process Church of Final Judgment, initially boasting some fifty-odd members, the cult called itself the "Four P" movement or "Four Pi," after the Process Church's "power sign" — four P's arranged in the shape of a swastika. The sect's leader, dubbed the "Grand Chingon" or "Head Devil," was said to be a wealthy California businessman of middle age, who exercised his power by compelling younger members to act as his slaves and murder random targets on command. The central object of the cult was to promote "the total worship of evil."

Organized in northern California during 1967, the Four Pi movement held its secret gatherings in the Santa Cruz Mountains, south of San Francisco. Rituals were conducted on the basis of a stellar timetable, including the sacrifice of Doberman and German shepherd dogs. Beginning in June 1968, authorities in San Jose, Santa Cruz, and Los Gatos began recording discoveries of slaughtered canines, skinned and drained of blood without apparent motive.

As the director of the Santa Cruz animal shelter told Sanders, "Whoever is doing this is a real expert with a knife. The skin is cut away without even marking the flesh. The really strange thing is that these dogs have been drained of blood."

If we accept the word of self-described witnesses, the missing blood was drunk by cultists in their ceremonies. So, according to reports, was *human* blood, obtained from sacrificial victims murdered on a dragon-festooned altar. Death was the result of stabbing with a custom-made six-bladed knife, designed with blades of varied length to penetrate a victim's stomach first, before the heart was skewered, causing death. Each sacrifice allegedly was climaxed by removal of the heart, which cultists then divided up among themselves to eat. The evidence of murder was incinerated in a portable crematorium, mounted in the back of a truck.

According to reports from self-styled members of the Four Pi cult, sacrificial victims were typically hitchhikers, drifters and runaways, with an occasional volunteer from the ranks. One such, a young woman, reportedly went to her death with a smile in November 1968, near Boulder Creek. But even sacrifice of willing victims is a risky business, and the cult was said to mount patrols around its rural meeting places, using guards with automatic weapons and attack-trained dogs to insure privacy.

In 1969, the cult reportedly moved southward, shifting operations to the O'Neil Park region of the Santa Ana Mountains, below Los Angeles. The move produced — or was occasioned by — a factional dispute within the group, one segment striving to re-emphasize Satanic ritual, while more traditional adherents clung to Lucifer and human sacrifice. The group apparently survived its schism and expanded nationwide, with author Maury Terry citing evidence of a thousand or more members across the country by 1979. One hotbed of activity appeared to be New York, where 85 German shepherds and Dobermans were found skinned in the year between October 1976 and October 1977.

Along the way, the Four Pi movement has apparently rubbed shoulders with a number of notorious killers, feeding — or perhaps inspiring — their sadistic fantasies. Cannibal killer Stanley Baker, jailed in Montana for eating the heart of one victim, confessed to other murders perpetrated on orders from the "Grand Chingon." (His bloody fingerprints were found at the scene of a San Francisco murder in April 1970, but charges were dismissed in that case, on grounds that Baker was denied a "speedy" trial.) Recruited from a college campus in Wyoming, Baker remained unrepentant in prison, organizing fellow inmates into a Satanic coven of his own, but his testimony brought lawmen no closer to cracking the cult.

Charles Manson and his "family" reportedly had contact with the Four Pi movement, prior to making headlines in Los Angeles. Ed Sanders reports that some of Manson's followers referred to him — in Sanders's presence — as the "Grand Chingon," distinguished from the original article by his age and the fact that Manson was jailed while the real "Chingon" remained at large. Likewise, "family" hacker Susan Atkins has described the sacrifice of dogs by Manson's group, and searchers digging for the last remains of Manson victim Shorty Shea, reported finding large numbers of chicken and animal bones at the family's campsite — a peculiar form of garbage for a group reputedly composed of vegetarians.

Convicted serial killer David Berkowitz — more famous as the "Son of Sam" who terrorized New York in 1976 and '77 — has also professed membership in the Four Pi cult, revealing inside knowledge of a California homicide allegedly committed by the group. In 1979, Berkowitz smuggled a book on witchcraft into his prison cell, with passages on Manson and the Four Pi movement underlined. One page bore a cryptic notation in the killer's own handwriting: "Arlis Perry. Hunted, stalked, and slain. Followed to California." As researched by Maury Terry, the Berkowitz note points directly to an unsolved murder committed at Stanford University in mid-October 1974.

On October 11 of that year, co-ed Arlis Perry was found in the campus chapel at Stanford, nude from the waist down, a long candle protruding from her vagina. Her blouse had been ripped open, and another candle stood between her breasts. Beaten and choked unconscious by her assailant, she was finally killed with an ice pick, buried in her skull behind the left ear. In subsequent conversations and correspondence, Berkowitz alleged that Perry was killed by Four Pi members as "a favor" to cultists in her native North Dakota, whom she had apparently offended in some way. Her slayer was named by Berkowitz as one William Mentzer, a.k.a. "Manson II," a professional killer "involved with the original Manson and the cult there in L.A."

As for Mentzer himself, he presently resides on California's death row at San Quentin Prison, condemned for his role in the 1983 murder of New York celebrity movie producer Roy Radin, abducted and killed during a visit to Los Angeles. Maury Terry had described the Radin murder as a cult-related crime in 1987, more than a year before Mentzer's arrest, and L.A. police confirmed Mentzer's participation in "some kind of hit squad." Named as the probable triggerman in several other slayings, Mentzer was convicted of the Radin murder in July 1991 and sentenced to die.

Despite the testimony of reputed Four Pi members, authorities have yet to build a case against the cult. Some suspects, named by witnesses, have died in "accidents" or "suicides" before they could be questioned by police. Another obstacle appears to be the use of code names, which prevent cultists from identifying one another if questioned by police. The group itself apparently relies on varied names from place to place, with New York members meeting as "The Children," while Alabama hosts "The Children of the Light" (suspected of involvement in two dozen murders by 1987). A faction called the "Black Cross" is said to operate as a kind of Satanic "Murder Incorporated," fielding anonymous hit teams for cultists nationwide, disposing of defectors and offering pointers on the fine art of human sacrifice. If law enforcement spokesmen are correct, the cult is also deeply involved in white slavery, child pornography, and the international narcotics trade (exemplified by Bill Mentzer's participation in a Florida cocaine assassination).

"Frankford Slasher" — Pennsylvania (1985-90)

Philadelphia's Frankford district is the hard scrabble neighborhood chosen by Sylvester Stallone as the setting for his first *Rocky* film. Rocky Balboa had gone on to bigger, better things by the late 1980s, however, when Frankford earned a new and unwelcome celebrity, this time for the presence of a vicious serial killer who slaughtered at least seven women.

The mystery began on August 28, 1985, when two transit workers reported to their job at a Frankford Avenue maintenance yard, around 8:30 a.m.. Within moments, they found a woman's lifeless body sprawled between two heaps of railroad ties. She was nude from the waist down, legs splayed, her blouse pushed up to show her breasts. An autopsy report enumerated 19 stab wounds, with a gaping slash between the victim's navel and vagina, nearly disemboweling her. She was identified as Helen Patent, 52, well known in many of the bars on Frankford Avenue.

Just over four months later, on January 3, 1986, a second mutilated corpse was found on Ritner Street, in South Philadelphia, 10 miles from the first murder scene. Neighbors were surprised to see the door of 68-year-old Anna Carroll's apartment standing open, and they found her dead inside, on the floor of her bedroom. Like Helen Patent, this victim was also nude below the waist, her blouse pulled up. She had been stabbed six times, her abdomen sliced open from breastbone to pubis.

No more was heard from the stalker for nearly a year — until Christmas night, in fact — when victim number three was found on Richmond Street, in the Bridesburg neighborhood, three miles from where Helen Patent was killed. Once again, it was worried neighbors who found the corpse, investigating an open apartment door to find 74-year-old Susan Olzef dead in her flat, stabbed six times in the back. Like Helen Patent, Olzef was a familiar figure on Frankford Avenue, police speculating that her killer may have known her from the neighborhood.

Thus far, Philadelphia's finest had little to go on, and they naturally resisted the notion of a serial killer at large in their town. As Lieutenant Joe Washlick later told reporters, in an effort to explain the oversight, "The first three slayings happened in different parts of the city. We could almost give you a different suspect for each job."

Almost... but not quite. In fact, there were no leads and had been no arrests by January 8, 1987, when two Frankford Avenue fruit vendors found a woman's corpse stuffed underneath their stand, around 7:30 a.m. The latest victim, 28-year-old Jeanne Durkin, lay face-down and she was nude below the waist, legs spread. She had been stabbed no less than 74 times, with several wounds gashing her buttocks.

With four corpses and no end in sight, authorities officially linked the Patent and Durkin murders, later connecting all four and creating a special task force to hunt the man Philadelphia journalists were already calling the "Frankford Slasher." For nearly two years, the task force spun its wheels, making no apparent progress until November 11, 1988. That morning, 66-year-old Marge Vaughn was found dead on Penn Avenue, stabbed 29 times in the vestibule of an apartment building from which she was evicted the previous day. She died less than three blocks from the Durkin murder site, half a mile from the spot where Helen Patent was found... and this time, there was a witness of sorts.

A Frankford Avenue barmaid recalled seeing Vaughn around 6 p.m. the previous day. Vaughn had been drinking with a round-faced, middle-aged Caucasian man who wore glasses and walked with a limp. Several sketches of the unknown subject were prepared and published, but despite predictable false leads and finger-pointing by uneasy or malicious neighbors, the police appeared no closer to their man than they had been in 1985.

Two months later, on January 19, 1989, 30-year-old Theresa Sciortino left a Frankford Avenue saloon at 6 o'clock in the evening. She was last seen alive moments later, walking down the street with an unidentified middle-aged man. Around 6:45, Sciortino's neighbors heard sounds of an apparent struggle inside her apartment, followed shortly by footsteps creeping down the stairs, but they failed to call police, and it was 9:00 p.m. before they spoke to the apartment manager. He, in turn, waited past midnight to check on his tenant, then found Sciortino sprawled on the floor of her kitchen, nude but for socks, stabbed 25 times. A bloody footprint at the scene provided homicide detectives with their best lead yet, and while they initially focused on Sciortino's boyfriend, calling him "a good suspect," he was finally cleared when police checked his shoes, reporting them "similar, but not identical" to the killer's.

Another 15 months elapsed before the killer struck again. Patrolman Dan Johnson was cruising his beat in the predawn hours of April 28, 1990, when he saw a woman's nude, eviscerated corpse in the alley behind a Frankford Avenue fish market. The latest victim had been stabbed 36 times, slashed open from her navel to vagina, with her left nipple cut off. A purse, found nearby, identified the woman as 45-year-old Carol Dowd, and a preliminary canvass of the neighborhood turned up a witness who had seen her walking along Frankford Avenue with a middle-aged white man several hours before she was found.

It looked like another dead end until detectives got around to questioning employees of the fish market several days later. One of them, 39-year-old Leonard Christopher, had already spoken to reporters, describing the alley behind his workplace as "a hooker's paradise" and frequent scene of drug deals. Questioned by authorities about his movements on the night Carol Dowd was murdered, Christopher replied that he had spent the evening with his girlfriend. The lady in question, however, denied it, insisting that she spent the night at home, alone. Suspicious now, investigators took a closer look at Leonard Christopher. They found a local mailman who reported seeing Christopher and Dowd together in a bar the night she died. Another witness — this one a convicted prostitute, allegedly saw Christopher and Dowd walking together, down the street. A second hooker told police she saw Christopher emerge from the Frankford Avenue alley around 1:00

a.m. on April 28. According to her report, Christopher had been "sweating profusely, had his shirt over his arm, and a 'Rambo knife' was tucked into his belt."

On the strength of those statements, Christopher — a black man who bore no resemblance to the "Frankford Slasher" sketches or the middle-aged Caucasian seen with Carol Dowd the night she died — was arrested for murder and held without bond, his trial date set for December. A search of his apartment failed to turn up any useful evidence: one pair of slacks had a tiny bloodstain on one leg, but it was too small to be typed, much less for any tests involving DNA.

While Christopher sat in jail, the Frankford Slasher — or a skillful copycat — struck again, in early September. It was 1:00 a.m. on September 8, when tenants of an Arrott Street apartment house complained of rancid odors emanating from the flat occupied by 30-year-old Michelle Martin. The manager used his passkey and found Martin dead on the floor, nude from the waist down, her blouse pushed up to bare her breasts. Stabbed 23 times, she had been dead for roughly two days, last seen alive on the night of September 6, drinking with a middle-aged white man in a bar on Frankford Avenue.

Ignoring their apparent dilemma, prosecutors went ahead with Leonard Christopher's trial on schedule, in December 1990. Their case was admittedly weak — no motive or weapon, no witness to the crime itself, no evidence of any kind connecting the defendant to the murder scene — but jurors were persuaded by the testimony describing Christopher's "strange" behavior and lies to police. On December 12, he was convicted of murder, later sentenced to life imprisonment. From his cell, Christopher still maintains, "I was railroaded."

And what of the Frankford Slasher, described for years as a middle-aged white man? What of the near-identical murder committed while Christopher sat in jail?

Lieutnant Washlick seemed to shrug the problem off, telling reporters, "Surprisingly, we still get phone calls. Leonard Christopher is a suspect in some of the killings, and we have additional suspects as well. Last year, we had 481 homicides in the city, and we solved 82 percent of them."

But not the Frankford Slasher case. The perpetrator of those crimes is still at large.

"Freeway Phantom" — Washington, D.C. (1971-72)

A puzzling case recorded from the nation's capital, this murder series stands officially unsolved despite conviction of two defendants in one of seven similar homicides. Authorities have speculated on solutions in the case, asserting that "justice was served" by the roundup of suspects on unrelated charges, but their faith was shaken by an outbreak of lookalike murders in **Prince Georges County, Maryland**, during 1987. At this writing, some students of the case believe the "Phantom" has eluded homicide detectives altogether, shifting his field of operations to a more fertile hunting ground.

The capital stalker's first victim was 13-year-old Carole Denise Sparks, abducted on April 25, 1971 while en route to a neighborhood store in Southeast Washington. Her strangled, ravaged body was recovered six days later, a mile and a half from home, lying on the shoulder of Interstate Highway 295, one of several freeways passing through Washington east of the Anacostia River.

Ten weeks passed before 16-year-old Darlenia Denise Johnson disappeared, on July 8, from the same street where Carole Sparks was kidnapped. Strangled to death, she was found on July 19, within 15 feet of the spot where Sparks was discovered on May 1. In the meantime, a third victim, 14-year-old Angela Denise Barnes, had been abducted from Southeast

Washington on July 13, shot to death and dumped the same day at Waldorf, Maryland. Brenda Crockett, age 10, disappeared two weeks later, her strangled corpse recovered on July 28 near an underpass on U.S. Highway 50.

The killer took a two-month break in August and September, returning with a vengeance to abduct 12-year-old Nenomoshia Yates on October 1. Familiar marks of strangulation were apparent when her body was found six days later, discarded on Pennsylvania Avenue, near the Maryland state line. At 18, Brenda Denise Woodward was the oldest victim, kidnapped from a Washington bus stop November 15, stabbed to death and dumped the next day on an access road leading to Prince Georges County Hospital. A mocking note, its contents still unpublished, was discovered with the body, signed "The Freeway Phantom" in accordance with the nickname coined by journalists. In a macabre twist, FBI experts reported that Woodward had written the note herself, in a steady hand, betraying no hint of tension or fear.

For once, police had ample evidence of pattern, from the victims' race — all black — to the peculiar fact that four were named Denise. There also seemed to be a geographical connection, both in the abduction and disposal of remains, but speculation brought authorities no closer to their goal of an arrest. Black Washington was up in arms, demanding a solution to the case, intent on proving that a white man was to blame, but angry rhetoric did nothing to advance the murder probe.

Ten months elapsed before the Phantom claimed his final victim, abducting 17-year-old Diane Williams on September 5, 1972. Her body was found the next day along I-295, five miles from the point where Carole Sparks was discovered in May 1971. Again, police noted striking similarities with the other crimes — and again, they found no evidence that would identify a suspect in the case.

In late March, Maryland state police arrested two black suspects — 30-year-old Edward Leon Sellman and 26-year-old Tommie Bernard Simmons — on charges of murdering Angela Barnes. Both suspects were ex-policemen from Washington, and both had resigned in early 1971, before completion of their mandatory probation periods. Investigators now divorced the Barnes murder from other crimes in the Freeway Phantom series, filing additional charges against both suspects in the February 1971 abduction and rape of a Maryland waitress. Convicted of murder in 1974, both defendants were sentenced to life.

Meanwhile, a federal grand jury probing the Phantom murders focused its spotlight on "a loosely knit group of persons" suspected of luring girls and young women into cars — sometimes rented for the hunt — then raping and/or killing their victims for sport. Suspects John N. Davis, 28, and 27-year-old Morris Warren were already serving life on conviction for previous rapes when a new series of indictments was handed down in December 1974. Warren received a grant of limited immunity in return for testimony against Davis and another defendant, 27-year-old Melvyn Sylvester Gray.

As a government spokesman explained, "The ends of justice can be served just as well if the person is convicted and sentenced to life for kidnapping, than if he is jailed for the same term for murder."

Critics questioned the wisdom of that advice, 13 years later, when a new series of unsolved murders was reported from neighboring Maryland. Again, the female victims were young and black, abducted and discarded in a manner reminiscent of the Freeway Phantom's style. Authorities refuse to speculate upon a link between the crimes, and so both cases are considered "open," officially unsolved.

Gay murders — California (1974-75): See **"Doodler"**

Gay murders — California (1988)

A sadly underreported case from San Diego, California, involves the shooting deaths of three presumed homosexual victims in November 1988. Authorities report that two of those murdered were transients, and "at least two" were gay, although the press and public have been left to guess at which is which. David Sino, age 31, was the first known victim in the series, killed by multiple head shots in Balboa Park, his corpse found on November 19. Six days later, 60-year-old Edward Hope was discovered, gunned down in identical circumstances, not far from the scene of Sino's murder. On November 26, Balboa Park was once again the scene of homicide, with 36-year-old Bryan Poole cut down by multiple shots to the head. At this writing, no charges have been filed in the case, no suspect identified.

Gay murders — Canada (1988-93)

Montreal's homosexual community has been plagued for years by reports and rumors of a serial stalker at large, knifing victims to death in their homes after casual meetings in various local gay bars. Police responded to the spreading alarm in 1991 with a task force designed to investigate a dozen murders of gay men in Montreal since 1988. At least eight of the 12 had been stabbed, several with their throats slashed and skulls crushed by heavy blows. Three of the slayings were ultimately solved, and while authorities stopped short of blaming the rest on a serial killer, they did issue a warning, in autumn 1991, asking gays to "be careful."

The investigation seemed to help, at least for a time, as no more slayings of the same type were reported in 1992. Then, in January 1993, two more victims were stabbed to death like the earlier victims — one in his Montreal apartment, the other at his home in suburban Chomedey. Still, police spokesmen refused to apply the "serial" label. As Pierre Sangollo, head of Montreal PD's major crimes division told reporters, "There are still some steps before we can say, 'Yes, a serial killer.'" At the same time though, he acknowledged that "there is a certain pattern that links them together." Whatever that may be, it remains a closely guarded secret at police headquarters... and the killer of gay men in Montreal is still at large.

Gay murders — Italy (1997)

In August 1997, Italian police announced that a serial killer might be on the prowl in their country, targeting older gay men. The declaration followed the bludgeon slayings of two prominent homosexuals, one each in Rome and Florence. The first victim, 56-year-old Louis Inturrisi, was an American who divided his time between teaching university classes and writing for the *New York Times*, found beaten to death in his own apartment, in Rome. The killer's second target was an Italian nobleman, 72-year-old Count Alvise di Robilant, a former managing director of Sotheby's Italia. Found beaten to death in his Renaissance home, in Florence, under circumstances "similar" to Inturrisi's murder, the count was well known for his female conquests, but authorities reported that he had begun a homosexual love affair shortly before he was killed. Thus far, no suspects have been charged or publicly identified in either case.

Gay murders — Maryland (1996-97)

Between October 1996 and January 1997, five gay black men in Maryland were murdered by an unknown home-invader who left no signs of forced entry at the crime scenes. Homicide investigators, working backward, came to suspect a serial killer when it was learned that all five victims frequented certain popular gay bars — the Bachelor's Mills, "360," and the Full House — in nearby Washington, D.C. As Corporal Diane Richardson, spokesperson for the Prince Georges County police, told reporters, "At some point they all frequented the same clubs, but we have not established that they knew each other."

The first to die — and the only victim killed alone — was 42-year-old Anthony Barnes, found stabbed to death in his Bladensburg home on October 6, 1996. Ten weeks later, on December 21, 33-year-old Jimmy McGuire and 27-year-old James Williams were shot execution-style in the home they shared, in Clinton, Maryland. The last two victims were 22-year-old Derrick Hilliard, a D.C. resident, and 41-year-old John Whittington, of Hyattsville, found shot in a ground-floor room at the Motel 6 in Camp Springs, Maryland. To date, no suspects have been named by homicide investigators, and no more slayings have been added to the list.

Gay murders — New York (1973)

In January 1973, a series of brutal stabbings cast a pall over New York City's free-wheeling homosexual community, sparking angry demands for police protection in quarters where officers are normally viewed as the enemy. Targeting denizens of the gay "leather" scene, a faceless butcher mutilated seven victims in a little over three weeks' time, ending the murder spree as suddenly and mysteriously as it began.

The first slaying was recorded on January 4, when neighbors found 29-year-old Ronald Cabo knifed to death in his apartment, laid out on a burning sofa. Four days later, on the Lower East Side, 40-year-old Donald MacNiven and his next-door neighbor, 53-year-old John Beardsley, were slaughtered in MacNiven's apartment, discovered by firemen called out to extinguish an arson fire at the scene. Police confirmed that all three victims were "leather boys," well known in sadomasochistic circles, but rumors of other mutilation deaths were dismissed as "grossly exaggerated."

On January 18, victim Robben Borrero, 23, was pulled from the Hudson River off Greenwich Village, along with the body of a young "John Doe." Nine days later, the killer scored his last double-header in Brooklyn Heights, invading the apartment that schoolteacher Nelson Roberts shared with his male lover. Neighbors used a pass key to investigate a blaring radio and stumbled on a scene of carnage. In the living room, hands bound behind his back, Roberts lay covered with a blanket, killed by multiple stab wounds in the back. His roommate was discovered in the bedroom, hog-tied, with a broken neck. The couple's pet, a miniature poodle, had been drowned in the sink.

The slayer's premature "retirement" after seven murders left police without a single piece of valid evidence. An undercover officer was fitted out with leather gear to infiltrate the seamy world of S&M, and while his exploits helped inspire the movie *Cruising,* starring Al Pacino, they did not result in apprehension of the killer.

Gay murders — New York (1985-86)

On March 21, 1986, Pedro Gonzalez, a 43-year-old restaurant worker, was found tied up and strangled in his Corona, Queens apartment. Six days later, homicide detectives told the press his death bore similarities to two other homicides in Queens, committed since July of 1985. All three victims were dark-skinned Hispanic homosexuals, known to frequent the same two bars in Queens and Manhattan. Each victim was beaten to death or asphyxiated in his own apartment, with the lights left on and a radio blaring loud music. Objects stolen by the still-unidentified killer included two videocassette recorders and a portable radio.

Gay murders — New York (1993):
See **"Last Call Killer"**

Gay murders — Virginia (1987-95)

Reporters in Virginia suspected the presence of a serial killer, stalking gay men in Chesapeake and environs, as early as September 1993. Eight victims had been stabbed to death by that time, but authorities required another twenty months — and two more dead — before they finally acknowledged the obvious in May 1995. By that time, the murders had dragged on for nearly eight years, the only promising lead had gone up in gun smoke, and police were no closer to an arrest than they had been when the first corpse was found.

That first victim, 18-year-old Charles Smith, was found in Chesapeake on July 17, 1987, knifed to death, clad only in his jeans and sneakers. Two days later, and again in Chesapeake, the knife-scarred body of Joseph Ray was found discarded along Interstate Highway 64. The killer took a breather after that, returning to murder 21-year-old Stacy Reneau in Chesapeake on January 7, 1989. After a three-year lull, he struck again, hacking the life from John Ross Jr., a 37-year-old ironworker from North Carolina. On July 2, 1992, 32-year-old Billy Lee Dixon — a sometime "model" for gay magazines — was found murdered in neighboring Isle of Wight County. Reginald Joyner's body was found in Suffolk County on March 7, 1993, and Ray Bostick, a 27-year-old unemployed truck driver in Chesapeake, joined the list three months later, on June 6. Another Chesapeake victim, 24-year-old Robert Neal, was found slashed to death on September 8, 1993.

The press started making connections at that point, despite stony silence from authorities. Aside from the obvious pattern of death by stabbing, inflicted on gay men (or "straights" with numerous gay friends), it was also known from autopsy results that four of the last five victims — Ross, Dixon, Joyner and Bostick — had snorted cocaine a short time before they were killed. By year's end, police had staked their hopes on a young man said to possess crucial information on the case, but their "non-suspect" was found shot to death in a Moyock, North Carolina mobile home, in the spring of 1994. Local authorities called it a suicide, while press reports described the circumstances as "suspicious."

Whatever he may have known, the dead man clearly was not Chesapeake's gay stalker. Five months after his death, the killer returned with a vengeance, on September 16, 1994. That afternoon, 24-year-old newlywed Garland Taylor left home to buy some lunch in Portsmouth and never returned. His mutilated corpse was found next day, in rural Suffolk County, relatives insisting he was "straight," although a number of his closest friends were gay.

The final homicide to date, which forced police to acknowledge grudgingly what the press had known since 1993, occurred on February 14, 1995. Samuel Aliff, age thirty-one, was found knifed to death in Tidewater, prompting Richard Black of the Chesapeake Police Department to admit, "At this point, we feel we have enough of a pattern that we can say it's a serial killer."

In fact, police already had an FBI profile of the stalker, vaguely described as an attractive, personable and outgoing white man, age 30 to 35 years. Spokesmen for the Chesapeake gay community suggested that the killer would turn out to be a bitter "closet case," killing his chosen partners in an effort to erase his private shame at being homosexual. Larry McCann, with the Virginia State Police, announced, "I'm sure the person responsible for these homicides has let a lot of people go. I'm sure he has interacted with a lot of potential victims over the years, but for one reason or another didn't kill them. As for why, we'll have to ask him when we catch him."

And there, of course, was the rub. Chesapeake police called a press conference on July 21, 1995, announcing that while several suspects were being examined, no arrest was imminent. The bottom line: "We're no closer now than we were three months ago." Or three *years* ago, for that matter. At this writing, no new murders in the series have been publicly acknowledged, and the man (or men) responsible for snuffing out 10 lives in southeastern Virginia remains at large.

Gay murders — Washington, D.C. (1971)

On March 3, 1972, police in the District of Columbia announced that 10 of 1971's 38 unsolved murders were "homosexually motivated or related." Hesitant to speculate about connections in the crimes, investigators did report that they were searching for a single suspect, pictured in a photograph with 55-year-old victim James Williams, found stabbed to death in his Northwest apartment on April 13, 1971. The snapshot was taken by a photographer known only as "Bill," who ignored official pleas for help in solving the case. At last report, the suspect remains unidentified, the 10 murders unsolved.

Gilmore Lane Convalescent Hospital — California (1984-85)

Two days before Christmas 1985, California state authorities announced that an investigation was under way in the cases of 11 "suspicious" deaths at the Gilmore Lane Convalescent Hospital, in Oroville. (Several more patients died after being transferred to Oroville Hospital for emergency treatment.) The deaths, initially ascribed to unknown "illness," all occurred in January 1985, at a time when Justice Department officials were already probing the cases of 38 elderly patients, lost between January and April 1984. Health officials reportedly failed to perform autopsies in the 49 cases, leaving prosecutors to start from scratch with victims already buried or cremated. At this writing, no final result of the investigation has been published, no suspects in the rash of deaths identified.

Good Samaritan Hospital — Illinois (1979-80)

Ellen O'Hara, age 92, was awaiting surgery at Good Samaritan Hospital, in the Chicago suburb of Downer's Grove, when she died on October 19, 1979. Autopsy surgeons blamed her death on hypoglycemia — abnormally low blood sugar — induced by unknown causes. O'Hara's body was routinely cremated, but hospital administrators were startled when patient Vivian Brown died with identical symptoms on February 8, 1980. Neither patient had a prior history of hypoglycemia, and the police chief of Downer's Grove called Brown's death "highly suspicious." Physicians agreed, concluding in May 1980 that her condition was caused by an "externally administered dose of insulin." In retrospect, they thought it likely that Ellen O'Hara had been the victim of a similar lethal injection.

In early June, hospital administrators suspended 24-year-old nurse Linda Kurle from her post on the night shift at Good Samaritan. Both patients had shown their first symptoms of hypoglycemia during Kurle's shift, and while she professed no memory of Ellen O'Hara, Kurle recalled finding Vivian Brown in "serious straits" in the predawn hours of February 8. Her treatment of the patient, Kurle insisted, had been strictly by-the-book. No charges were filed, and the case of the mysterious insulin injections at Good Samaritan Hospital remains unsolved at this writing.

Grand Rapids murders — Michigan (1994-97)

Authorities in Kent County, Michigan, hesitate to blame a serial killer for the murders of 11 women — eight of them known prostitutes — since early 1994, but Lieutenant Carol Price, spokesperson for a fifteen-member task force assigned to the case, has told reporters, "We're not denying it's a possibility. But we don't concentrate on that theory to the exclusion of others."

Thus far, sadly, no theory has brought police any closer to a solution in the case that has Grand Rapids residents glancing over their shoulders in grim apprehension.

The first known victim, 25-year-old prostitute Lesa Otberg, was abducted from Grand Rapids, her body discarded in Muskegon, 40 miles to the northwest on March 28, 1994. Eight months later, on November 6, a second corpse — still listed on the record as "Jane Doe," age 35 to 50 years old — was found in neighboring Ottawa County, to the west. Authorities believe she was murdered in the spring or early summer of 1994. Number three, 33-year-old hooker and drug addict Pamela Verile, was found beaten to death on June 1, 1995, in a thicket near Walker, on the western outskirts of Grand Rapids. Gale Cook, a 37-year-old convicted drug user from Lansing and fugitive from a prison work-release program, was the next to die, found strangled in Grand Rapids Township on October 4. Local prostitute Dawn Shaver, age 25, was beaten and strangled before she was dumped in a creek north of town, her body recovered on November 21, 1995. No cause of death was determined for Michelle Becker, a 36-year-old convicted prostitute, found dead in downtown Grand Rapids on August 9, 1996. Sonyia Compos, 27, was a hooker from Wyoming, found near Walker on September 21; once again, the cause of death was undetermined. The same was true on October 1, for a "Jane Doe" corpse discovered north of town, in Plainfield Township. Thirty-year-old Sharon Hammack, another convicted junkie-prostitute, was killed two days later, discarded on the fringes of suburban Kentwood.

A 14-member task force was organized to investigate the murders on October 10, 1996. Three days later, an anonymous phone tip led police to a tenth victim — yet another "Jane Doe," age 40 to 55 years old — in a field behind a south Grand Rapids factory. Number 11, 29-year-old Victoria Moore, was found two weeks later, on October 27, her decomposing body dumped beside a country road, 20 miles north of Grand Rapids. By that time, a pattern of sorts had emerged, police acknowledging that Moore and at least four other recent victims had contacted the Rose Haven Ministry, a local sanctuary for prostitutes. Rose Haven's director, Brenda Dalecke, told reporters, "I'd be really surprised if it wasn't a serial killer. It's too much of a coincidence."

Local authorities, for their part, were less certain. "We're not ready to use the big 'S' word yet," said Police Chief Walter Sprenger, in nearby Walker. "So far, we haven't found the common thread that links all these victims together."

Of course, police weren't discounting the theory, either. Captain Kevin Belk, chief of detectives for Grand Rapids P.D., conceded that "There are enough similarities to lead us to believe that the majority or all of these homicides are related." Still, he added, "We're not prepared to say one person was responsible. We have several tips and leads, but we're not focusing on any prime suspect."

Two years later, the manhunt is no more focused than it was in 1996, and the killer(s) of Grand Rapid prostitutes is still at large.

"Green River Killer" — Washington (1982-84)

One of America's most prolific unidentified killers is credited with 40 homicides around Seattle and Tacoma, Washington, in two years' time; another eight suspected victims are officially described as missing, since remains have not been found. Vaguely described as a white male in his late twenties or early thirties (at the time of the murders), the elusive killer draws his popular nickname from the fact that several victims were discarded in or near Washington's Green River. All of his victims were women, and many were prostitutes, working the infamous "Sea-Tac Strip." At this writing, police say the slayer has claimed no new victims in Washington since autumn 1984, but they have no idea why he stopped, or where he may have gone.

The killer's first known victim, 16-year-old Leann Wilcox, from Tacoma, was found strangled in a field near Federal Way, eight miles south of Seattle, on January 21, 1982. The absence of a pattern in the case prevented homicide detectives from establishing connections to the string of later deaths, and nearly two years would elapse before Leann was finally acknowledged as a "Green River" victim, in November 1983. Likewise, number two, 36-year-old Amina Agisheff, was simply a missing person when she vanished on July 7, 1982, her skeletal remains recovered and identified in April 1984.

The first "official" victim, 16-year-old Wendy Coffield, was reported missing from her foster home on July 8, 1982, her body fished out of the Green River seven days later. On August 12, 23-year-old Deborah Bonner was dragged from the water, a half-mile upstream from where Coffield was found. Three days later, the Green River yielded three more victims, including 31-year-old Marcia Chapman, 17-year-old Cynthia Hinds, and 16-year-old Opal Mills.

Detectives realized they had a problem on their hands, and it was growing by the day. Two 17-year-olds, Karen Lee and Terri Milligan, went missing in late August (with Milligan's remains identified on April 1, 1984). Debra Estes, age 15, joined the missing list on September 14, followed by 19-year-old Mary Meehan a day later. (Their skeletal remains were found in May 1988 and November 1983, respectively.) Gisele Lovvorn, age 17, became "official" victim number six when she was found September 25, two months after running away from home.

According to police, the six known dead had all been working prostitutes, but the killer also showed a taste for runaways and hitchhikers. Shawndra Summers, 17, disappeared on October 7, 1982, her remains identified by authorities in mid-August 1983. Becky Marrero, a 20-year-old friend of Debra Estes, was last seen alive on December 2, 1982. Alma Smith, 19, picked up her last "trick" in Seattle on March 3, 1983; her skeletal remains were found with Terri Milligan's on April 2, 1984. Two weeks later, 16-year-old Carrie Rois vanished from Seattle, her remains discovered almost two years later, on March 10, 1985. Kimi Pitsor, 16, joined the missing list on April 28.

Through it all, the murders maintained a certain ritualistic quality. Like Ted Bundy before him, the Green River killer seemed to prefer certain dumpsites for multiple victims. At least four such locations were used, the killer alternating sporadically, despite police surveillance. Many of his victims were covered with loose brush and branches, several stretched out beside fallen logs. Pathologists found small, pyramid-shaped stones inserted into the vaginas of several Green River victims, their significance unknown to this day. At least one corpse was left by the killer with a dead fish draped across one thigh.

The killer scored a double-header on May 8, 1983, picking off 21-year-old Carol Christenson in Seattle and dumping her body near Maple Valley, then rebounding to snatch 16-year-old Joanne Hovland, shortly after her release from juvenile detention in the town of Everett. On May 5, he killed Martina Authorlee, 18, hiding her remains so well that they would not be found until November 1984. Yvonne Antosh, a 19-year-old from Vancouver, British Columbia, vanished in Seattle on May 20, her decomposed remains identified on October 18, 1983. On June 8, Constance Naon, a 20-year-old prostitute, was reported missing, her bones recovered in October. Four days later, on June 12, the killer found 27-year-old Kimberly Reames on the Sea-Tac Strip, her body discovered the next afternoon. April Buttram, 17, left home for the last time on August 4, 1983, and she remains among the missing, included on the official task force list of victims.

Debbie Abernathy, 26, was the first victim in September, murdered on the fifth, her skeletal remains discovered on March 31, 1984. Nineteen-year-old Tracy Wilson was reported missing one week later, on September 12, and Maureen

Feeney, another 19-year-old, disappeared on September 29. (Her remains were found on May 3, 1986.) October's victims included Kelly Ware, a 24-year-old hooker, and 25-year-old Mary Bello, from Enumclaw, Washington. (Bello's remains were discovered a year and a day after her disappearance, on October 12, 1984.)

The killer took a break that autumn, returning to business as usual on February 6, 1984, with the murder of 16-year-old Mary West, abducted en route to a neighborhood market, her skull identified in September 1985. Patricia Osborn, a 19-year-old prostitute, had been reported missing by her family on January 24; her name made the "Green River" victims list on February 11.

And the list kept growing, as investigators searched their files on missing women. Victims added with the benefit of hindsight included: Colleen Brockman, 15; Alma Smith, 18; Sandra Gabbert, 17; Cheryl Wyms, 18; Denise Bush, 24; Shirley Sherrill, 19; Marie Malvar, 18; Tammy Liles, 16; and Kelly McGuinness, 18. By April 1984, authorities had listed 24 known dead and 13 missing in the case, with 12 new skeletons unearthed since New Year's Day. By January 1986, the list of dead had grown to 34; it rose to 40 in the spring of 1988, with new discoveries, and there were still eight women which were unaccounted.

There was also, apparently, a survivor, mistakenly left for dead by the killer in haste. Still unidentified for her own protection, the lucky woman helped police prepare a sketch of the Green River killer that was broadcast on national TV in 1989, but none of the tips received led detectives to a viable target. Back in Seattle, various "prime suspects" included a cab driver and a part-time law student, each certifiably "weird" in the eyes of police, each finally exonerated as the case dragged on... and on... and on.

If nothing else, police drew consolation from the fact that their killer had apparently "retired," with no new victims missing from Seattle or Tacoma since 1984. At the same time, speculation is rampant that the Green River killer may have taken his show on the road, with authorities from neighboring **Spokane**, Washington, to **San Diego**, California hinting at possible "Green River" involvement in their own gruesome series of prostitute murders. Whatever the truth in those cases, one indisputable fact remains: the Green River killer has yet to be identified and punished for his crimes.

"Guangzhou Ripper" — China (1991-92)

Hard-line communist societies face a built-in disability in dealing with serial killers, since state propaganda denies the existence of crime in a "workers' paradise." Russian authorities learned the grim truth over a span of two decades, from butchers like Gennadiy Mikhasevich (36 victims), Andrei Chikatilo (52 dead), Nikolai Dzhumagliev ("at least 100" slain), and "Ivan the Ripper" (never publicly identified), but the notion of serial killers was still new to Red China in 1991, when a faceless stalker surfaced in Guangzhou (formerly Canton).

The slasher's first victim was reportedly found on February 22, 1991, described vaguely as a woman in her early 20s. Her genitals were carved out with a knife, but the mutilation did not prevent police from finding unspecified "evidence of sexual intercourse." Five more slayings followed in the next six months, each victim reportedly subjected to a sexual assault, then smothered, stabbed, or strangled, after which the bodies were dismembered, stuffed in rice bags, and dumped on rubbish heaps in the bleak suburbs where Guangzhou's "floating population" lives in dismal squalor. And then, the murders stopped.

Thus far, there had been no press coverage of the crimes in China, marking the case as a "success" in terms of propaganda, even though the murderer remained at large. Chinese authorities ran out of luck in March of 1992, when a seventh victim washed ashore in the nearby British colony of Hong Kong. As described in the *South China Morning Post,* number seven had been slit from throat to stomach, then crudely stitched shut again, her fingers severed almost as an afterthought. Because no women were reported missing from Hong Kong, it was assumed the corpse had floated in from mainland China, and thus the "Guangzhou Ripper" was belatedly exposed.

Even then, it was impossible for homicide investigators, reared from childhood under communism, to believe that their system would spawn such a monster. Zhu Minjian, head of Guangzhou's provincial Criminal Investigation Department, told reporters, "In all my thirty years with the force, I have never come across anything like this. Perhaps he copied from the West."

Zhu said there had been "progress" in the case, but he was not prepared to share the details. "We're putting a lot of effort into this case," he declared. "We've got to solve it."

Or, maybe not. Six years after the first press report of the crimes, Chinese authorities have yet to name a suspect (or a victim, for that matter) in the string of crimes that shocked them so. Unless the killer has been secretly detained — unlikely on its face, considering the rash of prior publicity — we must assume that Guangzhou's Ripper has performed a disappearing act.

Gunness, Belle

America's first "black widow" of the 20th century was born Brynhild Paulsdatter Storset, on November 11, 1859, in the fishing hamlet of Selbu, on Norway's west coast. The daughter of an unsuccessful merchant, Brynhild immigrated to the United States in 1881; three years later, she settled in Chicago, Americanizing her given name to "Belle" (or sometimes "Bella"). In 1884, at age 25, she married a Norwegian immigrant, Mads Sorenson.

The couple opened a confectioner's shop in 1896, but the business was wiped out by fire the following year. Belle told her insurance agents that a kerosene lamp had exploded, and the company paid off on her policy, although no lamp was found in the wreckage. The Sorensens used their found money to purchase a home, but fire leveled the house in 1898, bringing further insurance payments. Bad luck dogged the couple, and a second house burned down before they found a home that met their needs, on Alma Street.

As everything Belle touched was soon reduced to ashes, so her family began to dwindle in the latter 1890s. Daughter Caroline, her oldest child, went first, in 1896. Two years later, Axel, her first son, was laid to rest. In each case, the children were diagnosed as victims of "acute colitis," demonstrating symptoms which — in hindsight — may have indicated they were poisoned.

On July 30, 1900, Mads Sorenson died at home, exhibiting the classic symptoms of strychnine poisoning. Belle admitted giving her husband "a powder," in an effort to "help his cold," but the family physician did not request an autopsy. With Mads under treatment for an enlarged heart, his death was automatically ascribed to natural causes.

The widow Sorenson collected her insurance money and departed from Chicago, settling outside La Porte, Indiana, with three children under her wing. Two were natural daughters: Myrtle, born in 1897, and Lucy, born in 1899. The new addition, Jennie Olsen, was a foster daughter, passed along to Belle by parents who, apparently, were tired of dealing with the child.

In April 1902, Belle married a Norwegian farmer named Peter Gunness. Less durable than Sorenson before him, Gunness lasted only eight months. On December 16, 1902, he was killed when a heavy sausage grinder "fell" from its place on a shelf, fracturing his skull. A son, named Philip, was born of the brief union in 1903, and Jennie Olsen vanished from the farm three years later. When neighbors inquired, Belle explained that her foster child had been sent "to a finishing school in California."

Widowed for the second time, with only two children to assist her on the farm, Belle started hiring drifters who would work for a while and then, apparently, move on. She also started placing "lonely hearts" ads in Norwegian-language newspapers throughout the Midwest, entertaining a series of prospective husbands at her farm. Somehow, none of them measured up to her standards... and none of them were ever seen again.

On April 28, 1908, the Gunness homestead was leveled by fire. Searchers, digging through the rubble, found a quartet of incinerated bodies in the basement; three were clearly children, while the fourth — a woman's headless corpse, without the skull in evidence — was taken for the last remains of Belle. The local sheriff arrested handyman Ray Lamphere, employed by Belle from 1906 until his dismissal in February 1908, on charges of arson and murder.

The case became more complicated on May 5, when searchers started finding *other* bodies on the Gunness ranch. Dismembered, wrapped in gunny sacks and doused with lye, a few reduced to skeletons, the corpses told a graphic tale of wholesale slaughter spanning years. The final body count has been a subject of enduring controversy. Without citing its source, the *Guinness Book of World Records* credited Belle with 16 known victims and another 12 "possibles." The local coroner's report was more modest, listing — in addition to the basement bodies — 10 male victims, two females, and an unspecified quantity of human bone fragments. Belle's suitors were buried together, in the muck of a hog pen, while her female victims had been planted in a nearby garden patch.

Only six of the victims were positively identified. Jennie Olsen was there, far removed from the mythical finishing school. Farm hands Eric Gurhold and Olaf Lindblom had ended their days in the hog pen, beside farmers John Moo, of Elbow Lake, Minnesota, and Ole Budsberg of Iola, Wisconsin. Both of the latter had answered Belle's newspaper ads — and so, presumably, had their six anonymous companions in death. The single "Jane Doe," buried beside Jennie Olsen, is an anomaly, unexplained to this day.

A coroner's inquest was launched on April 29, and witness depositions taken through May 1 reflect a standard hearing "over the dead body of Belle Gunness." After May 5, with the discovery of new corpses, official documents began describing the headless woman as "an unidentified adult female," assuming that Belle might have faked her own death to escape from the scene. A futile search for the missing skull was begun on May 19, resulting in discovery of Belle's dental bridge, complete with anchor teeth attached. Ignoring the various unanswered questions, the coroner issued his final report on May 20, declaring that Belle Gunness had died "at the hands of persons unknown."

Ray Lamphere, from his cell, was adamant in claiming that Belle was still alive. On April 28, he said, once Belle had set the house on fire, he drove her to the railway station at Still-well, Indiana. Police initially took his story at face value, arresting an innocent widow, Flora Heerin, en route from Chicago to visit relatives in New York City. Hauled off the train at Syracuse and briefly detained as Belle Gunness, Heerin retaliated in a lawsuit charging Syracuse police with false arrest.

Charged with four counts of murder and one count of arson, Ray Lamphere's case went to the jury in November 1908. On November 26, he was convicted on the arson charge alone, suggesting that the jurors felt Belle's death had not been proven "beyond a reasonable doubt." Surviving for two years in prison, Lamphere talked endlessly about the case, crediting Belle with 49 murders, netting more than $100,000 from her victims between 1903 and 1908. The basement victim, he contended, had been found in a saloon, hired for the evening, and murdered to serve as a stand-in. Belle had promised she would get in touch with Lamphere, after she was settled elsewhere, but it seemed that she had changed her plans.

The first reported sighting of a resurrected Belle was logged on April 29, six days before the new bodies were found at her farm. Conductor Jesse Hurst was certain Mrs. Gunness went aboard his train at the Decatur, Indiana station. She was bundled on a stretcher, Hurst recalled, and seemed quite ill.

Perhaps, but what are we to make of the reported sighting at La Porte, on April 30? While visiting Belle's closest friend, Almetta Hay, a local farmer claimed he saw the missing woman sitting down to coffee. When Almetta died in 1916, neighbors picking through the litter in her crowded shack retrieved a woman's skull, wedged in between two mattresses. In spite of speculation that it might belong to the decapitated basement victim, the intriguing lead was not pursued.

More "sightings" were recorded through the years. In 1917, a childhood neighbor recognized Belle Gunness on admission, as a patient, to the South Bend hospital where he was working as a student nurse. He called police, but Belle had slipped away before detectives reached the scene. In 1931, a Los Angeles prosecutor wrote to La Porte's sheriff, claiming that murder defendant Esther Carlson — charged with poisoning 81-year-old August Lindstrom for money — might be Belle Gunness. Carlson carried photographs of three children resembling Belle's, but La Porte could not afford to send its sheriff west in those Depression days, and the suspect died of tuberculosis before trial, leaving the question forever open.

As late as 1935, subscribers to a magazine allegedly recognized Belle's photograph as the likeness of a whorehouse madam in Ohio. Confronting the old woman and addressing her as "Belle," one amateur detective was impressed by the vehemence of her reaction. Pursuing the matter through friends, he was urgently warned to let the matter rest... and so it has.

If Gunness did, in fact, survive her "death," she stands with **Bela Kiss** in that elite society of slayers who — although identified, with ample evidence to win convictions — manage to escape arrest and so live out their lives in anonymity. Her legacy is rumor, and a snatch of tawdry rhyme that reads, in part:

> There's red upon the Hoosier moon
> For Belle was strong and full of doom;
> And think of all those Norska men
> Who'll never see St. Paul again.

"Headless murders" — Pennsylvania (1925-39)

While homicide detectives in Ohio stalked Cleveland's "**Mad Butcher of Kingsbury Run**" through the latter 1930s, they were periodically distracted by reports of unsolved slayings from the area of New Castle and West Pittsburgh, Pennsylvania. No solid link between the crime sprees was established, but coincidence of timing, the proximity of common railway lines, and the unanimous decapitation of victims in both states have produced some tantalizing theories. No two reports agree on the number of New Castle victims, and several accounts make surprisingly detailed references to nonexistent crimes. A retrospective survey in the local paper, published in December 1971, refers to eleven victims between 1921 and 1940, but a detailed review of newspaper records reveals only five murders, spanning a period of fourteen years.

The first victim, a young man, was found in a marshy area between New Castle and West Pittsburgh — later dubbed the "murder swamp" — on October 6, 1925. Nude on discovery, the man had been dead at least three weeks when he was found, and discovery of his severed head on October 8 provided no clue to his identity. As with the other Pennsylvania victims, he remains unidentified.

On October 17, 1925, a headless male skeleton was found in the swamp. The matching skull was unearthed two days later, with that of a woman killed at least a year earlier. Neither victim was identified by authorities, and no trace of the woman's body was ever found.

The local "headless murders" were a fading memory by July 1, 1936, when a man's decapitated body turned up on a slag dump of the Pittsburgh & Lake Erie Railroad, at New Castle Junction. The victim's head was never found, and he remains anonymous. Newspapers, spread beneath the body, included issues from Pittsburgh and Cleveland, dating from July of 1933.

On October 13, 1939, another headless, decomposing man was fished out of the swamp near West Pittsburgh. Charred newspapers surrounding the body included month-old copies from Youngstown, Ohio, and the victim's head was found nearby, in an abandoned boxcar, five days later.

Were the Pennsylvania crimes and Cleveland's murder spree connected? Did Ohio's "Mad Butcher" first try his hand in New Castle, taking a decade off before he resumed activities in Cleveland? Detective Peter Merylo, stalking the Ohio headhunter into retirement, blamed one man for both sets of murders, plus 20 to 30 more kills, nationwide. The final truth has managed to elude police for 60 years, and it may well lie buried in the Pennsylvania "murder swamp."

"Highway Killer(s)" — Canada (1973-81)

For the best part of a decade, between 1973 and 1981, Canadian authorities were baffled by a series of unsolved sex-murders along the Trans-Canada Highway, spanning the provinces of Alberta and British Columbia. Victims ranged in age from 12 years old to 35, and while published sources could never agree on a body count — citing various totals from 11 to 33 victims — the most frequent tally lists 28 slayings spread over eight years. Many of the victims were apparently hitchhikers, sexually assaulted before they were beaten, strangled, or stabbed to death, with some of the bodies revealing postmortem mutilations.

Generally acknowledged as the first "highway" victim, 19-year-old Gale Weys was thumbing her way home to Kamploops, from a job in Clearwater, when she met her killer on October 19, 1973. Her naked, decomposing corpse was found a few miles south of Clearwater on April 6, 1974.

By that time, the killer had claimed another victim, picking off 19-year-old Pamela Darlington, at Kamploops, on November 6. Her ravaged body was fished out of the Thompson River the next day, and a train crew reported sighting a man with "messy blond hair" near the scene of the crime, but the vague description led detectives nowhere.

Colleen McMillan, 16, was last seen alive on August 9, 1974, thumbing rides near Lac La Hache. A month later, on September 4, her nude, decomposing remains were found some 35 miles away. Police suspected a drug addict, who confessed to the murder and then recanted before committing suicide. The case remains officially unsolved.

On January 9, 1976, 16-year-old Pauline Brazeau was found stabbed to death, outside Calgary. Six months later, on July 1, 19-year-old Tera White disappeared from Banff, her skeletal remains discovered near Calgary in March 1981. Marie Goudreau, 17, was murdered near Devon on August 2, 1976, and 20-year-old Melissa Rehorek was murdered near Calgary on September 15, her body discarded 12 miles from the spot where Pauline Brazeau was discovered.

Barbara McLean, age 26, traveled all the way from Nova Scotia to meet her death near Calgary, strangled by persons unknown on February 26, 1977. Monica Jack, 14, disappeared while bicycling near Merritt, on May 6, 1978, and she has not been seen since, though her bike was found at the bottom of a highway embankment. On September 26, 1979, 12-year-old Susan Duff went biking near Penticton and never returned, her body recovered from the outskirts of town on October 21. Mary Jamieson, 17, disappeared while hitchhiking near Davis Bay, on August 7, 1980; nine days later, when her body was discovered in the nearby woods, the cause of death was listed as asphyxiation.

On February 28, 1981, victim Oanh Ha — a 19-year-old immigrant from Vietnam — was raped and strangled near Golden, her body mutilated after death. Two months later, on April 22, 15-year-old Kelly Cook was reported missing, her body found near Taber, Alberta, on June 29. The only male victim in the series, transvestite Frederick Savoy, was parading in drag when the killer apparently mistook him for a woman, knifing him to death in a Vancouver parking lot. Maureen Mosie, generally described as the last "highway" victim, was beaten to death at Kamloops on May 8, 1981.

Six months later, authorities convened a special summit meeting to discuss 33 of Canada's 200 unsolved murders, and while they generally agreed that they were seeking several killers — possibly as many as 18 — in the "highway" series, no clear suspects were identified. A ray of hope broke through in 1983, with the marathon confessions of serial slayers Henry Lucas and Ottis Toole including vague references to "several" Canadian victims, but no charges have been filed to date, and the long string of murders remains unsolved.

"Highway Killer" — Massachusetts (1988)

Between April and early September of 1988, at least nine women from New Bedford, Massachusetts were abducted and murdered by an unknown serial killer who dumped their bodies near highways surrounding the city. Two other women, reported missing from New Bedford in the same time period, are presumed to be victims of the same human predator. Several of the victims were known prostitutes, while others were described by the police as drug-addicted "semi-pros." At least six knew each other in the months before they died, frequenting the same saloons, sometimes walking the same streets in search of tricks.

The first hint of a killer on the loose around New Bedford came on July 2, 1988, when a motorist stopped to urinate in some bushes near the Freeport exit ramp of Interstate 140. Instead of a quiet rest stop, he found the partially clad skeleton of a woman, identified five months later as 30-year-old Debra

Madeiros, last seen alive on May 27, when she left her boyfriend's apartment in the wake of a lover's quarrel.

Four weeks later, on July 30, more decomposed remains were found near the Reed Road exit ramp from I-195, six miles west of New Bedford. The victim was identified, on December 7, as one Nancy Paiva, a 36-year-old heroin addict last seen alive on July 11. Despite her addiction and various run-ins with the law over drugs, Paiva's relatives denied she was a prostitute, and she had no arrests for hooking on her record.

A little more than three months passed before the next grim discovery, on November 8, 1988, when the remains of yet another woman were discovered near the Reed Road exit on I-195. Two days after Christmas, the body was identified as that of Deborah DeMello, a 34-year-old fugitive from justice who had fled a prison work-release program in June while serving time for prostitution. Last seen alive on July 11, DeMello was found with some clothing and other personal items identified as belonging to victim Nancy Paiva.

Eleven days after DeMello was found, on November 19, a road crew clearing brush along I-195 discovered the nude, decomposed corpse of Dawn Mendes, a 25-year-old New Bedford resident missing since September 4. Her remains were identified by fingerprints, which matched her record of arrests for prostitution.

Less than two weeks passed before discovery of the next victim, on December 1. By that time, police were out searching with dogs, and their effort paid off with the report of a skeleton found near Interstate 140, two miles south of the point where Debra Madeiros was found in July. This time, the skeleton was fully clothed, with a sack of extra clothing found nearby. Three full months would pass before the victim was identified, on February 28, 1989, as 25-year-old Deborah McConnell, missing from New Bedford since May.

By the time McConnell was identified, police had a sixth victim on their hands, found December 10 by hunters, at an abandoned gravel quarry half a mile north of the Reed Road exit on I-195. Nine days later, the skeleton was identified as that of 28-year-old Rochelle Clifford, last seen alive on April 27, 1988, in company with an ex-convict known as Nancy Paiva's sometime live-in lover. An automatic suspect in two of the murders to date, the man was investigated and apparently cleared on both counts, as no charges were filed.

The first "highway" victim of 1989 was found on March 28, on the southbound side of I-140, directly opposite the spot where Debra Madeiros was found nine months earlier. The skeleton had a full set of teeth, and identification was made the next day, naming victim number seven as Robin Rhodes, a 28-year-old single mother last seen alive in April 1988. While not a working prostitute, according to her family and friends, Rhodes *was* acquainted with victims Clifford, Paiva, and Mendes, from hanging out in local bars.

Rhodes was also a friend of the next victim found, 26-year-old Mary Santos, whose skeleton was found along Route 88 on March 31, 1989. The dumpsite placed her miles from the first seven victims, but the killer otherwise held to his patter, hiding the body in brush some 20 to 25 feet from the roadway. Last seen alive in New Bedford on July 15, 1988, Santos was a known heroin addict, also friends with victims Clifford, Paiva, and Santos.

The last victim found, on April 24, 1989, was identified as Sandra Botelho, discarded without any clothes beside I-195, eight miles east of New Bedford. A 24-year-old college dropout, junkie, and hooker, Botelho was last seen alive on August 11, 1988, leaving her apartment for a night on the stroll. She had never returned, and her fate was a mystery for eight months, until her skeletal remains were found.

By that point in their search for clues, authorities had listed two more missing women as probable victims of the elusive "Highway Killer." Nineteen-year-old Christine Monteiro, an addict with arrests for prostitution on her record, had vanished in May 1988, while her next-door neighbor, 34-year-old Marilyn Roberts, disappeared from New Bedford the following month. At this writing, both women are still missing and presumed dead.

By late November 1988, local and state authorities were trying to coordinate their manhunt for the Highway Killer. Sadly short of evidence, they concentrated first on rumors that a knife-wielding rapist had been terrorizing hookers in New Bedford for a year or more. Police had a vague description of the suspect and his white pickup truck, but they were getting nowhere fast until December 13, 1988, when one alleged victim spotted the pickup again and recorded its license number. Detectives traced the vehicle to Neil Anderson, a 35-year-old unemployed trucker and fish-cutter who lived with his mother, boasting convictions for assault and battery with a dangerous weapon (1978), attempted breaking and entering (1981), plus various arrests concerning drugs and alcohol. Arraigned December 15 on rape charges, Anderson was initially held on $20,000 bond, subsequently convicted on one count of sexual assault and sentenced to a prison term of three to five years. No evidence was found connecting him with any of the "highway" murders in New Bedford.

Another alleged hooker rapist in town was known to his victims as "Flat Nose," identified in January 1989 as one Tony DeGrazia. Seventeen prostitutes allegedly named DeGrazia as their rapist before he was hauled in for questioning, on April 19. He denied any wrongdoing, but reportedly admitted to police that "everyone" suspected him of murdering the Highway Killer victims. Formally arrested on May 4, DeGrazia was held in a mental hospital for testing, while various forensic samples from his body, home, and pickup truck were rushed to the FBI lab in Washington. Those test results were a mixed blessing for investigators: DeGrazia was eliminated as a murder suspect in New Bedford, but hairs recovered from his vehicle appeared to match with several alleged rape victims. Released on $37,500 bond in January 1990, DeGrazia was still awaiting trial a year later, when he was arrested once more, charged with raping yet another prostitute. He denied that charge, as well, but sat in jail until July 1991, when he finally made bond on the latest charge. A few days after his release from custody, DeGrazia committed suicide with an overdose of antidepressant medication.

Long before that time, however, local cops and prosecutors had focused on another suspect as their most likely candidate for the "Highway Killer" title. Kenneth Ponte was a practicing attorney, honorary sheriff's deputy for Bristol County, and a known associate of murder victim Rochelle Clifford. On April 3, 1988, before she disappeared, New Bedford police found Ponte in possession of a pistol, accused of threatening a man he claimed had raped Rochelle, but Clifford disappeared a short time later, with the case still unresolved. On June 7, police questioned Ponte again, after they found him sitting with a young woman in a parked car, on a street notorious for prostitutes. Ponte claimed the woman had "lured" him there, and a quick search led to her arrest for possession of drug paraphernalia. Ponte, for his part, was carrying a gun. His permit was at home, he told the officers, and while he promised to retrieve it for them, Ponte never reappeared. On June 8, he was charged with possessing and unlicensed weapon, but the charge was thrown out one day later by a New Bedford magistrate.

Apparently tired of the hassles, Ponte closed his law practice in September 1988 and moved to Florida a month later. Police called the move suspicious, noting that Ponte sold his house at a reported price $100,000 below the fair market value, making just enough on the deal to cover some outstanding debts. Three days after Christmas, when Ponte missed a scheduled interview with New Bedford police concerning the recent murders, one detective allegedly threatened to "screw him in the media." True or not, the first front-page story naming Ponte as a suspect in the Highway Killer case broke nine days later, police describing their search of the attorney's former home and office. According to authorities, a dog trained to sniff out human corpses had scored a "hit" on the carpet in Ponte's old office. A day later, on January 7, a local drug dealer supposedly approached police, ratting Ponte out as a regular patron from 1984 through 1987.

Troubles began to multiply for Ponte, with the new rash of publicity. On January 18, he was back in court, charged with assault for the April 1988 gun-waving incident. Five days later, a New Bedford prostitute regaled police with stories of Ponte's alleged sexual exploits and drug abuse. Before the month was out, however, Ponte scored his first legal victory, winning indefinite postponement on the firearms charge, because a judge found the police collection of blood and hair samples (for use in the Highway Killer investigation) unreasonable in a case of simple assault.

A special grand jury was impaneled to investigate the Highway Killer case, and its first session was held on March 2, 1989, continuing sporadically through July 1990. Most of the testimony focused on Ponte, resulting in his March 29, 1990 indictment (with three codefendants) on charges of conspiring to possess cocaine. Back in Florida, on June 11, 1990, Ponte was jailed for leaving the scene of an accident, after a neighbor claimed he tried to hit her with his car. Riding with Ponte at the time of his arrest was a young woman sought by police for violating probation. In custody, the officers noted bruises on her neck, and she soon accused Ponte of assaulting her on two separate occasions, within the week before his latest arrest. On June 12, Ponte was slapped with brand-new felony charges, including aggravated assault, aggravated battery, false imprisonment, and using a firearm in commission of a felony. Two days later, Ponte's accuser recanted in court, telling the judge her statement was extorted by police withholding medication until she agreed to press false charges. It should have been a win for Ponte, but on June 15 the judge *increased* his bond to a whopping $205,000, citing the arrival of a Massachusetts police affidavit, naming the lawyer as a murder suspect.

New Bedford's special grand jury finally got around to indicting Ponte on one count of first-degree murder — for victim Rochelle Clifford — on August 17, 1990. Ponte pled not guilty at his arraignment, and bond was set at $50,000. Local authorities seemed confident at first, but it was all for show. In March 1991, special prosecutor Paul Buckley was appointed to investigate the Highway Killer case from scratch. Four months later, he announced that Kenneth Ponte's murder charge would not be tried.

"It would get to the judge," Buckley told reporters, "and he would rule as a matter of law that there is no evidence."

The charge was formally withdrawn by New Bedford's district attorney on July 29, 1991, and Ponte returned to the practice of law, cleared of any lingering suspicion by the FBI forensics lab. (One of his first clients was Tony DeGrazia's mother, pursuing a wrongful death claim against New Bedford's D.A.) At this writing, the case of Massachusetts's most lethal serial killer since the Boston Strangler remains unsolved, with no suspect in sight.

Highway murders — Germany (1935)

In September 1935, authorities in Berlin were plagued by a sudden rash of unexplained — and unsolved — violent crimes. While firemen were kept busy with an outbreak of arson incidents, blamed on "malignant maniacs," other culprits were stretching taut wires across rural highways by night, wrecking cars and injuring or killing their occupants. Robbery was suspected in one or two of the incidents, but for the most part, victims were not molested after their vehicles crashed.

According to the local press, "The similarity of the method of fastening the wires leads the police to believe a maniac is the chief culprit."

Without motives or suspects, investigators could do little but stand by and watch as the body count rose. Berlin auto dealers were more resourceful, cashing in on the panic while it lasted by offering their customers saw-toothed attachments for the front of their cars, designed to clip cables on impact.

Hit-and-run murders — California (1991)

On December 19, 1991, authorities in Porterville, California, announced that two female joggers and one male bicyclist had recently been killed in separate hit-and-run attacks, apparently deliberate and carried out at random. Eyewitnesses described a vehicle with two male occupants, but at last report, police had no firm leads on the identity of their local road warriors, and the thrill-killers remained at large.

Hollywood murders — California (1982)

On the afternoon of July 30, 1982, the bodies of two dead boys were discovered within 100 yards of each other, on an embankment of the Hollywood Freeway. Three weeks passed before the victims were identified as 13-year-old Raymond Davis from Pittsburg, California, and 16-year-old Robert Avila of Los Angeles. Davis had disappeared while visiting his mother in the neighborhood of Echo Park, and forensic tests attributed his death to strangulation. Robert Avila lived 12 blocks away from Davis's mother, although they did not know each other, and no cause of death was determined in his case. Medical examiners reported that the boys had died a month apart, but the disposal of their bodies in such close proximity points to a single hand in both cases. Neither victim has thus far been credited to southern California "freeway killers" William Bonin (executed February 23, 1996 for 10 murders) or Randy Kraft (awaiting execution for sixteen homicides, suspected of 51 others).

"Honolulu Strangler" — Hawaii (1985-86)

It was, perhaps, inevitable that America's vacation spot would share the notoriety of other states where random killers have made headlines, claiming innocent victims at will. As residents of Anchorage, Alaska, learned from savage stalker Robert Hansen during 1983, mere geographic isolation does not guarantee immunity against the modern murder epidemic. Unlike the Hansen case, however, Hawaii's first case of serial murder remains unsolved, the slayer still at large.

Vicky Purdy, 25 years old, was first to die. A twice-married housewife, employed at a local video shop, she was abducted and strangled by persons unknown on May 29, 1985. When found, Purdy still wore her jumpsuit and jewelry, with no indications of robbery or sexual assault.

On January 15, 1986, 17-year-old Regina Sakamoto vanished on her way to school, moments after phoning her boyfriend to say she had just missed her bus. Strangled and raped, her partially nude body was fished out of Keehi Lagoon a month later.

Denise Hughes, a 21-year-old navy wife, failed to report for her regular job on January 30, 1986. Listed as a missing person, she was found in a drainage canal on February 1, strangled to death, hands bound behind her, body wrapped in a blue plastic tarp.

Two months later, on March 26, the killer claimed 25-year-old Louise Medeiros, a single mother three months pregnant at the time she died. Lost en route to her boyfriend's apartment, Medeiros was found dead on April 2, hands tied behind her back, wearing only a blouse. Authorities did not release the cause of death.

Linda Pesce, 36, was last seen alive a month later on April 29, reported missing by her roommate the following day. On May 3, her body was found at Sand Island, arms bound behind her back, the cause of death once more remaining secret at the wish of homicide investigators who insist one killer is responsible for all five murders.

A "profile" of the slayer, drawn up by FBI agents, describes him as a white man in his late 30s or early 40s, driving a light-colored cargo van. Six days after Linda Pesce's body was discovered, Honolulu officers detained a 43-year-old suspect for questioning, but he was released without charges after 10 hours of interrogation. At this writing, the case remains open, with no arrest in sight.

Hospital for Sick Children — Canada (1980-83)

Between June 1980 and March 1981, the cardiac ward at Toronto's Hospital for Sick Children experienced a traumatic 616 percent leap in infant mortality, with the number of actual deaths pegged between 21 and 43 babies in various police and media reports. The first "suspicious" death was that of 18-day-old Laura Woodstock, lost on June 30, 1980. Two months later, after 20 deaths, a group of nurses on the ward voiced their concern to resident cardiologists, and a fruitless investigation was launched on September 5, in the interest of resolving "morale problems."

Still, the deaths continued, and on March 12, 1981, a staff physician aired his personal suspicions in a conversation with Toronto's coroner. An autopsy of the latest victim, 27-day-old Kevin Garnett, found 13 times the normal level of digoxin — a drug used to regulate heart rhythm, itself fatal if taken in too large a dose. On March 21, following more deaths and discovery of elevated digoxin levels in two more corpses, the coroner met with police and hospital administrators in an emergency session. Members of the cardiac nursing team were placed on three days' leave while officers began to search their lockers, comparing work schedules to the dates and times of suspicious deaths.

On March 22, with the locker searches under way, another baby died on the cardiac ward at Sick Children. Justin Cook is generally named as the last victim in a bizarre string of slayings, his death attributed to a massive digoxin overdose, inflicted by persons unknown. Three days later, police arrested nurse Susan Nelles on one count of murder, adding three identical charges to the list on March 27. As "evidence" of her involvement in the crimes, officers referred to certain "odd" remarks and facial expressions mentioned by other nurses, noting that 24 of the suspicious deaths occurred on Nelles's shift, between 1:00 and 5:00 A.M.

With Nelles on leave pending trial, bizarre events continued at the hospital. In September 1981, nurse Phyllis Trayner found capsules of propanolol — another heart regulator — in the salad she was eating for lunch, and a second nurse spooned more capsules out of her soup. Administrators had no explanation for the incident, and rumors flourished of a "phantom" or a "maniac" stalking the hospital corridors.

A preliminary hearing in the case of Susan Nelles opened on July 11, 1982, with prosecutors citing sixteen other "carbon copy" murders in addition to the four already charged. Four months later, on May 21, the pending charges were unconditionally dismissed, the presiding judge describing Nelles as "an excellent nurse" with "an excellent record." At the same time, he noted that five of the hospital deaths were apparently murders, committed by persons unknown.

Fresh out of suspects, the state launched its first judicial probe of the case on May 25, requesting assistance from the Atlanta-based Centers for Disease Control four months later. CDC's report on 36 submitted cases called 18 deaths "suspicious," with seven listed as probable homicides; another 10 cases were "consistent" with deliberate digoxin poisoning, but there was insufficient evidence for a definitive conclusion.

A new judicial inquiry was ordered on April 21, 1983, and Gary Murphy, six months old, died on the cardiac ward two days later, his passing notable for "elevated digoxin levels" discovered in postmortem testing. Murphy's death was excluded from the "official" list when hearings began on June 21, with testimony pointing vaguely toward a different suspect on the staff. By February 1984, cardiac nurses were voicing suspicions against Phyllis Trayner, one reporting that she saw Trayner inject infant Allana Miller's I.V. bottle with an unknown drug three hours before the baby died, on March 21, 1981. Trayner flatly denied all charges of impropriety, and the commission left her denials unchallenged, refusing to name a suspect in its January 1985 report. That document describes eight infant deaths as murders, while another 13 are listed as "highly suspicious" or merely "suspicious." Fifteen years down the road, a solution to the case is improbable at best.

"House of Horrors" murders — Texas (1990-92)

On July 25, 1990, Houston police were dispatched to 703 Pacific Street, in the affluent Montrose district, to investigate foul odors emanating from a stylish townhouse. Patrolmen recognized the stench of death, and forced their way inside when there was no response to pounding on the door. They found the living room equipped with a ceiling-mounted winch and chain, complete with gleaming metal hook attached, and trailed the sickly odor to a bedroom, where a metal coffin lay atop a sturdy wooden table, sealed with duct tape. Opening the casket, they found a dead man swathed in plastic, later identified as 25-year-old James Robert Lutz, sought by authorities for violating his parole on a 1988 narcotics conviction. Scattered around the death scene, police also found leather garments, chains and handcuffs, all suggestive of some sadomasochistic bondage ritual. Postmortem testing ruled the death a homicide by means of suffocation.

Houston, like any other large metropolis, hosts a more-or-less identifiable gay community, where police are more often viewed as enemies than as defenders of alternate life styles. The Montrose district was renowned as such an area, but certain residents were willing to discuss the latest murder with authorities, referring vaguely to a group of S&M devotees who had dubbed themselves the "Brotherhood of Pain." Such rumors led police to speculate on possible occult involvement in the murder, but their only solid lead quickly proved to be a dead-end. The owner of the townhouse, one Ted Lenz, was openly gay, but he also had an air-tight alibi for the time of the murder: he had been hospitalized, recuperating from brain surgery. Questioned by police, he denied any knowledge of James Lutz, the casket in his bedroom or the events leading to his untimely death. In fact, Lenz told investigators, he had no idea how a coffin had come to reside in his bedroom.

There the matter rested for the next two years, until Houston police were called out on another "dead body" report. This time, the address was 600 Fargo Street, and they found their man in the attic. Ted Lenz was nude, except for a leather belt around his waist and a clamp on his penis, surrounded by bondage magazines and traces of white powder that proved to be cocaine. Autopsy results attributed his death to heart failure, triggered by coke, and the case was written off as one more example of autoerotic misadventure, leading to an early grave.

There was no accident involved three months later, on September 23, however, when patrolmen were called back to Lenz's former residence. Incredibly, another corpse was waiting for them in what some wags had begun to call the "house of horrors." Nude, hog-tied and beaten to death by persons unknown, the latest victim was identified as 49-year-old Robert Williams. While it is clear that Lenz, himself deceased for 60 days, had no link to the latest murder in his former digs, that is the *only* thing police can state with any certainty about the sadomasochistic homicides committed at 703 Pacific Street. To date, six years and counting since the second murder, they are still without a suspect or coherent motive in the grisly crimes.

Human sacrifice — Florida (1989)

For more than three decades, police investigators, occult researchers and self-described practitioners of ritual magic have discussed the problem of modern human sacrifice reported from five continents. One common feature of such reports — dismissed by skeptics as a gruesome flight of fantasy — is the removal and consumption of a sacrificial victim's heart. Despite outspoken disbelief in certain quarters, there can be no doubt that such crimes have occurred, committed both by self-styled Satanists and by adherents of the Afro-Caribbean *palo mayombe* cult. In Wyoming, during 1970, Satanist Stanley Baker (a confessed member of the sinister **"Four P" movement**) was sentenced to life in prison for murdering a game warden and eating his victim's heart. Two decades later, in 1989, 14 members of the Mexican cult led by Adolfo Constanzo were imprisoned for a series of nearly identical murders, committed outside Matamoros.

Four months after the discovery of Constanzo's heart-eating cult, a similar case was reported from the Florida Keys. In July 1989, 39-year-old Sherry Perisho was found floating in the ocean with her heart cut out. A short time earlier and 10 miles away, 20-year-old Lisa Sanders had been found in a rock grotto on No Name Key, strangled and robbed of her heart.

As homicide detectives told the press, concerning that still-unsolved crime, "All we can determine is that someone killed her for her heart."

Thus far, officials in the Sunshine State are disinclined to speculate on whether the slayings have ceased... or, perhaps, that the heart-hunting killers have found a more efficient method of disposal.

Human sacrifice — Mexico (1987-??)

Mexico, home of the heart-harvesting Aztecs, has also experienced its share of human sacrifice in modern times, from the ritual bloodletting of the Hernandez brothers in the 1960s to the grisly deeds of Adolfo Constanzo, linked with at least 23 sacrificial murders between 1987 and 1989. Police in Mexico City investigated the ritual slayings of 60 adults and

14 infants during the same period, with more grisly deaths reported from around Vera Cruz. With the exposure of Constanzo's cult, it was tempting to blame him for all such crimes, but in fact, the ceremonies have continued since his death in a shootout with police.

As prosecutor Guillermo Ibarra explained, "We would like to say, yes, Constanzo did them all, and poof, all those cases are solved. And the fact is, we believe he was responsible for some of them, though we'll never prove it now. But he didn't commit all of those murders, which means someone else did. Someone who is still out there."

A lead to the identity of one such practitioner was offered to police by surviving associates of the Constanzo cult. In June of 1989, the sister of Constanzo disciple Martin Quintana (killed in the same showdown with authorities) told investigator's that Adolfo's first *madrina* ("godmother") was still at large and practicing her blood magic around Guadalajara. And from jail, shortly before he died of AIDS, cult killer Omar Orea declared, "I don't think that the religion will end with us, because it has a lot of people in it. They have found a temple in Monterey that isn't even related to us. It will continue."

Human sacrifice — Nigeria (1987-??)

In parts of Africa, practitioners of *ju-ju* typically sacrifice goats and other animals, but they also have ritual uses for man — "the animal that eats salt." Rampant promiscuity encouraged during periodic harvest festivals results in the birth of "throwaway babies" who are sometimes donated to the cult by their unmarried mothers, subsequently murdered by *ju-ju* priests and processed into various potions, powders, soaps and lotions. Adult victims are preferred for the ritual of *iko-awo,* in which a man or woman is flayed alive, then gutted, the liver preserved in a plastic box, while the corpse is washed and hung in a portable wardrobe, then taken home as a "spirit slave" by the client who sponsored the sacrifice.

Retired *ju-ju* priest Isaiah Oke describes one such ritual in which he assisted, performed on behalf of a colonel in the Nigerian army. In July 1987, *Nigerian Tribune* reported the case of a man who hired a *ju-ju* priest to sacrifice his own 13-year-old nephew. The boy was decapitated, his body dumped in a canal, while his head resided in a box at his uncle's home. The relic was later introduced as evidence in court, with the uncle and his parents — the victim's grandparents — convicted of murder. Six months later, in Onitsha, Nigeria, a 34-year-old man was found at home with his throat cut, his ears and genitals removed, and the room "sprayed with blood." A ritually decorated machete lay beneath a cushion, near the corpse.

In May 1988, the *African Guardian,* published in Lagos, Nigeria, declared that native shamans were using human blood, plus the breasts and pubic hair of murdered women, to produce magic charms. A short time later, Nigerian essayist Wilson Asekombe wrote, "human sacrifice will soon become the number two cause of accidental death in West Africa, second only to automobile accidents."

Human sacrifice — Peru (1940-??)

Ritual sacrifice of human beings remains a daily fact of life in Peru, dating back to the time of the Inca Empire. For some practitioners, the offering of human lives is believed to insure bountiful crops, control the weather, and prevent natural catastrophes such as floods and earthquakes. Such rituals, called "paying the earth," are also employed by wealthy businessmen, ranging from mine owners to beer distributors, to guarantee continued prosperity. Various local festivals and holidays demand a human sacrifice, and regional narcotics smugglers — as in Mexico and elsewhere — rarely make a move without spilling blood to appease the gods in advance. In parts of Peru, a sect of cultists called *liquichiri* devote themselves solely to the extraction of fat from human victims. The end product, called *cebo,* is believed to be especially useful in rituals aimed at acquiring new vehicles, ranging from automobiles to airplanes and even spacecraft.

While isolated cases have been documented throughout Peru from the 1940s to the present day, some *yatiri* — shamans for hire — have traditional killing grounds of their own. One such, near Puno, is Mount Santa Barbara, the site of several gruesome sacrifices in the early 1980s. A female victim, killed there in 1982, was found with her breasts cut off, her vagina slashed, and her face painted black.

Around Yunguyo, ritual murders are so common that Mayor Horacio Benavides circulated a petition in May 1988, calling on the provincial prosecutor's office to investigate. Signed by local nuns, together with civil and military authorities, the petition charged that "around these places there are abnormal elements or people who are practicing paganism or perhaps the narcotrafficker *pistacos* [vampires]."

To date, despite several well-publicized cases resulting in prosecution and occasional convictions, the ceremonial murders continue.

"Ironman" — South Africa (1970s)

Time and distance make the details sketchy for this South African case, involving a killer who ambushed late-night strollers in the small township of Atteridgeville, near Pretoria, beating at least seven persons to death with an iron bar, afterward robbing their corpses. The grisly crimes amplified paranoia in a region that has seen more than its share of unsolved serial murders, since the depredations of the **"Atteridgeville Mutilator,"** some two decades earlier. "Ironman" has apparently retired, his crime spree ended, but police still have no clue to his identity, and no solution to the murders is anticipated.

"I-35 murders" — Texas (1976-81)

Interstate Highway 35 covers some 740 miles from Salina, Kansas, in the north, to Laredo, Texas, on the Mexican border. More than half the highway's length — in excess of 420 miles — runs north-to-south across the Lone Star State, past Gainesville, Denton, splitting to accommodate the twin giants of Dallas-Fort Worth, reuniting above Hillsboro for the long run south, through Waco, Temple, Austin, San Antonio. Between 1976 and 1981, the Texas stretch of I-35 was the hunting ground for a killer (or killers) who preyed on hitchhikers and motorists in trouble, claiming at least 22 victims in five years' time. Some officers believe the stalker is at large today.

The first "official" victim was 21-year-old Lesa Haley, found two miles north of Waxahachie, Texas, on August 23, 1976. Bound for Oklahoma City, traveling by thumb, she was last seen climbing into a van at Waco. Haley was stabbed in the neck with an awl before she was dumped on the shoulder of I-35.

On the night of November 5, 1978, 19-year-old Frank Key and 18-year-old Rita Salazar ran out of gas on a date in Austin. Next morning, Key was found north of Georgetown, shot nine times with a .22-caliber pistol, including four postmortem shots in the back of the head. Salazar's body, shot six times with the same gun, was found on a frontage road near Waco.

Sharon Schilling, age 27, was found on a street in San Marcos, Texas, on Labor Day 1979, a few blocks from I-35. Shot once in the abdomen with a .410-gauge shotgun, she died on September 13, without regaining consciousness. Less than a month later, Sandra Dubbs was kidnapped after her car broke down on the drive from St. Louis to San Antonio. Her body, stabbed 35 times, was discovered in Travis County, Texas. On Halloween, the strangled body of a "Jane Doe" victim, nude except for a pair of orange socks, was found in a highway culvert near Georgetown.

On June 23, 1980, victim Rodney Massey, shot four times, was found in a field near Temple, Texas, 70 miles north of the state capital at Austin. On July 9 of that year, an Hispanic "Jane Doe" was discovered near Pflugerville, stabbed 27 times with a screwdriver; her pants had been pulled down, although there was no evidence of sexual assault. In May 1981, yet another "Jane Doe" was found near New Braunfels, shot six times in the head with a .25-caliber pistol.

Authorities convened in Austin to discuss the murders on October 30, 1981, but their review of the case produced no solid results. Two years later, serial slayers Henry Lucas and Ottis Toole confessed to most of the I-35 murders — and Lucas was sentenced to die on conviction in the "orange socks" case — but subsequent recantation of the Lucas confessions, in 1985, returned several cases to the "unsolved" column. Texas authorities remain divided on the subject of Lucas's guilt, or the involvement of multiple killers in the I-35 murder series.

"I-45 Killer" — Texas (1982-97)

In the 15 years from 1982 to 1997, 42 teenage girls and young women have been kidnapped from small towns and suburbs along Interstate Highway 45, between Houston, and Galveston, Texas. Many of those were later found dead, described by local authorities and FBI agents as the victims of one or more serial killers prowling the 50 miles of wide-open highway. Despite the four-year focus of police attention on a single suspect, no evidence has been found to support an indictment, and by early 1998, it appeared that authorities had been mistaken in their choice of targets all along.

The most recent victim in the murder series was 17-year-old Jessica Cain, last seen alive while performing with a local theater group, one night in August 1997. Following the show, she left for home, driving alone down I-45, but she never reached her destination. Jessica's father found her pickup truck abandoned on the shoulder of the highway, and her name was added to the ever-growing victims list.

By that time, police believed they knew the man responsible. Their suspect, Robert William Abel, was a former NASA engineer and operator of a horseback riding ranch near League City, in Brazoria County. Abel first came under suspicion in 1993, when the corpses of four missing girls were found in the desert, near his property. FBI agents spent a grand total of two hours with League City police, sketching a psychological profile of the killer based on such traits as "intelligence level" and assumed proximity to the crime scene. Abel's ex-wife pitched in with tales of alleged domestic abuse ("externalized anger," in FBI parlance) and claims that Abel sometimes beat his horses (a charge that he staunchly denies). The punch line of the federal profile was direct and to the point — "Serial sexual offender: Robert William Abel."

That profile alone was deemed sufficient to support a search warrant, and police moved in, seeking — among other things — a cache of nude photos described by Abel's wife. In fact, they *did* find photographs, some 6,000 in all, of which precisely two depicted naked women, neither of them victims in the murder case. No evidence was found at Abel's ranch connecting him with any sort of criminal activity.

Frustrated in their search for clues, League City police took the unusual step of naming Abel publicly as a suspect in the I-45 murder case. He was "innocent until proven guilty," of course, but in the absence of alternate suspects, his life became a waking hell on earth, with death threats pouring in from neighbors and the relatives of sundry victims. One such, Tim Miller, having lost his daughter Laura to the I-45 killer, launched a personal crusade of daily "reminders" to Abel, including armed visits to his home and threats of murder recorded on Abel's answering machine. League City's finest, still convinced that Abel was their man, took no steps to prevent the harassment, and stalled when Abel volunteered to take a polygraph exam. In fact, while League City's assistant police chief publicly "welcomed" Abel's cooperation in the case, said cooperation only made matters worse, since such behavior is common among serial killers.

It was early 1998 before Robert Abel got to take his long-sought polygraph, courtesy of the *20/20* television show. In fact, two tests were administered by a retired FBI agent, with Abel denying any knowledge of the four victims found near his ranch in 1993. He hesitated in responding to one surprise question, dealing with rumors of a young victim's drug use, and was rated "untruthful" in respect to that answer, but a second test, administered without trick questions, found him to be truthful on all counts. FBI agents in Houston called the *20/20* test "extremely significant," admitting that the four-year-old profile of Abel was "poor quality" work on the part of their colleagues. In fact, they told the world, Robert Abel had been eliminated as a suspect in their eyes, and even Tim Miller appeared to repent his harassment of Abel, with a televised apology.

Not so the lawmen in League City. Abel may indeed be innocent, they say, but since they have no solid evidence to clear him by their own exacting standards, Abel "is still swimming in the pool of suspects." One is tempted to ask *what* pool, since vague local references to "other suspects" always stop short of naming alternative candidates. Texas courts have barred Abel from filing a lawsuit to clear his name, ruling that League City police are within their rights to publicize him as a suspect, even when the original FBI profile has been retracted. The *real* I-45 Killer, meanwhile, remains unidentified and presumably still at large.

"I-70 Killer" — United States (1992-94?)

In the spring of 1992, Midwestern merchants were briefly terrorized by a killer who roamed across three states, striking randomly at small "specialty shops" near Interstate Highway 70, stealing small amounts of cash and executing shop proprietors or employees. The murder spree ended as suddenly and mysteriously as it had begun, only to resume — some authorities say — a year later, in a different part of the country. Six murders are definitely linked to one unknown subject by ballistics evidence, while authorities suspect the same man (with different weapons) in at least four other homicides.

The first definite victim was 26-year-old Robin Fuldauer, gunned down on the job at an Indianapolis shoestore, on April 8, 1992. Three days later, in Wichita, Kansas, the same .22-caliber weapon was used to kill proprietor Patricia Magers, 26, and 23-year-old employee Patricia Smith, at a small bridal shop. The shooter was seen by at least one witness, who assisted in the preparation of a published sketch, but all in vain. On April 27, the only male victim in the series, Michael McCown, was shot and killed in a Terre Haute, Indiana, ceramics shop. Six days later, on May 3, Nancy Kitzmiller was slain in St. Charles, Missouri, at a shop specializing in Western boots. The last "official" victim, 37-year-old Sarah Blessing, was killed in a Raytown, Missouri, video store on May 7. Once again, there was a witness, who confirmed descriptions of the gunman seen in Wichita.

According to police in the five cities where the gunman struck, their suspect was a white male in his 20s or 30s, 5-foot-6 or -7, with sandy blond or reddish hair, sometimes sporting a day's worth of beard stubble. Ballistics tests confirmed a single weapon used in all six murders, and the small amounts of cash stolen in each case — never more than $400 from any one shop — convinced authorities that they were dealing with a serial killer who "cased" his targets in advance, searching for attractive brunette victims. (Police speculated that Michael McCown, who wore long hair and earrings, may have been mistaken for a woman as the killer watched him from a distance, through the windows of his shop.) In each case, the victims were found in the rear of their stores, shot in the back of the head, with no signs of a struggle at the scene. Though all but one of the victims were attractive females, there was never any sign of an attempted sexual assault.

The murders were a nine-day wonder across the Midwest, but official interest faded quickly in the stretch. Within a week of the final murder, St. Charles disbanded its task force, with Raytown following suit on May 21. Officially, law enforcement spokesmen promised that the crimes would be investigated "at nearly the same level" by individual detectives. But in fact, they had nothing to go on, admitting for the record that solution of the mystery would probably rely on some fatal mistake by the killer, rather than any great detective work.

A brief, faint ray of hope was seen in early June, when authorities in Dyersburg, Tennessee, announced a "possible link" between the I-70 murders and a local pair of homicides. Suspect Donnie Waterhouse, age 37, had been sought for questioning since February, when his mother and stepfather were found shot to death in their home. A trail of blood at the scene and more stains in an abandoned pickup truck suggested Waterhouse may have wounded himself somehow, while killing his parents. Dyersburg authorities noted Donnie's "resemblance" to the I-70 gunman — 5-foot-6, 145-155 pounds, blond and balding — but there was nothing else to link him with the Midwest slayings, and the slim lead ultimately came to naught.

By the first anniversary of the I-70 murders, police across the Midwest were beginning to relax, indulging in the wishful notion that their subject might be dead, or locked up on some unrelated charge. By summer's end, however, they had started hearing rumbles from the state of Texas, where another unknown gunman had begun to prey on lookalike victims, in strikingly similar settings.

The first to die in Texas was 51-year-old Mary Ann Glasscock, shot execution-style in her Fort Worth antique shop, on September 25, 1993. On November 1, after Amy Vess was killed in an Arlington dancewear shop. Texas authorities described a link to the I-70 murder series as "definitely possible." Before the month was out, another shop clerk was killed under similar circumstances, in Dallas, and January 15, 1994, witnessed the murder of a fourth Texas victim, this time in Houston.

Supporters of the linkage theory had no solid evidence of a connection in the crimes — ballistics did not match the Midwest homicides. But they pointed to the similarity of victims and targets: dark-haired women killed in shops adjacent to Interstate 35/45 — which, in turn, leads back to I-70 at Salina, Kansas, to the north. Captain Chris Dahlke, with the Indianapolis Police Department, was one who saw the connection, citing a "strong possibility" that the Texas murders were committed by the unnamed I-70 gunman.

Perhaps.

If lawmen in Texas and Indiana are correct, their quarry is responsible for at least 10 murders... and has dropped out of sight once again, with no new crimes reported since January 1994. If they are wrong about the link, then Texas has a random killer all its own — a circumstance that would be no surprise in one of the nation's five worst states for incidence of serial murder. Either way, the cases have remained unsolved, and barring a spontaneous confession from the killer(s), no solution is anticipated.

Infant murders — New York (1915)

On September 29, 1915, Joseph Miller, night watchman at a pier on South 11th Street, in the Williamsburg section of New York City, noticed two dark objects floating in the Hudson River. Scrambling into a boat, Miller followed the current and fished out the pieces of flotsam, appalled to discover that two baby girls had been thrown in the river to drown.

A coroner's report revealed the victims to be less than two days old. Worse yet, a scan of recent files told homicide detectives that a dozen other infants, three days old or less, had been recovered from the Hudson in the past six weeks. Found floating anywhere from South 11th Street to Broadway, most of the tiny victims had been tossed in the water naked to drown; a few were bundled up so tightly that they must have suffocated prior to entering the river, as no water was discovered in their lungs.

Without a single clue to work on, homicide investigators organized a special team to prowl the waterfront by night, but they were flying blind. A spokesman for the force announced that someone was "systematically engaged in the slaying of new-born babies," but a recognition of the problem offered no solution. With publicity, the grim parade of tiny corpses ceased... or, possibly, the killers simply found a new means of disposal.

"Jack the Ripper" — Georgia (1911-12)

In the 12 months between May 1911 and May 1912, black residents of Atlanta, Georgia, were terrorized by the activities of a knife-wielding maniac who preyed exclusively on women of color, leaving them with throats slashed and bodies mutilated after death. Inevitably, he was christened "Jack the Ripper" by the local press, and like his namesake in 19th-century London, he was never captured or identified. Unlike his predecessor, though, Atlanta's Ripper claimed an even 20 victims, while the original Jack had satisfied himself with five.

The early murders in Atlanta were committed with a shocking regularity, the slayer claiming victims on seven successive Saturday nights, between May 20 and July 1, 1911. White newsmen were quick to point out that the victims were all attractive, well-dressed mulattos, with no "out-and-out black women" slain by the stalker. In each case, there was evidence of the woman being choked unconscious, after which her throat was slit from ear to ear and "the carving of the victim — always in the same area of the body — begins."

None of the women had been raped, but from the nature of the mutilations, tactfully unspecified in media reports, it was apparent that the crimes were sexual in nature. As in the case of London's Jack (and nearly all his imitators), newsmen noted that the killer "seems to possess some knowledge of anatomy."

Number seven on the Ripper's hit list was 40-year-old Lena Sharp, slain in the late hours of July 1, her head nearly severed, her body "horribly mutilated" after death. Concerned when Sharp was late arriving home, her daughter started searching in the streets. She was accosted by a well-dressed black man, but his mannerisms frightened her, and as she turned to flee he stabbed her in the back. Escaping with her life, she offered homicide investigators a description of the man, but no arrest resulted from the lead.

The Ripper's first near-miss resulted in a change of schedule, slowing down his pace. He would require 10 months to claim another 13 victims in Atlanta, mutilating his last target — a "comely yellow girl" of 19 years — on Friday, May 10, 1912. A large reward collected by the black community produced no takers, and the case remains unsolved today. It is, perhaps, coincidental that the years 1911 and 1912 also witnessed the unsolved ax murders of 49 mulatto victims in Texas and Louisiana.

"Jack the Ripper" — New York (1915)

At five years old, Lenora Cohn was used to running errands for her mother. She was not required to leave the New York City tenement that housed her family, except on rare occasions, and her chores were never rigorous, but she was learning to rely upon herself. The lesson would have served her well, had she survived.

At 7:30 on the evening of March 19, 1915, Lenora's mother sent her for a pail of milk. It was a simple task — she merely had to run downstairs — and neighbors saw her toiling homeward with a brimming pail 10 minutes later. She was nearly home, already climbing toward the third-floor landing of her own apartment, when she passed out of their sight. At 7:45, Augusta Johnson heard what sounded like an infant's cry outside her door, directly opposite the stairwell. Peering out, she saw a small child lying on her face, apparently the victim of a fall. Concerned, Miss Johnson rushed to help. The child was cradled in her arms before she saw the dark blood welling out of ragged knife wounds, soaking through the tiny dress.

Police were summoned to the tenement, along Third Avenue, but they found little in the way of clues. Lenora's pail of milk was sitting at the bottom of the stairs, where she was found, and not a drop had spilled. Detectives scouring the tenement found drops of blood on two steps of another staircase, on the far side of the house, but their significance remains obscure. Lenora's left hand clutched a tuft of short, gray hair, and bruises on her throat reflected violent contact with a larger-than-average hand. She had apparently been choked unconscious, stabbed and mutilated afterward with something like a leather worker's knife.

As if the nightmare of a murdered child were not enough, Lenora's mother soon became the target of sadistic letters, written by an individual who claimed to be the killer. Picking up on garish headlines in the press, the author signed his letters "Jack the Ripper," after London's gaslight ghoul of 1888. The notes were handed over to police, who passed them on to United States postal inspectors. On April 29, a 27-year-old Austrian named Edward Richman was arrested in connection with the mailings, quickly cleared of actual involvement in the murder.

But Richman's arrest did not stop the letters. One day after he was jailed, another note was posted to Lenora's mother. It read:

> Dear Mrs. Cohn: Just a line to let you know that the person that is accused of writing letters to you is innocent. I am the fellow that wrote you the letters, and as I said before a man that keeps his ears open and mouth shut will always get along and never get caught. Some day thats if I get the chair I may confess. But as long as I am out they can never get me. Kindly give the enclosed letter to the police and tell them I wrote it. From
>
> H.B. RICHMOND, Jack-the-Ripper

Enclosed with the letter was a second envelope, marked "Give this to the police." Inside was a letter that read:

> Why don't you drop this case? You know that man can't get me in 100 years from now so its no youse in sirchen for me. I am a wise guy you know but wise guys never get caught. You may think that I am a fool to write you But I am writing just to show that I aint afraid. Mr.Richmond [sic] is innocent of the letter which you accuse him of writing to Mrs. Cohn. I am the one that wrote all of them. As I told you in one of my letters that is going to be the biggest murders to be committed in N.Y. that was ever known. Now do you see I am true.
>
> H.B. RICHMOND
> JACK-THE-RIPPER

Police initially suspected Edward Richman of attempting to divert suspicion from himself, and visitors who called on him in jail were shadowed as potential cohorts, but no link between the suspect and the final "Ripper" letters was established.

On May 3, the threat was realized. Charles Murray, four years old, did not respond when members of his family called him in from play at 7:30 in the evening. A hasty search was organized, uncovering his mutilated body tucked beneath a staircase in the family's First Avenue tenement. Police responding to the call announced that Murray's killer "very likely" was the same man who had slashed Lenora Cohn on March 19. The victim's sister, Mamie, offered a description of the killer, but police eventually dismissed it as the product of a child's imagination.

Meanwhile, homicide detectives and patrolmen fanned out through the neighborhood in search of clues. Five doors up the street, they met the frantic parents of Louisa Niedig, six, who had apparently escaped the killer's clutches moments earlier. While playing on the street outside a bakery, waiting for her aunt to get off work, Louisa was approached by a neatly dressed man wearing a black derby hat and sporting a dark mustache. When she refused to speak with him, he grabbed her arm and dragged Louisa through an open doorway, but her screams brought neighbors on the run and her attacker fled before she suffered any harm.

At 47th Street and Third, Patrolman Curry was approached by several girls, aged eight to 12, who said two men were chasing them with knives. Just then, the suspects came around a corner, stopping short at sight of Curry's badge. When Curry ordered them to halt, they rushed him, drawing blades and slashing him across the hand before he battered one assailant to the ground. The other fled, abandoning a stunned James Daly to his fate, but no connection was established to the Ripper crimes.

Reports kept pouring in, but all of them were vague, and none contained the crucial information that would crack the case. At Stuyvesant Park, 12- and 13-year-old girls informed detectives that a stranger with a dark mustache and Van Dyke beard had been "annoying" them for several months. Inspector Joseph Faurot told reporters that "the ripper type... is one of the shrewdest and most elusive of criminals," an opinion seconded by Coroner Israel Feinberg. More murders were expected, Feinberg said, unless the killer could be found "within 10 days."

The panic spread. On May 8, 50 men and boys attacked a Ripper suspect after two small boys accused him of "suspicious" actions. Rescued by police, the bloodied victim proved to be a Polish shoemaker, visiting friends on the street where he once had his shop.

On Sunday, May 9, two neighborhood housewives found crude, penciled notes on their doormats, signed "The Ripper Jack." In each, the author threatened death to children in the target families; they would be killed on Monday afternoon, the letters said, or kidnapped from their homes that night if all else failed. There were no incidents on Monday, and on May 12 officers secured confessions from two girls who wrote the notes "for fun." That afternoon, another "Ripper" note was traced to its author, an 18-year-old, who had threatened her employer's children out of spite.

Exposure of such childish hoaxes did not ease the local atmosphere of tension. On the evening of May 15, six-year-old Anna Lombardi was lured into a basement by a man who raped her there. A mob went looking for the suspect, but police — who claimed to know his name — denied a link between the rape and murders. Two days later, when patrolmen arrested Stephen Lukovich for beating his wife and child, rumors spread that "a ripper" was in custody, drawing 1,000 outraged vigilantes to the street outside the precinct house.

Nor was the Ripper scare confined to New York City. On June 22, Inspector Faurot visited Philadelphia, where a man in custody had recently confessed to murdering a child "on 15th Street." Detectives had no knowledge of the crime, but young Charles Murray had been slain near 16th Street, and so the suspect warranted an interview. Faurot found his man confined in the mental ward of a local hospital, coming away from the interrogation convinced of his innocence in the Ripper crimes.

In August, Lieutenant Patrick Gildea was dispatched to Baltimore, where Ripper suspect Edward Jones was being held on charges of defrauding his landlady. Informant Grace Elliott had denounced her common-law husband as the slayer, and while the woman's own behavior seemed erratic and irresponsible, New York authorities were notified. It was revealed that Jones and Elliott had lived in New York City when the homicides occurred, but there was nothing to connect them with the crimes. Interrogated by Gildea, Grace Elliott withdrew the charges, denying earlier statements that Jones had "confessed" the murders in her presence. Rather, she decided he was simply interested in reading articles about the crimes.

The trail grew cold, and local panic faded over time. Despite assignment of 100 homicide detectives to the case, interrogation of innumerable "witnesses" and suspects, no solution was forthcoming in the case. As with Atlanta's Ripper — and his several predecessors of the 19th century — the New York crimes remain unsolved.

"Jack the Stripper" — England (1959-65)

Seventy years after Jack the Ripper murdered and disemboweled prostitutes in London's East End, a new generation of hookers learned to live with the ever-present fear of a lurking killer. This "Jack" carried no knife and penned no jaunty letters to the press, but he was every bit as lethal (claiming eight victims to the Ripper's five) and possessed of far greater longevity (operating over nearly six years, compared to the Ripper's 10 weeks). At the "conclusion" of the case, both slayers shared a common attribute: despite a wealth of theories and assertions, neither "Jack" was ever captured or identified.

On June 17, 1959, prostitute Elizabeth Figg, 21, was found floating in the Thames, clad only in a slip, her death attributed to strangulation. Four and a half years passed before discovery of the next murder, with the skeleton of 22-year-old Gwynneth Rees unearthed during clearance of a Thames-side rubbish dump, on November 8, 1963. The cause of death was difficult to ascertain, and homicide investigators later tried to disconnect both murders from the "Stripper" series, but today the better evidence suggests that these were practice runs, the early crimes committed by a killer who had yet to hit his stride.

Thirty-year-old Hannah Tailford was the next to die, her naked corpse discovered in the Thames by boatmen on February 2, 1964. Her stockings were pulled down around her ankles, panties stuffed inside her mouth, but she had drowned, and the inquest produced an "open" verdict, refusing to rule out suicide, however improbable it seemed.

On April 9, 1964, 20-year-old Irene Lockwood was found naked and dead in the Thames, floating 300 yards from the spot where Tailford was found. Another drowning victim, she was four months pregnant when she died. Suspect Kenneth Archibald confessed to the murder later that month, then recanted his statement, blaming depression. He was subsequently cleared at trial.

Helen Barthelemy, age 20, was the first victim found away from the river. On April 24, her naked body was discovered near a sports field in Brentwood, four front teeth missing, with part of one lodged in her throat. Traces of multi-colored spray paint on the body suggested that she had been kept for a while after death in a paint shop, before she was dumped in the field.

On July 14, 21-year-old Mary Fleming was discarded, nude and lifeless, on a dead-end London street. Witnesses glimpsed a van and its driver near the scene, but none could finally describe the man or vehicle with any certainty. Missing since July 11, Fleming had apparently been suffocated or choked to death — as opposed to strangled — and her dentures were missing from the scene.

Margaret McGowan, 21, had been missing a month when her nude corpse was found in Kensington, on November 25, 1964. Police noted the familiar traces of paint on her skin, and one of her teeth had been forced from its socket in front. The last to die was 27-year-old Bridget O'Hara, last seen alive on January 11, 1965, her body found on February 16, hidden in some shrubbery on the Heron Trading Estate, in Acton. Her front teeth were missing, and pathologists determined she had died on her knees. The corpse was partially mummified, as if from prolonged storage in a cool, dry place.

Despite appeals to prostitutes for information on their "kinky" customers, police were groping in the dark. Inspector John Du Rose suggested that the last six victims had been literally choked to death by oral sex, removal of the teeth in four cases lending vague support to the hypothesis. A list of suspects had supposedly been narrowed down from 20 men to three, when one of those committed suicide, gassing himself in his kitchen and leaving a cryptic note: "I cannot go on." It might mean anything — or nothing — but the murders ended with the nameless suspect's death, and so police seem satisfied, although the case remains officially unsolved.

Who *was* the Stripper? Suspects range from a deceased prize fighter to an unnamed ex-policeman, but Du Rose favored a private security guard on the Heron Trading Estate, his rounds including the paint shop where at least some of the victims were apparently stashed after death. The only "evidence" of guilt is the cessation of similar crimes after the suspect's suicide, but numerous serial killers — from the original Ripper to the **Zodiac** and **Babysitter** — have "retired" once they achieved a certain body count. The best that we can say for Scotland Yard's solution is that it is plausible... but unconfirmed.

"Jane/John Doe" murders — California (1980)

On June 12, 1980, members of a highway construction crew discovered the nude bodies of two white males, both in their early 20s, near the Ventura Freeway's exit ramp for Forest Lawn Drive. Cause of death was undetermined, the bodies bearing no marks aside from superficial scratches suffered in their slide down the embankment, after they had been ejected from a vehicle. At this writing, both victims remain unidentified.

A month later, on July 19, a woman's decomposing body was found beside a church basketball court in Pasadena, stuffed inside a cardboard box. Listed in official records as "Jane Doe," the victim had first been sighted on June 17, mistaken for a dead animal with only hair visible at first glance.

On September 10, Orange County authorities were summoned to Oak Creek Horse Ranch, where the bodies of a man and woman had been unearthed from a shallow grave. Unlike the other recent victims, these were fully clothed and had been killed by close-range shotgun blasts. Like those who went before, they remain unidentified, their killer(s) still at large.

Jersey Shore murders — New Jersey (1965-66)

Between September 1965 and August 1966, the Jersey Shore of Monmouth and adjoining Ocean County was the scene of half a dozen unsolved murders, marked in nearly every case by similar — if not identical — techniques. Three decades later, homicide investigators are no closer to a suspect in the case than when the crimes began.

The slayer's first target was 18-year-old Mary Klinsky, a high school senior in West Keansburg, killed in what detectives called an "especially vicious attack." The victim left her home at 9:00 P.M. on September 15, bound for the corner mailbox with a letter to her fiancé; seven hours later, her nude and battered body was discovered by motorists near the entrance to Garden State Park.

Joanne Fantazier, a 17-year-old dropout, was next, found on the ice of Yellow Brook in Cold Neck Township on February 11, 1966. Fully clothed, with no sign of sexual assault, Fantazier had been fatally beaten and thrown off a highway bridge, her impact failing to break the ice as her killer plainly intended.

A month later, on March 17, 16-year-old Catherine Baker left her home in Edison Township, trekking toward the neighborhood bakery a block away. Her semi-nude body was found on May 14, floating in a branch of the Metedeconk River, in a remote area of Jackson Township. Death was attributed to multiple skull fractures, the result of a vicious beating.

The first male victim, five year-old Paul Benda, was discovered on June 21, in the high grass bordering an unpaved road near Raritan Bay. Sexually abused before death, he had also been beaten, tortured with lit cigarettes, and finished off with five strokes of an ice pick. The body was nude on discovery, his clothes piled nearby.

Another male, 18-year-old Ronald Sandlin, was abducted from his job at a Lakewood service station on August 7, beaten to death with a tire iron and dumped in a ditch in Manchester Township. Three days later, 44-year-old Dorothy McKenzie was found shot to death in her car, the vehicle mired in sand near a diner on Route 9. The latest victim was fully clothed, her purse untouched on the seat beside her.

In the absence of a suspect or a clear-cut motive, officers could only say that the McKenzie murder, with its use of firearms, seemed to break the chain. Or did it? As with Joanne Fantazier, there had been no sexual assault, and if one slayer was responsible for all five of the recorded deaths, he had already shown his "versatility" by raping boy and girl alike, abstaining when it suited him. It would have been no trick to swap his tire iron for a gun, but we may only speculate, because the case remains unsolved, no suspects in sight.

Jessup child murders — Georgia (1980-81)

Within a period of 16 months, from June 1980 to October 1981, authorities in Jessup, Georgia, logged the sudden deaths of four related children, all of which remain unsolved today. Successive coroner's reports could find no cause of death in any of the cases. As Detective Joel Smith explained to reporters, "We have no idea what killed them. It's hard not to think there's some foul play in it, but we have no proof."

The first to die was four-year-old Olympia Reddish, found in her bed on June 28, 1980 after playing outside in the yard. A year later, on July 14, 1981, Phyllis Worley was checking another of her children, nine-month-old Tiffany Reddish, when she found the infant stretched out in her crib, not breathing. Three days later, Tiffany was pronounced dead in the intensive care unit of a local hospital.

That same morning, July 17, 19-month-old April Gaston — a half-sister to the Reddish girls — refused to eat her breakfast, returning to bed in midmorning as if she felt ill. Looking in on the child a bit later, Ola May Gaston found her daughter dead.

The final casualty, two-year-old Latoia Reddish, displayed similar symptoms on October 13, 1981, refusing breakfast, complaining of a headache and stomach pains. Packed off to bed by her mother, Latoia was dead within the hour, leaving medical examiners without a clue to help explain her fate.

Authorities reported that all four girls had the same father, although he resided with none of them. Paternal visits were infrequent, and the man had not been close to any of his children on the days they died. A physical examination of the father and his sole surviving child revealed no traces of hereditary illness to explain the sudden deaths. Detectives hold to their conviction of foul play, but there appears to be no likelihood of a solution in this baffling case.

Johannesburg child murders — South Africa (1997-98)

South African police suspect a serial killer in the deaths of two children and the disappearance of 11 more from Orange Farm township, a shanty town south of Johannesburg. Although they have no suspect, and most of the presumed victims are still missing, authorities have theorized that the case may involve "muti" — a form of traditional religious "medicine" that incorporates human body parts as primary ingredients.

Even the body count is vague in this unsettling case, with the first public announcement of a police investigation aired on January 20, 1998, reporting that 13 children had vanished from Orange Farm "over the past five months." The actual manhunt began two days earlier, with the discovery of six-year-old Bukeka Nhlonetse's headless body, discarded on a rubbish dump at nearby Ennerdale. On January 20, six-year-old Zanele Nongiza's severed limbs (missing head, torso and feet) were found near her Orange Farm home. It was unclear whether the skull and rib of an unidentified young girl, found in the same general area, belonged to either victim, but police said the latest find had "been in the area for a considerable length of time."

Thinking back, detectives recalled the case of yet another young girl, whose mutilated corpse was found on the veld near Finetown, in February 1997. Subsequent news reports named two more girls — Nompumelelo Kgamedi and Edith Aron — found "last year," near the site where the latest remains were located. Overall, that made at least four murders in the district, and possibly six (depending on the published source), while the *Mail & Guardian* (on February 6) referred to "sixteen children who disappeared and were later found dead in Fine Town and Orange Farm in the past few months."

In the wake of the police announcement, local reporters combed missing-persons dockets and produced 26 cases, 13 of them involving subjects below the age of 18. Investigating officer Mshengu Tshabalala told journalists that most of the children had vanished around Christmastime. The case took an odd turn on January 22, when two "missing" boys — Bongani Ngubeni and Mpho Lebese — recognized their photos in the newspaper and contacted police. Apparently, they had returned home shortly after their parents reported them missing, but no one thought to advise police of the fact.

That left at least seven children unaccounted for around Orange Farm, and while some skeptics waited for the rest sheepishly to present themselves, no further living runaways have been identified. Police are hampered in their search, meanwhile, by what Captain Thabang Letlala of the Vaal Rand police describes as negligent and untrained officers around Orange Farm.

"We are having trouble there," Letlala told the press, "because these people do not have the right skills to do basic police investigative work, but attempts are being made to bring them up to speed."

An internal investigation has also been launched, Letlala said, to find out why authorities ignored reports of 13 missing children until bodies started turning up. Zanele Nongiza's mother complained that when she went to report her daughter missing on January 3, a policeman slapped her on the buttocks and asked her for sex. Authorities ignored the case, meanwhile, until Zanele's mangled remains were found.

Police downplayed the "muti" angle in their statements to the press, but that did not prevent angry locals from venting their wrath on various suspects. By February 7, at least four men had been driven from their homes in the Vaal Triangle, as armed mobs scoured the countryside for an elusive killer. Anxiety increased two days later, when an eight-year-old girl was snatched from her home in Portlands by a man who told her she was "never coming back." The child kicked her assailant and managed to escape, but the prowler was long gone before police arrived.

Curiously, by that time, authorities already had a suspect of sorts in custody, arrested on January 30 and vaguely described to the press as "a middle-aged man" who had tried to lure three children away from the Nomini Primary School.

According to the principal who spotted him initially, the man showed certain photos to the kids "and told them of his club, which he wanted them to join."

At sight of the approaching principal, the stranger fled, but he was run down by a howling mob and only rescued by the prompt arrival of police. As for his link to the murders and disappearances of children at Orange Farm, police spokesmen would only tell reporters that "After we have done all the investigations, we will take him to court."

Kiss, Bela

A family man and amateur astrologer, Hungarian Bela Kiss began his career as a serial murderer relatively late in life. In February 1912, at 40 years of age, Kiss moved to the village of Czinkota with his wife Marie, some 15 years his junior. Within a matter of weeks, Marie had found herself a lover, one Paul Bikari, and in December 1912, Kiss sadly told his neighbors that the couple had run off together, leaving him to pine alone. In place of his wife, Kiss hired an elderly housekeeper. She, in turn, learned to ignore the parade of women who came to spend time with Czinkota's newly eligible bachelor.

Around this same time, Kiss began collecting large metal drums, informing the curious village constable that they were filled with gasoline, expected to be scarce with the approach of war in Europe. Budapest authorities, meanwhile, were seeking information on the disappearance of two widows, named Schmeidak and Varga, who had not made contact with their friends or relatives for several weeks. Both women had last been seen in the company of a man named Hoffmann dwelling near the Margaret Bridge in Budapest, but he had also disappeared without a trace. Czinkota's constable was generally aware of the investigation, but he saw no reason to connect Hoffmann with the quiet, unassuming Bela Kiss.

In November 1914, Kiss was drafted into military service, leaving for the front as soon as he was sworn into the ranks and issued gear. Another 18 months would pass before officials in Czinkota were informed that Kiss had died in combat, one more grim statistic for the casualty rosters in that bloody spring of 1916. He was forgotten by the townsfolk until June, when soldiers visited Czinkota in a search for stockpiled gasoline.

The village constable remembered Kiss, his cache of metal drums, and led a squad of soldiers to the dead man's home. Inside the house, the searchers turned up seven drums... but they contained no gasoline. Instead, each drum contained the naked body of a woman, strangled and immersed in alcohol. The drawers of Kiss's bureau overflowed with cards and letters from women responding to newspaper advertisements, purchased by Kiss in the name of Hoffmann, a self-described "lonely widower seeking female companionship."

Czinkota's constable recalled that there had been more drums — and many more, at that. A search of the surrounding countryside revealed another 17, each with a pickled corpse inside. Authorities from Budapest identified the missing widows, and Marie Kiss occupied another drum. Her lover, Paul Bikari, was the only male among the 24 recovered victims.

Police theorized that Bela Kiss had slain his wife and her clandestine lover in a jealous rage, disposing of their bodies in a fashion that — he thought — eliminated any possibility of subsequent discovery. The crime apparently unleashed some hidden mania, and Kiss spent the next two years pursuing lonely women with a passion, bilking several of their savings prior to strangling them and sealing them inside his makeshift funeral vaults. It was a grisly case, but Kiss had gone to face a higher court.

Or, had he?

In the spring of 1919, Kiss was sighted on the Margaret Bridge in Budapest, "Herr Hoffmann's" antebellum stomping ground. Police investigation proved that Kiss had switched his papers with a battlefield fatality, assuming the dead man's identity to make good his escape. That knowledge brought detectives no closer to their man, however, for Kiss had slipped the net again.

The futile search went on. In 1924, a deserter from the French Foreign Legion told officers of the Surete about a fellow legionnaire who entertained the troops with tales of his proficiency with the garrote. The soldier's name was Hofman, and he matched descriptions of Bela Kiss, but the lead was another dead end. By the time Hungarian police were informed, Legionnaire "Hofman" had also deserted, vanishing without a trace.

In 1932, a New York homicide detective, Henry Oswald, was convinced that he had sighted Bela Kiss, emerging from the Times Square subway station. Nicknamed "Camera Eye" by colleagues, after his uncanny memory for faces, Oswald was unshakable in his belief that Kiss — who would have been approaching 70 — was living somewhere in New York. Unfortunately, Times Square crowds prevented Oswald from pursuing Kiss, and he could only watch in helpless rage as his intended quarry disappeared.

In 1936, a rumor spread that Kiss was working as a janitor, in some apartment building on New York's Sixth Avenue. Again, he managed to evade police — if he was ever there at all — and there the trail grew cold. Whatever finally became of Bela Kiss remains a mystery, beyond solution with the passage of more than six decades. In Hungary, he is remembered as the one who got away. [See also: **Belle Gunness**]

"Last Call Killer" — New York (1992-93)

Each decade seems to bring at least one psycho-stalker to afflict the gay community in New York City. And the 1990s were no exception, as Big Apple gay bars became the hunting ground of a predator dubbed the "Last Call Killer." Police speculated on motives ranging from morbid homophobia to brutal "revenge" for infection with AIDS, but proof of any single theory requires a known suspect, and manhunters are still empty-handed in this puzzling case.

The killer's first known victim, in July 1992, was 56-year-old Thomas Mulcahy, a traveling salesman. Stabbed in the heart and "neatly" dismembered with a hacksaw, his remains found July 10 in trash bags scattered along highways in Ocean County, New Jersey, Mulcahy was identified from the contents of his briefcase, left at one dump site. Last seen alive at the Townhouse — a Manhattan gay bar — on July 8, Mulcahy left a wife and three grown children, none of whom professed to know that he was homosexual. The skilled dissection of his corpse convinced Manhattan homicide detectives that their quarry "knows something about joints and human anatomy."

Ten months later, 44-year-old male prostitute Anthony Morrero became number two, his dismembered remains sealed in six plastic trash bags, dumped along New Jersey highways, where they were found on May 10, 1993. Although Morrero had no fixed address, he was known to work the streets of Manhattan, turning bargain-basement "tricks" for as little as 10 dollars.

Michael Sakara Jr. stood six-foot-four and weighed 250 pounds, but his bulk didn't save him in July 1993, when the slayer picked him off in Greenwich Village. A 56-year-old Manhattan typesetter, Sakara was last seen in a restaurant in the early morning hours of July 30. His severed head and arms were found at 11:00 A.M. on July 31, in a sidewalk trash can in Rotterdam, New York. The rest of his body has never been found, but Sakara's identity was confirmed — as in Mulcahy's case — by a briefcase left at the scene.

As police investigated the latest rash of homicides, they also perused older files, including that of 54-year-old Peter Anderson, a Philadelphia resident murdered on a visit to Manhattan in May 1991. Last seen alive at the Townhouse — victim Mulcahy's final pit stop — on May 3, Anderson was found two days later, his remains stuffed into eight trash bags, deposited in garbage cans along the Pennsylvania Turnpike, in Lancaster. Although twice married, Anderson was known among his hometown friends as being gay, and while the circumstances of his death bore striking similarities to the other "Last Call" murders, authorities hastened to declare, "We're not trying to say there's a serial killer."

That tune had changed by mid-August 1993. Initially, police blamed the Last Call Killer for a total of five murders — including the July 1992 dismemberment of Schenectady resident Guillermo Mendez, found in trash bags at a Rotterdam cemetery — but in the absence of a proven link to Manhattan, Mendez was officially dropped from the list. And there the matter rests, despite a "vague" sketch of a limping suspect allegedly seen with Michael Sakara by a neighborhood beggar. To date, there have been no arrests, no more "official" slayings in the series. It is business as usual in New York, with the Last Call Killer still at large.

Latino murders — California (1980)

On November 6, 1980, the Los Angeles Police Department asked for public help in their pursuit of three Hispanic men connected to a string of robberies, assaults, and fatal stabbings in the San Fernando Valley area. Lieutenant William Gaida said of the elusive trio, "They seem to derive sadistic pleasure out of stabbing people. Apparently robbery is the primary motive, but the suspects stabbed the victims in almost all cases; stabbed them even if the victim complied with all their demands."

The reign of terror began on May 17, 1980, when three separate victims were slain and a fourth gravely wounded over a period of three hours and 15 minutes. A task force was organized to handle the case on September 29, and by October 30, when 19-year-old Jesus Solis was knifed to death by assailants matching the suspect descriptions, police credited the trio with a minimum of seven murders.

Two of the elusive suspects were described as Latino men between the ages of 25 and 30 years, while no description was available for their companion. The killers reportedly lurked in restrooms of taverns or loitered outside, choosing Hispanic males as their primary targets of robbery and murder. No solution to the case has yet been announced by LAPD.

"Lisbon Ripper" — Portugal (1992-93)

A modern bogeyman in the tradition of 19th-century London's "Jack the Ripper," this stalker of drug-addicted prostitutes in Lisbon has inspired police investigators to connect him — albeit tentatively — to murders in six nations, on both sides of the Atlantic Ocean. Unfortunately, none of those cases (ranging in number from three to 18, depending on the source) has yet been solved, and the killer remains at large.

Lisbon's nightmare began in July 1992, when some factory workers found a young woman's body discarded in a shed. Her throat was slashed, and she had been disemboweled with a broken bottle, found at the scene. By March 1993, two more victims were found in similar condition — the third within 50 yards of the first murder scene — all identified as prostitutes and addicts in their twenties. Two of them were HIV-positive, prompting speculation that the killer might be a "john" infected with AIDS, venting his rage on prostitutes as a group.

In March 1993, Lisbon detectives visited New Bedford, Massachusetts, where a still-unidentified "**Highway Murderer**" had slaughtered 11 prostitutes between April and September 1988. Techniques varied, and several Massachusetts victims had been found as skeletal remains, but the large Portuguese population in New Bedford prompted detectives in both countries to suspect that the "Highway Murderer" may have "gone home" to continue the hunt, after heat around New Bedford became too intense. In the absence of suspects, however, the theory could never be proved, and Lisbon authorities came away from their visit with little more than sympathy for their plight.

Back in Europe, meanwhile, the same killer — or one with a remarkably similar M.O. — had apparently taken his act on the road. Between 1993 and 1997, authorities in Belgium, Denmark, the Czech Republic and the Netherlands reported one "nearly identical" murder of street girls in each of their countries. Police now speculate that their hypothetical AIDS victim-cum-psycho slasher is also a long-haul truck driver, thus granting him access to victims throughout Europe. Predictably, expansion of the hunting ground did nothing to improve the odds of capture, and the "Lisbon Ripper" case remains unsolved today.

London (Ontario) murders — Canada (1967-69)

In the summer of 1997, police in Ontario, Canada, organized a task force code-named "Project Angel" — reportedly drawing its name from "guardian angel" — to review the evidence in 20 unsolved murders reported from the city of London, between 1956 and 1983. The task force held its first press conference on February 4, 1998, and while one UPI report claimed that "police suspect the 20 cases may be linked and could be the work of one or two serial killers," the truth was less dramatic. In fact, while refusing to offer specifics, Ontario Provincial Police Detective Inspector Mike Coughlin, assigned to lead Project Angel, told reporters that *three* of the murders were probably linked, and possibly connected to two more slayings outside the immediate London vicinity. All three "connected" murders, Coughlin emphasized, had occurred between 1967 and 1969, indicating that "the killer's either died, been locked up or moved away to some other part of the country."

While authorities refused to name the three victims allegedly slain by one killer, they did provide a list of the cases subject to renewed investigation. Victims logged during the relevant period include:

- Glenda Teball, 16, last seen walking "into a bush" near her Thedford, Ontario, home on Halloween 1967. She is presumed dead, although her body has never been found.
- Jacqueline Dunleavy, also 16, strangled and beaten to death in January 1968, her violated body found in a driveway near the London Hunt and Country Club.
- Frankie Jensen, age nine, who vanished on his way to school in February 1968. Two months later, his body was

dragged from the Thames River near Thorndale, a fractured skull listed as the cause of death.

- ➲ Scott Leishman, 16, reported missing from Thorndale three months before his corpse was found, on May 15, 1968. Cause of death was undetermined, and while some of Leishman's clothes were disarranged, tests for sexual assault were inconclusive.
- ➲ Helga Beer, age 31, last seen leaving a friend's London apartment with an unknown man on August 6, 1968, subsequently found in the back seat of her own car, raped, strangled, and beaten to death.
- ➲ Nineteen-year-old Lynda White, a college student, vanished from the University of Western Ontario campus on November 13, 1968, her remains found five years later in a shallow grave near St. Williams, in Norfolk County. Her clothing was never found, and cause of death remains unknown.
- ➲ Jane Wooley, 62, had been dead for three days when her battered, semi-nude corpse was found in her London apartment, on February 3, 1969. Police report no evidence of sexual assault.
- ➲ Patricia Ann Bowin, 22, strangled and stabbed to death on April 24, 1969, in the London apartment she shared with her two young sons.
- ➲ Robert Stapylton, 11, vanished from his London home on June 7, 1969, his corpse recovered from a wooded lot four miles away, in London Township. Once again, the cause of death remains unknown, and there was no clear evidence of any sexual assault.
- ➲ Jacqueline English, 15, last seen entering a car outside a London shopping mall on October 4, 1969, her nude body found five days later in Big Otter Creek, near Tillsonburg. English had been sexually assaulted and killed by a blow to the head.

Armchair detectives were left to draw their own conclusions from the victim list, which included four teenage girls, three male victims, and three adult females. Detective Inspector Coughlin, meanwhile, told the press, "We're going to give it our best shot at solving some of these murders. I'll guarantee you we'll solve as many as we can."

To date, sadly, the solution rate remains at zero.

London-Colchester murders — England (1987)

In June of 1987, Wendy Krell, a 25-year-old shop manager, was raped and murdered in her London flat. Five months later, on November 24, with that case still unsolved, police received a missing-person report on 20-year-old Caroline Pierce, a London restaurant manager. Her body was found near St. Mary, on December 15, and police publicly speculated on a connection between the two killings.

On November 29, an unnamed suspect in the death of Wendy Krell was charged with rape, but his incarceration did not halt the rash of murders. Three days after Caroline Pierce was discovered, searchers at Colchester — 50 miles northeast of London — retrieved the decomposing remains of 18-year-old Fiona Gallant from the slope of a highway embankment. As in London, the Colchester case was believed to be linked with an ongoing series of rapes in the area.

At this writing, no solution has been announced for the murders in London and Colchester. Police refuse to speculate on possible links between Fiona Gallant's death and the crimes in London, while the killer (or killers) remains at large.

Los Angeles murders — California (1982)

Between the months of August and October 1982, Los Angeles police were mobilized to track a prowling gunman who selected random motorists as targets, imitating New York's "Son of Sam." Before the rampage ended — with the gunman still at large — two victims had been killed and three more wounded in a spate of sudden, unprovoked attacks.

The first two victims, killed in August, were a local oceanographer and a vacationing student from Princeton University. On September 4, 51-year-old Jack Listman was wounded by shots fired through a window of his car, while he was waiting for the light to change at a Los Angeles intersection. In the week of October 11 to 15, two Beverly Hills women were wounded, in separate shooting incidents, apparently by the same gunman.

Detective Sherman Oakes could offer little hope for a solution in the case when he addressed the media in mid-October. Describing the gunman's technique, Oakes said, "He just walks up, never says a word, and starts shooting. Once the victim is dead, he then goes through the victim's pockets."

Moving on or tiring of his game with the October shootings, L.A.'s phantom gunman faded from the scene, still unidentified, to be replaced by other random killers in the coming months.

"Lover's Lane" murders — Georgia (1977)

While homicide detectives in New York were stalking the elusive "Son of Sam," their counterparts in Georgia were attempting to identify a killer with a similar M.O., who preyed on couples parked on darkened lanes, attacking from the shadows, interrupting passion with the searing blasts of point-blank gunfire. In Manhattan, officers eventually bagged their quarry; in Atlanta, there was no such luck. As this is written, Georgia's phantom gunman remains unidentified.

The stalker's one-man war began on January 16, 1977, when police were summoned to the scene of a peculiar auto accident. A single vehicle had veered across an intersection, terminating its erratic course when it collided with a traffic sign. Inside, a naked man lay slumped behind the steering wheel, his face and body streaked with blood. A woman — also nude and bloody — lay behind him, in the back seat, covered by a coat.

The victims were identified as LaBrian Lovett, 26, and Veronica Hill, age 20. Lovett had been shot four times — in the head, stomach, right leg, and left arm; his companion had suffered two wounds, in the left leg and abdomen. Both died at the hospital, but investigators determined they were shot while making love in nearby Adams Park.

Police were playing the percentages, investigating jealous friends and lovers, when the killer struck a second time, attacking in the predawn hours of February 12. This time, his target was a teenage couple necking in West Manor Park, three miles northwest of Adams Park. Approaching their car at 2:45 A.M., the assailant — described as a large black man — fired six shots into the car before trying to open the locked doors. Frustrated, he fled on foot, leaving both victims with nonfatal chest wounds.

Jealousy went out the window as a motive when ballistics tests revealed that the same .38-caliber weapon had been used in both recent shootings. Likewise, the gunman seemed to have no interest in robbing his victims, nor in raping the women. Detectives were still puzzling over the motiveless crimes when their adversary made his third appearance in Atlanta.

On the night of March 12, 20-year-old Diane Collins was cuddling with her fiancé in Adams Park. They had announced their engagement a few days earlier, taking in a movie that evening before stopping in the park. Distracted, neither saw the gunman as he approached their vehicle, pumping six rounds through the window on the passenger's side. Diane was killed instantly, her fiancé wounded in the head. Despite the spurting blood that nearly blinded him, he put the car in motion, and drove home on instinct to telephone for help.

Police were baffled, but at least they had the bare suggestion of a pattern now. Twenty-seven days had elapsed between the first two attacks, 28 between the second and third shootings. If their man was hunting on a four-week cycle, homicide investigators theorized, they stood a decent chance of catching him by staking out local parks on April 6-8.

The plan was logical enough, but it was wasted as the gunman vanished, calling off his lethal feud as suddenly and inexplicably as it began. Weeks lengthened into months without a new attack, and by the time a local newsman wrote a two-year retrospective article about the shootings, in March 1979, police were frank in their admission that they had no leads, no suspects in the case. Atlanta's phantom gunman — like the "ripper" who preceded him in 1912 — is one of those who got away.

"Mad Butcher of Kingsbury Run" — Ohio (1934-??)

The gully known as Kingsbury Run lies like a scar across the face of downtown Cleveland, Ohio. Sixty feet deep in places, the ancient creek bed is lined with 30-odd pairs of railroad tracks serving local factories and distant cities, bearing cargo to Pittsburgh, Chicago, or Youngstown, whisking commuters to posh bedroom communities like Shaker Heights. During the Great Depression, Kingsbury Run was also a favorite camp site for hoboes, and a playground for children with time on their hands. In the latter 1930s, it became the focal point of America's most fascinating murder mystery — a puzzle that endures to this day — though, in fact, the case had its origins elsewhere, on the shores of Lake Erie.

On September 5, 1934, a driftwood hunter found the lower portion of a woman's torso buried in sand at Euclid Beach, eight miles east of downtown Cleveland. The victim's legs were severed at the knees, her skin discolored by the application of a chemical preservative. A coroner extrapolated height and age from the pathetic evidence available, but victim number one did not resemble any of Cleveland's known missing women. She was never identified, police adding insult to injury by their stubborn refusal to count her as an "official" victim once a pattern of crime became apparent.

A year later, on September 23, 1935, boys playing in Kingsbury Run found two headless male bodies, nude but for stockings worn by the younger victim. Both had been emasculated, and their severed heads were found nearby. The older victim, unidentified, had died at least five days before the younger, and his skin possessed a reddish tinge from treatment with a chemical preservative. The younger man, identified as 29-year-old Edward Andrassy, was a bisexual ex-convict with a long record of petty arrests in Cleveland. Retraction of the neck muscles on both corpses pointed to decapitation as the likely cause of death.

On January 26, 1936, a Cleveland butcher was alerted to the presence of "some meat in a basket" behind his shop. Investigating, he was stunned to find two human thighs, one arm, and the lower half of a woman's torso. The upper torso, lower legs and missing arm were found behind a vacant house on February 7, several blocks away, but fingerprints had already identified the victim as Florence Polillo, a 41-year-old prostitute. Her severed head was never found.

Four months later, on June 5, two boys found the severed head of a man in Kingsbury Run, a mile from the spot where Andrassy and his nameless companion were found in September 1935. Railroad workers found the matching body on June 6, but victim number five remained anonymous, despite publication of numerous distinctive tattoos. His fingerprints were not on file in Cleveland, and he had not been reported missing.

On July 22, 1936, the naked, headless body of an unknown man was found beside Big Creek, in the suburb of Brooklyn, across town from Kingsbury Run. The only victim slain on Cleveland's southwest side, this new "John Doe" would also be the only victim killed where he was found. Decomposition foiled all efforts to identify the corpse.

A hobo spotted number seven — or, a portion of him — in Kingsbury Run on September 10, 1936. The dismembered remains were floating in a stagnant pond, and police divers were called to retrieve two halves of the torso, plus the lower legs and thighs. The severed head, along with arms and genitals, was never found. Decapitation had not been the cause of death, but medical examiners could not identify another cause.

Soon after the discovery of victim number seven, Detectives Peter Merylo and Martin Zalewski were assigned to the "torso" case full-time. Over the next two years, they investigated hundreds of leads, cleared scores of innocent suspects, jailed dozens of perverts and fugitives — all without bagging their man. The press, meanwhile, ran banner headlines on the futile search for Cleveland's "Mad Butcher," speculating endlessly on motives, the identity of the victims, and the killer's supposed surgical skill.

On February 23, 1937, the upper half of a woman's torso was found at Euclid Beach, almost precisely where the first (still unacknowledged) victim was discovered in September

1934. The lower trunk was found in Lake Erie, off East 30th Street, on May 5, while the head, arms and legs remained forever missing.

On June 6, the skeleton of a black woman — missing one rib, plus the bones of arms and legs — was found beneath the Lorain-Carnegie Bridge. The victim was decapitated, and Coroner Samuel Gerber placed her death sometime in early June of 1936. In April 1938, the son of Rose Wallace "identified" his mother's remains on the basis of dental work, but problems remained. Wallace had disappeared in August 1936, two months after the victim's estimated date of death, and her Cincinnati dentist was deceased, his files destroyed, rendering positive identification impossible. Detective Merylo accepted the shaky I.D., but it brought him no closer to the arrest of a suspect.

Exactly one month after number nine was found, the lower torso of a man was sighted in the Cuyahoga River, underneath the Third Street Bridge. Police retrieved the upper trunk and severed thighs that afternoon, but other pieces surfaced in the days to come. By July 14, authorities had everything except the nameless victim's head, and that was never found.

On April 8, 1938, a woman's lower left leg was fished out of the Cuyahoga, behind Public Square. The missing left foot, both thighs, and two halves of the torso were hauled ashore, wrapped in burlap, on May 2, but the victim's head, right leg and arms remained at large.

The last "official" victims — male and female, killed at different times — were found on August 16, 1938, by workmen at a lakeside rubbish dump. The new "John Doe" was nothing but a skeleton, decapitated in familiar style, missing two ribs, plus both hands and feet. Murdered no later than February 1938, he may have died as early as December 1937. The female victim was cut into nine pieces, but all were accounted for. She had been killed sometime between February and April

1938, her identity forever disguised by advanced decomposition.

In January 1939, the Cleveland *Press* reprinted the following letter, mailed from Los Angeles:

> Chief of Police Matowitz:
>
> You can rest easy now, as I have come to sunny California for the winter. I felt bad operating on those people, but science must advance. I shall astound the medical profession, a man with only a D.C.
>
> What did their lives mean in comparison to hundreds of sick and disease-twisted bodies? Just laboratory guinea pigs found on any public street. No one missed them when I failed. My last case was successful. I know now the feeling of Pasteur, Thoreau and other pioneers.
>
> Right now I have a volunteer who will absolutely prove my theory. They call me mad and a butcher, but the truth will come out.
>
> I have failed but once here. The body has not been found and never will be, but the head, minus the features, is buried on Century Boulevard, between Western and Crenshaw. I feel it my duty to dispose of the bodies as I do. It is God's will not to let them suffer.
>
> "X"

No buried heads were found in Los Angeles, and the manhunt shifted back to Cleveland. On July 5, 1939, sheriff's deputies arrested a Slavic immigrant, 52-year-old Frank Dolezal, and launched a marathon interrogation of their suspect. Dolezal eventually confessed to murdering Andrassy and Polillo, flubbing many details that were "corrected" in later confessions. He later retracted all statements, charging detectives with third-degree tactics, and suspicious stains found in his flat were identified as animal blood. On August 24, Dolezal "committed suicide" in his cell, found hanging from a wall hook shorter than he was, and the autopsy revealed four ribs broken by beatings in jail. Today, no one regards him as a serious suspect in the "torso" case.

On May 3, 1940, three male corpses were discovered in abandoned box cars at McKees Rocks, Pennsylvania, outside Pittsburgh. All had been decapitated, and the heads were missing; one was otherwise intact, while two had been dissected at the hips and shoulders. Killed in the cars where they lay, the men had been dead from three to six months, and all three bodies had been scorched by fire. The most "complete" victim was identified as 30-year-old James Nicholson, a homosexual ex-convict from Wisconsin. The killer had carved the word "NAZI" on Nicholson's chest, inverting the "Z" by accident or by design. Authorities unanimously blamed the crimes on Cleveland's butcher, tracing the movements of the box cars to pinpoint the murders in Youngstown, Ohio, during December 1939.

Journalist Oscar Fraley, in his book *4 Against the Mob,* contends that Eliot Ness — then Cleveland's director of public safety — not only identified the Mad Butcher in 1938, but also brought him to a semblance of justice. Tagged with the pseudonym of "Gaylord Sundheim," the suspect was described as a homosexual premed student and member of a prominent Cleveland family. Interrogated by Ness in autumn 1938, "Sundheim" allegedly escaped prosecution by committing himself to a mental hospital, where he died around 1940 or '41. In the interim, he tormented Ness with a barrage of obscene, menacing notes, which terminated with his death.

The tale deserves consideration, inasmuch as Ness preserved the "greeting cards" — all carefully anonymous — and they are viewable in Cleveland archives. But, do taunting notes provide a viable solution to the torso murders? Why did experts on the case insist the Butcher claimed three victims in December 1939, when "Sundheim" had been out of circulation for a year or more? If Ness was certain of the killer's whereabouts, why did he allow "suspect" Frank Dolezal to be abused (and possibly murdered) by sheriff's officers in 1939? If the case was solved in 1938, why did Detective Merylo pursue the Butcher into retirement, blaming his elusive quarry for fifty-odd murders by 1947? Tantalizing as it is, the Fraley story falls apart on close examination, failing every test of common sense.

There is a grisly postscript to the Butcher's story. On July 23, 1950, a man's headless body, emasculated and dismembered, was found in a Cleveland lumber yard, a few miles from Kingsbury Run. The missing head turned up four days later, and the victim was identified as Robert Robertson. Coroner Samuel Gerber, responsible for handling most of the Butcher's "official" victims, reported that "The work resembles exactly that of the torso murderer."

In retrospect, it is clear that the Mad Butcher murdered at least 16 victims between 1934 and 1939. He may have slaughtered the 1950 victim as well, and speculation links the same elusive suspect with a series of "**headless murders**" around New Castle, Pennsylvania, between 1925 and 1939. No firm connections were established in that case, and the number of New Castle victims has been wildly inflated by sensational journalists, but the crimes *were* committed in close proximity to rail lines serving Cleveland and Youngstown. None of the New Castle victims were ever identified, and the identity of their killer — like the whereabouts of the Mad Butcher's eight trophy heads — remains a mystery.

"Mad Trapper" — Alaska (1930-31)

In January 1931, it was announced that the United States Attorney General's office was committing federal agents to the search for an elusive killer, blamed for 15 murders and a string of unsolved disappearances in the territory of Alaska. All of the killings and disappearances were reported in the wilderness area in the southeastern part of the territory. Hunters and fishermen lived in constant fear of the nameless slayer who struck without warning, trailing his victims to isolated killing grounds, leaving little or no trace of himself behind. In every case, it was reported that the killer "slipped away with ghost-like ease."

In fact, though, there was a trace, if anything could be determined from the meager evidence. The latest confirmed murder victim, fish buyer John Marshall, had been found a few miles outside Ketchikan on October 20, 1930. The victim was still in his anchored boat, laid out where he fell after crushing blows shattered his skull. Clutched in one stiff hand, for what they might be worth, were several strands of human hair.

If Marshall was the last known victim, he was not the latest local resident to disappear, and terrified survivors counted every missing soul as a fresh "Mad Trapper" victim. John Wickstrom had gone out trolling in a small boat, shortly before Marshall's murder and at the same spot, only to vanish without a trace. Since Marshall's death, at least three more locals had disappeared. Albert Anderson, hunting from his skiff, was named among the missing. More recently, Albert Farrow and L.C. Davis had disappeared from their small boat, found anchored in a lonely cove and partly swamped with water.

On January 18, 1931, a federal marshal was reportedly en route to an isolated part of Prince of Wales Island, tracking an unnamed suspect in the case, but the progress of his search was never reported, and no files on the investigation have survived. The haunting case remains unsolved today.

Maranháo murders — Brazil (1994-97)

At last report, in 1997, Brazilian police were still hunting an unidentified serial killer blamed for the death of seven young boys since 1994, in the state of Maranháo. The most recent victims, both 10 years old, were found in northeastern Maranháo, with their genitals mutilated. One child had died from a broken neck, while the other's cause of death was undisclosed. Authorities reported that neither boy had been sodomized.

In fact, the grisly double event was only the latest in a string of child murders around Maranháo. A spokesperson for the state police told reporters, "We believe the boys may have been the victims of the same person who killed another three boys in Paco do Lumiar in the last three years. The other three were also sexually mutilated, and their bodies were also found in wooded areas." In addition to those five slayings, two more boys with "similar" mutilations were found in 1996, on the outskirts of São Luis, the state capital. At this writing, no suspect has been identified, and the crimes remain unsolved.

"Maxwell's Silver Hammer" — California (1970-??)

Keith Montgomery could have done without the Sunday shift, but holidays threw everything off schedule. If you let the good times roll, somebody had to clean up afterward, and it was his turn, pulling morning duty in the chemistry department of the University of California at Santa Barbara. Montgomery left his Isla Vista digs at half-past eight, and 15 minutes later he was trudging by himself along a bluff that overlooked the beach. No sweat. He still had time.

But he was going to be late.

At first, the figures huddled in their sleeping bags seemed perfectly natural. Hundreds of students and locals had thronged the beach last night — July 4, 1970 — to watch the freebie fireworks show. Some joints and pills changed hands, and there was always lots of beer around. If anything, Montgomery was surprised that only three of those who turned out for the show had stayed behind to sleep it off.

It took a second, closer look to tell him there was something wrong about those figures on the sand. The sun was shining in their faces now, but only one of them was moving, more like twitching feebly in his sleeping bag than getting up to meet the day. Montgomery squinted, raised a hand to shade his eyes, and realized the dark smears on the camper's face were blood.

He ran back toward the campus, found a call box for security, and summoned the police. The first responding officer confirmed two were dead and one was in critical condition, barely hanging on. Before he radioed for help, he told Montgomery, "This is the most brutal thing I've ever seen."

Physicians at Goleta Valley Community Hospital agreed. Two of the victims, 17-year-old Thomas Dolan and 23-year-old Larry Hess, were dead on arrival at emergency receiving. Dolan had been stabbed four times in the chest, with numerous lacerations and several compound fractures of the face suggesting a ferocious beating. Hess had suffered five stab wounds in the back and two in the chest, before or after someone pulped his face and smashed his skull.

The lone survivor, 19-year-old Thomas Hayes, clung to life after five hours of surgery to repair internal injuries. When he was fit for questioning, he told police that he was on his way to San Francisco with his friends, when they had camped out on the beach, within a hundred yards of the UCSB marine biology lab. His memories of the attack were vague, but they included waking up to find himself surrounded by a ring of chanting figures dressed in hooded, flowing robes.

Police, meanwhile, were at a loss to understand the savage crime. They had no suspects, and there was no evidence of robbery, with cash and watches left behind. No weapons were discovered at the scene, but measurement of wounds told homicide detectives they were looking for a cleaver or machete, plus at least one knife that had a 12-inch blade.

Worse yet, the massacre was Santa Barbara's third beach killing of the year. On February 22, John Hood and his fiancé Sandra Garcia were found, beaten and stabbed to death in similar fashion on East Beach, a short distance from Santa Barbara Cemetery. Three months later, on May 24, Erwin Faulmann was sleeping on the beach at Isla Vista when a pair of strangers tried to cut his throat. He managed to escape and call police, but no arrests were made.

One possible solution for the unsolved crimes emerged from the Charles Manson murder trial, then under way in Los Angeles. On July 27, author Ed Sanders was lunching with defense attorney Ron Hughes and Mansonite Catherine "Gypsy" Share — herself jailed for robbery and attempted murder a year later — when he mentioned the Santa Barbara slayings and evoked an immediate, excited reaction. Gypsy Share was animated as she talked about the murders, crediting the series of attacks to a Satanic cult called "Maxwell's Silver Hammer," presumably after a popular Beatles song of the same name. No members of the cult were ever publicly identified, and they presumably remain at large today. The beachfront crimes are still officially unsolved.

Menarik, Carl

A native of Vienna, born October 2, 1889, Carl Menarik immigrated to New York in 1914, obtaining a job at the German Odd Fellows Home, in Yonkers, during July of that year. Using the name of "Frederick Mors," Menarik worked for six months at the home, arousing no suspicion as he went about his duties. Patients came and went throughout his tenure, several leaving in a hearse, but they were old and no one gave a second thought to their demise before the early days of February 1915.

On the afternoon of February 2, "Mors" presented himself at the district attorney's office, dressed in a corduroy hunting outfit, complete with knee-pants and a feathered alpine cap. Approaching the desk sergeant, Menarik spontaneously confessed to the murders of eight "superannuated octogenarians," killed in order to "make room for more inmates" at the Odd Fellows Home. A phone call confirmed the eight deaths — all listed as natural — and Menarik was taken into custody.

In jail, Menarik's story underwent a sudden shift. The homicides had not been his idea, he now proclaimed, but rather had been ordered by officials at the home, who described the elderly victims as "a lot of trouble and no good anyhow." On February 5, the home's superintendent and three more employees were clapped into jail as material witnesses, with the Odd Fellows lodge refusing to post their bail.

Although authorities refused to order exhumation of remains, an investigation seemed to bear out Carl Menarik's tale of inmates killed with chloroform and arsenic. Menarik had warned patient Elizabeth Houser of her impending death a day in advance, and a mortician recalled red markings — similar to chloroform burns — on the face of alleged victim Henry Horn. A teenage inmate of the home informed police about an errand she had run on January 4, delivering a bottle of chloroform from employee Max Ring — jailed as a material witness — to "Mors," in the room occupied by patient Ferdinand Scholz. Scholz died the same day, and other inmates suspected "Mors" of sabotaging the painter's scaffold that dropped Jacob Groh to his death on December 14.

The list went on, but prosecution was deferred in favor of a psychiatric test. Described as "not well mentally," Menarik was committed to Poughkeepsie's Hudson River State Hospital for the Insane. His employer and coworkers were released, the case dismissed with a host of questions still unanswered. On May 10, 1916 — a week before his scheduled deportation to Austria — Menarik escaped from the hospital in Poughkeepsie and disappeared. He was never recaptured, but authorities took the loss in stride, announcing that the fugitive was "not considered dangerous." With **Belle Gunness** and **Bela Kiss**, Menarik ranks as one of those who wriggled through the net of justice, even though identified by the authorities.

Mons murders — Belgium (1997)

Authorities in Mons, near the French border, strongly suspect a common hand at work in the murders of four women, whose dismembered bodies were retrieved from roadside ditches and the River Haine in 1997. The first discovery, in March, involved several trash bags containing the severed limbs of three women, found on the side of a highway approaching the city. One day later, yet another trash bag was discovered, this one weighted with a "surgically dissected" female torso. Some of the limbs seemed to match, and the timing of discovery forced police to theorize that one man — or, perhaps, one *group* — was responsible for all three murders. Postmortem tests revealed that one victim had been killed within a week before being found; the other two, with limbs apparently frozen at some point in time, may have been killed as far back as 1995.

Authorities immediately discounted any speculative link between the dismemberment slayings and killer-pedophile Marc Dutroux, whose kiddy porn ring, recently exposed, had slain at least four children. The latest Belgian stalker clearly preferred adult victims, and he also seemed to possess a wicked sense of humor, discarding body parts at sites with names like Rue du Depot (Dump Street), Chemin de l'Inquietude (the Path of Worry), or beside the Rivers Haine (Hate) and Trouille (Jitters).

As far as technique was concerned, detectives stated that the killer's victims were dismembered with "remarkable precision," prompting speculation that their man might be a surgeon or a butcher. The habitual disposal of remains on weekends makes police believe their man is gainfully employed, a nine-to-fiver, but further details of a psychological profile prepared by FBI experts remain under wraps at this writing. On June 3, 1997, a report was broadcast that authorities were looking into a religious motivation for the murders — perhaps Satanism — since "The treatment of the bodies is very methodical, which is often the case with satanics involved in ritualistic killings."

In fact, as the report made clear, the stalker's victims were not merely dismembered, but were chopped into pieces, each exactly 12 inches long. This fact suggested that the psychopath might be employing a machine, such as an automated log-cutter, to whittle down his prey. The last of 30 bags containing severed body parts was found on Rue St. Symphorien, named for a beheaded Third-Century martyr, whose remains lie in a nearby church. The June report also dismissed early reports of the killer's surgical skill, opting instead for someone with heavy equipment and the privacy in which to use it.

Three of the killer's victims have thus far been identified. Martine Bohn, a 43-year-old French transsexual and "retired" prostitute had disappeared on July 21, her torso found floating in the Haine, both breasts removed. The other positive I.D. was 21-year-old Nathalie Godart (no details available), while the third presumed victim, 33-year-old Jacqueline Leclercq, had last been seen alive on January 23, 1997. Study of an unknown woman's pelvis, found across the border in France, has so far failed to cinch connections with the Belgian murder spree.

Psychologists in Mons describe their stalker as a meticulous anal retentive, whose murders are committed "very neatly, very precisely, the work of an obsessive." The only suspect named to date was cleared upon substantiation of his alibi, and subsequently left the country. To date, Belgian police have no leads on the real killer or killers, waiting grimly to see if the next crime — assuming there *is* a next murder — will offer the critical evidence needed to make an arrest.

"Monster of Florence" — Italy (1968-85)

The countryside surrounding Florence, Italy, has long been favored as a prime vacation spot for campers, hikers, nature-lovers. In the summer months, warm breezes, starry skies, and rolling meadows make the area a perfect trysting spot for lovers, honeymooners, and couples seeking to rekindle a romantic flame in their relationships. In the latter half of this century, however, Florence acquired a different sort of reputation on the side, as the selected hunting ground of a sadistic killer who preferred to prey on couples, randomly selecting victims for a yearly sacrifice of blood. Three decades after the commencement of the terror, homicide detectives still cannot lay claim to having solved the case.

The Florence slayer's first appearance was recorded on August 21, 1968, when Barbara Locci and her adulterous lover, Antonio Lo Bianco, were shot to death as they lay on the front seat of an automobile, parked beside a rural lane. In the back seat, the dead woman's six-year-old son slept through the murder undisturbed, suggesting that the killer may have used a silencer. Despite a lack of any solid evidence, the crime appeared routine to local homicide investigators, and Locci's husband was convicted in a hasty trial. Six years elapsed before his innocence was proven, when the killer struck again.

The second set of victims, slain in September 1974, were shot with the same .22-caliber Beretta automatic pistol used in 1968; once more, the gunman used distinctive copper-jacketed Winchester bullets, manufactured in Australia in the 1950s. Unlike the first crime, however, this time the female victim was sexually mutilated after death, a grim addition that would become the Florence slayer's trademark.

Another long hiatus in the murders followed, but was broken in June and October 1981 when two more couples were killed with the same Beretta automatic. Mutilation of female victims remained a trademark of the killer. Stefani Pettini, killed on June 6, was stabbed more than 300 times, a severed grapevine thrust into one of her wounds. Susana Cambi, killed October 23, had her genitals sliced away like Carmela De Nuccio in 1974.

Each year from 1981 to 1985, the faceless hunter returned to kill one couple camped or parked within a 19-mile radius of Florence, shooting both victims before savaging the women with a knife. The pattern has been broken only once, in 1983, when two West German men were shot while sleeping in a camper, killed by the familiar Winchester bullets fired at point-blank range. Police believe the long blond hair of one young man confused the killer, making him believe one victim was a woman.

Recreation of the "Monster's" crimes revealed a striking similarity in every case. Each of the double murders occurred on moonless nights, between the hours of 10 o'clock and midnight. In each case, police believe the man was murdered first, the woman subsequently shot and mutilated as the killer exorcised his private frenzy. Fingerprint examinations of the murder scenes indicate the gunman typically wore rubber surgical gloves, and homicide detectives freely admitted they had no leads in the baffling case. As described by Francisco Fleury, the district attorney in charge of the investigation, "The man could be your respectable next-door neighbor, a man above suspicion."

Like so much else about the crimes, the six- and seven-year delays between the first three sets of murders remains unexplained.

Investigators thought they had a solid lead in 1985, when two French tourists camping in a tent were murdered on September 8. The woman's body had been slashed at least 100 times, her left breast severed. On the morning that the bodies were discovered, a copper-jacketed Winchester bullet was found on the sidewalk in front of a hospital close by the murder site. The hospital's proximity, together with evidence of surgical gloves and a scalpel employed in the crimes, led detectives to question members of the hospital staff, but no suspects were identified. The next day, police received an envelope addressed with letters clipped from a newspaper; inside, they found a portion of the murdered woman's genitalia, a mocking gift from their elusive quarry.

Three movies have been made, so far, about the "Monster" and his crimes, ranging from a pornographic feature to a documentary. One film was in production in September 1985, and members of the crew rushed to the latest murder site, shooting new scenes to update their story. Police, meanwhile, were fearful that increased publicity might prompt the killer to become more active, or encourage "copycats" to emulate his crimes. In fact, however, the slayer appeared to retire from the game, with no confirmed kills since 1985.

Italian police questioned more than 100,000 persons and briefly charged six different suspects in the Florence case, before they identified their best suspect yet, in 1993. Arrested on January 17 of that year, 71-year-old Pietro Pacciani was a semi-literate farmhand and amateur taxidermist, convicted in 1951 of murdering a traveling salesman caught "in an affectionate embrace" with Pacciani's girlfriend. (Following the murder, Pacciani made the woman lie next to the corpse, and raped her there.)

Paroled after 13 years in prison, Pacciani remained a ne'er do well, arrested for beating his wife, and served four more years (1987-91) in prison for molesting his two daughters. Convicted of seven double murders in November 1994, Pacciani still maintained that he was "as innocent as Christ on the cross," and an appeals court overturned his conviction on February 13, 1996.

Ironically, Pacciani's release from prison came within hours of police arresting his good friend, 70-year-old Mario Vanni, on charges of murdering a French couple in 1985. Authorities soon adjusted their previous theory, deciding that the "Monster of Florence" was, in fact, a gang, led by Pacciani, with members including Vanni, 77-year-old Giovanni Faggi, and 54-year-old Giancarlo Lotti. Ten months after Pacciani's release from prison, on December 12, 1996, the Italian Supreme Court reversed the appellate court's decision and ordered a new murder trial for Pacciani. His three alleged accomplices went to trial in Florence on May 21, 1997, charged with five double murders, while their supposed ringleader was ordered to remain in his home town of Mercatale, shadowed by police as a "socially dangerous character." Pacciani died of natural causes on Sunday, February 22, 1998, one day before closing arguments were scheduled to begin in the trial of his three alleged confederates.

Montreal child murders — Canada (1984-85)

Between November 1984 and June 1985, parents in Montreal, Canada, were terrorized by the specter of an anonymous child-killer stalking their city, selecting his male victims at random, brutalizing and sexually assaulting them before discarding their bodies like so much rubbish. Although police made every normal effort to detect the killer, he remains at large, the case unsolved.

The first to die were 12-year-old Wilton Lubin and his playmate, eight-year-old Sebastien Metivier, reported missing on November 1, 1984. Lubin was pulled from the St. Lawrence River a month later, his throat slashed, but Sebastien Metivier has never been found. On December 2, four-year-old Maurice Viens was reported missing from his home; discovered in a vacant house five days later, the boy had been sexually abused, then killed by heavy blows to the back of his head. Twelve-year-old Michel Ethier disappeared on Christmas Day 1984, turning up in the St. Lawrence, a reported drowning victim. Denis Roux-Bergevin, age five, had been missing for three days when hikers found his bludgeoned, violated body on the shoulder of a highway, 12 miles east of town.

Based on the existing evidence, authorities acknowledged a connection only in the Viens and Roux-Bergevin murders, but the frightened residents of Montreal were not so easily convinced. Gary Rosenfelt, who lost a child to sex-slayer Clifford Olson in the 1970s, told reporters, "Everything indicates that there is a serial killer in Montreal, and the police do not seem to even acknowledge it."

Speaking for his department, Detective Sergeant Gilles Boyer replied that all 16 members of the Montreal homicide squad were involved in the manhunt. "We are looking all over — in sewers, everywhere," he said. "The kids are not that big. They are easy to get rid of."

At this writing, the long search has produced no suspects and no leads.

"Moonlight Murderer" — Arkansas/Texas (1946)

America was still recovering from the trauma of World War II and the euphoria of V-J Day when headlines focused national attention on the town of Texarkana, straddling the Texas-Arkansas border. There, between March 23 and May 4, 1946, an unknown slayer claimed at least five victims, surfacing at three-week intervals to murder when the moon was full. His rampage brought hysteria to Texarkana and environs, causing citizens to fortify their homes or flee the town entirely, sparking incidents of violence when a paperboy or salesman was mistaken for a lethal prowler in the night. Despite five decades of investigation and production of a feature film about the case, it stands officially unsolved today, the so-called "phantom gunman" unidentified.

The killer's first attack, unrecognized for several weeks, took place on February 23. Jimmy Hollis, age twenty-four, was parked with his 19-year-old girlfriend, Mary Larey, on a lonely road near Texarkana, when a tall masked man approached their car with gun in hand. He ordered Hollis from the car and clubbed him to the ground, next turning on Larey and raping her with the gun barrel, tormenting her to the point that she begged him to kill her. Instead, he slugged her with the gun and turned back toward Hollis, allowing the young woman to escape on foot. Both victims managed to survive their ordeal, but the gunman would not be so lax a second time.

On March 23, 1946, 29-year-old Richard Griffin and 17-year-old Polly Ann Moore were killed on a lonely Texarkana lover's lane. Both victims were shot in the back of the head, Griffin kneeling underneath the dashboard, while his girlfriend sprawled in the back seat, but a blood-soaked patch of earth some 20 feet away suggested they had died outside the car. Both bodies were fully clothed, and recent reports deny any evidence of sexual assault. Contemporary rumors, however, featured mention of rape, torture and mutilation inflicted on Polly Moore.

Precisely three weeks later, on April 13, 17-year-old Paul Martin and 15-year-old Betty Jo Booker were ambushed in Spring Lake Park, following a late dance at the local VFW hall. Martin's lifeless body, shot four times, was found beside a rural highway on the morning of April 14. Booker's corpse was discovered six hours later and a mile away, shot in the face and heart. Again, the tales of fiendish torture spread through Texarkana, though a crop of modern journalists reject them as untrue.

The fanfare of publicity, complete with Texas Rangers on patrol and homicide detectives staked out in the guise of teen-age lovers, caused the killer to adopt a new technique for what was said to be his last attack. On May 4, 1946, 36-year-old Virgil Starks was shot through the window of his farmhouse, 10 miles from Texarkana, as he read his evening paper after supper. Emerging from a bedroom at the sound of breaking glass, his wife was wounded twice before she managed to escape and summon help from neighbors. In her absence, the intruder prowled from room to room, leaving bloody foot-prints behind as he fled, dropping an untraceable flashlight in the bushes outside. Tracking dogs were hurried to the scene, but they lost their man at the point where he entered his car and drove off.

Two days after the Starks attack, with Texarkana living in a state of siege, a man's mangled body was found on the railroad tracks north of town. While some reporters have suggested that he may have been the killer, capping off his murder spree with suicide, the coroner's report of May 7, 1946 reveals that victim Earl McSpadden had been stabbed to death before his body was dumped on the tracks, suffering further mutilation when a train passed over at 5:30 A.M. Today, it seems more likely that McSpadden was another victim of the "Moonlight Murderer," dispatched in an attempt to end the manhunt with a simulated suicide.

Arkansas lawman Max Tackett claimed to have captured the killer in the summer of 1946, basing his case on disjointed remarks from a convicted car thief and an inadmissible statement from the suspect's wife. At least one FBI agent also fingered the thief, later sentenced to life on unrelated charges, as a prime suspect in the murders, but he was never charged. If he *was* the killer, that fact somehow managed to elude Captain M.T. Gonzaullas, in charge of the Texas Rangers' investigation at Texarkana. As late as 1973, Gonzaullas listed the "moonlight" murders as his most baffling case, vowing that he would never stop hunting the killer as long as he lived. Today, the Ranger captain is no longer with us, and the case remains officially unsolved.

Mors, Frederick: See **Menarik, Carl**

Mpumalanga murders — South Africa (1997)

On March 18, 1997, police in South Africa's Mpumalanga district announced the possibility of a serial killer operating in their jurisdiction. Investigators went public with the warning six days after a young woman was found, raped and strangled to death with her own underwear, on the Grootvlei farm, near Delmas. A previous victim, assaulted and killed in identical fashion, had been found some fifty kilometers from Bethal, a short time earlier. At this writing, no further developments have been reported in the case.

Mythical murders

Unidentified serial killers at large are so frightening and fascinating — so "sexy," in media parlance — that some reporters apparently cannot resist fabricating cases of their own, for whatever reason. Sometimes, the fudging amounts to simple exaggeration of known body counts for well-established slayers, while in other cases the reporters go all-out, apparently manufacturing killers and victims out of thin air.

One of the earliest, most frequently exaggerated cases involves London's "Ripper," back in 1888. Authorities involved in the manhunt agreed that Saucy Jack killed five women — and only five — between August and November of that fateful year. Still, speculation on additional victims, ranging in number from seven to 20 or more, continues in various published accounts to the present day. Some of the "extra" victims really *were* killed in London during the Ripper's heyday, but in circumstances radically divergent from Red Jack's pattern, while others — generally noted only as anonymous statistics — are apparently figments of the individual author's imagination.

The "**Ax Man of New Orleans**" got a similar treatment from local papers, after he claimed his first two victims in 1918. Overnight, Crescent City newsmen "recalled" a similar series of murders in 1911 — including surnames of three victims — despite the fact that no such crimes are listed in police or coroner's reports for the year in question. Still, working primarily from front-page news reports, several authors accepted the 1911 murders as fact, over the next seven decades until I took the simple step of checking with authorities and published the truth in my book *Hunting Humans* (1990).

Far worse than the careless inflation of body counts — at least from the viewpoint of a serious researcher into crime — are the instances in which specific writers, for whatever reasons, publish books and articles on "unsolved" cases that have either been resolved with a conviction years before, or — worse yet — apparently never happened at all.

The late Joel Norris, a psychologist specializing in art therapy, was belatedly hailed as a preeminent expert on serial murder, featured on various tabloid talk shows, but his published work left much to be desired in terms of accuracy. Factual errors and typos aside, Norris created untold problems for academic researchers with his mangling — or outright fabrication — of unsolved serial murder cases. Some examples, from *Serial Killers: The Growing Menace,* (1988) include:

- The "Zodiac," described by Norris as a killer who "murdered and sexually assaulted several children in San Francisco" during 1974 (all false), and who was "[g]iven his name by the police because he carved the sign of the zodiac [sic] into the bodies of his victims." In fact, there were no mutilations as described by Norris, and the killer coined his own nickname, in letters to the press.
- "[T]he case of a cult killer of seven hitchhikers in Point Reyes Station, California," in 1980, with the killer "still at large." This hopelessly garbled account seems to address the so-called "Trailside Murders" of eight *hikers* around Point Reyes, between August 1979 and March 1981. Gunman David Carpenter faced trial on those charges in

1984 — four years before Norris's book went to press — and was sentenced to death.

- The "Skid Row Slasher" in Los Angeles, who — according to Norris — murdered eight victims in 1981. In truth, there were 10 victims, between 1964 and 1975. Killer Vaughn Orrin Greenwood was sentenced to prison for nine of the slayings in January 1977, a full 11 years before *Serial Killers* was published.
- Manhattan's "Midtown Slasher" case of 1981, described by Norris seven years later as "still open." Norris fails to note that the case was solved in July 1981, one day after the final stabbing, with the arrest of suspect Charles Sears. (Sears later pled guilty and was committed to a state hospital for the criminally insane.)
- The "Sunday Morning Slasher" case, curiously described by Norris as taking place "in Houston" during 1981… and, of course, "still open." In point of fact, the Slasher crimes occurred in Ann Arbor, Michigan, between April and July 1980, but they were solved in Houston, with the 1982 arrest and confession of serial slayer Coral Eugene Watts. Incredibly, Norris treats Watts in a separate entry, dubbing him "Carl Eugene Roberts" and misplacing his arrest in 1981!
- "Suspect unknown" in what Norris describes as the 1983 murders of "four White Plains, New York, women within seven months." This case remains a total puzzler, since my personal communication with lawmen, reporters, and librarians in White Plains has failed to turn up any record of such homicides, in 1983 or any other year.
- "Suspect unknown" once again, at a convalescent home in Galveston, Texas, where Norris describes police "investigating the deaths of 28 geriatric patients" in 1983. This case, apparently, *does* have some basis in reality, but it was not an example of serial murder. Rather, as I was told

by reporters on the scene in 1988, authorities investigated the "home" in question for chronic neglect of its inmates, resulting in several deaths.

➲ Again in 1983, the "Dunes Case" from Provincetown, Massachusetts, where — Norris tells us — "police are investigating the serial killer who left the bodies of twelve young women in sand dunes." A personal visit to Provincetown revealed that Norris had the date wrong, and had also tacked eleven nonexistent victims on to the killer's body count. Provincetown's "Lady of the Dunes," found with her hands and feet severed, was apparently the only victim of a slayer who remains unidentified today.

For all his flubs and fabrications, Norris still can't hold a candle to Jay Robert Nash, the much-touted "dean of crime writers," when it comes to botching the details of infamous cases, solved or otherwise. A prolific author of true-crime reference books, Nash plays fast and loose with the facts on various serial murder cases (and others), apparently preferring a "good story" to accurate reportage. Glaring bloopers in his work are so frequent and flagrant, in fact, that by the time Nash published his massive six-volume *Encyclopedia of World Crime* (1990), a prefatory note was included, warning would-be plagiarists that certain entries were deliberately "seeded with errors" to facilitate their subsequent prosecution. Certain lawyers may admire that stratagem, but any serious student attempting to use Nash's work as a reference for theses and such will recognize that such a tactic renders the material worthless, completely unreliable.

A few of Nash's problems with "unsolved" serial murder cases, deliberate or otherwise, include:

➲ The "Chicago Ripper," briefly described by Nash in his *Crime Chronology* (1984) as the unidentified mutilation-slayer of twenty female victims, the last killed in January 1906. Perusal of Chicago papers for that date reveal that the victim in question was *shot,* with no reported mutilations, and that her death was speculatively linked to *one* other slaying. No trace of the elusive Ripper or his "twenty" victims could be found in contemporary media sources.

- The "**Ax Man of New Orleans.**" Nash puts a weird spin on this unsolved case in *Bloodletters and Badmen*, reporting that: "Between 1916 and 1920 [suspect Joseph] Mumfre, on orders from the Mafia faction… systematically murdered, according to reports, twelve members of the Pepitone family, using an ax to bash in each victim's head." Nash offers no citation for said "reports," but they are clearly erroneous, since (a) the "Ax Man" murders began in 1918 (not 1916); (b) Joe Mumfre was in prison from 1911 until early 1918; (c) the stalker claimed a total of six lives (not twelve); and (d) only one of the six dead — the last victim — was named Pepitone, an innocent grocer with no apparent connection to organized crime.
- The "**3X**" case, involving a lover's lane gunman in Queens, New York, who killed two men and raped one woman in June 1930. Nash, in *Open Files* (1984) and the revised edition of *Bloodletters and Badmen* (1996), unaccountably describes the unknown shooter as a "mad bomber" who "terrorized the city in the early 1930s."
- "Ma" Barker's lesbian torture-slayings. Best known as the Depression-era mother who raised her sons to rob banks and kidnap wealthy businessmen, later dying in a shootout with FBI agents, Arizona ("Ma") Barker is described by Nash (in *Look for the Woman* [1981]) as a sadistic lesbian who kidnapped, tortured, and murdered countless young women, later ordering her outlaw sons and sidekick Alvin Karpis to dump their corpses in various Minnesota lakes,

where they presumably reside to this day. Nash's source for the tale is one "Blackie" Audett, an aging underworld informer of dubious veracity, but Nash repeats the tale, straight-faced, despite a total absence of supporting evidence. To date, there are no corpses, no reports of missing women from the area — nothing at all, in short, to imbue Audett's florid fantasy with any credence whatsoever.

- The "Tulsa bludgeonings," described by Nash in his *Encyclopedia of World Crime,* as the unsolved murders of four women (with two other victims surviving) between July 1942 and July 1948. The crimes were actually solved in 1949 — four decades before Nash published his version — with the arrest and confession of defendant Charles Floyd.
- The "Texas Strangler" case, reported by Nash (in *Open Files*) as a series of 12 unsolved murders committed in the late 1960s and early 1970s. In fact, at least two of the crimes listed by Nash were solved in 1972 — 12 years before the publication of *Open Files* — with the Odessa conviction of defendant Johnny Meadows. I personally advised Nash's editor of the Meadows conviction, but the case remained "unsolved" when Nash went to press with his subsequent *Crime Chronology.*
- The "Skid Row Slasher." Like Joel Norris (above), author Nash — in *Open Files* — reports this series of murders as unsolved... a full seven years after Vaughn Greenwood was sentenced to jail for the crime.
- Australian mutilation-murders. Described with lamentable brevity in Nash's *Crime Chronology,* this series of crimes allegedly included the "Ripper"-style slayings of at least seven women, between 1976 and 1979. While such murders are certainly plausible, repeated queries to police and newspapers in Australia since 1984 have thus far produced no documentation to suggest the crimes ever occurred.

- Moscow decapitation murders. Another brief entry in Nash's *Crime Chronology* alludes to the beheading of several women, their names and number undisclosed, around the Soviet capital in 1979. Strict communist censorship from that era makes the case impossible to document or disprove, but Nash's track record does not inspire confidence, particularly since the sketchy details offered fail to match the M.O. of any recognized Soviet serial killer to date. [See also: **"Soda Pop Slasher"**]

Nahanni Valley murders — Canada (1910-46)

A mystery of near-supernatural proportions haunts the beautiful but sinister Nahanni Valley, situated in the southern part of the Mackenzie mountain range, in Canada's vast Northwest Territories. Published reports differ on the number of victims slain in the Nahanni Valley and the dates of their murders, but all agree that the area is — or once was — stalked by an unknown headhunter who decapitated some of his victims, while others disappeared entirely. A compilation of Nahanni Valley cases, drawn from several sources, would include:

- Brothers Frank and Willie MacLeod, from Fort Simpson, found dead and decapitated in the valley around 1910. (Author Jay Robert Nash, in his less-than-reliable *Encyclopedia of World Crime,* adds an unnamed engineer to the MacLeod expedition, claiming all three victims disappeared in 1904, with their severed skulls found three years later.)
- Martin Jorgensen, found decapitated in a burned-out cabin, sometime in 1917.

- Annie Laferte, missing and presumed dead in the Nahanni Valley, circa 1926.
- Phil Powers, reportedly found burned to death inside his cabin, in 1932.
- Two unnamed prospectors reported missing from the valley in 1936, while a "John Doe" corpse was found, apparently unrelated to the missing men.
- Prospector Ernest Savard, who had previously emerged from the valley with rich ore samples, found dead in his sleeping bag in 1945, head nearly severed from his body.
- Another prospector, John Patterson, who missed a scheduled rendezvous with his partner in 1946, listed as missing and presumed dead.

A magazine article on the Nahanni Valley, published in 1950, names additional victims of the local "curse" as Joe Mulholland, from Minnesota; Bill Espler, of Winnipeg; Yukon Fischer; Edwin Hall; Andy Hays; and "one O'Brien," but no dates or details are provided for those cases, beyond a vague reference to "Canadian police records."

There are clearly varied reasons why a man or group of men might disappear in the Nahanni Valley — a rugged area sometimes used for survival training by elite military forces — but the record of at least six murders, most of them involving partial or complete decapitation, clearly indicate that the Nahanni once played host to a determined killer... one whose identity is obscured, perhaps forever, by the chill mist of the Great White North.

Newcastle murders — Australia (1979-94)

Details are sparse on this late-breaking case (March 1998), in which a task force has been organized to search for clues and corpses in the case of 12 young people lost around Newcastle — 100 miles north of Sydney, Australia — between 1979 and 1994. The case is also curious because it *may* be solved already, though police refuse to link their leading suspect with the several disappearances, or even to acknowledge that the missing youngsters may be victims of a random killer.

The new investigation, announced on March 22, is officially focused on only three victims — reported missing in 1979, 1993 and 1994, respectively — but authorities admit the disappearance of a dozen young hikers and campers in the area over the past two decades. Coincidentally or otherwise, the same region — including scenic Hunter Valley — had also served as a stalking ground for Australia's worst known serial killer Ivan Milat, convicted in July 1997 for the murders of seven young backpackers between 1989 and 1992. Authorities were quick to note that they are not attempting to clear old cases at random by pinning them on Milat; neither, in fact, are they willing to admit that the 12 missing youngsters were murdered by *anyone*. Still, the search continues with a significant allocation of manpower... and solutions to the grim mystery remain elusive.

New Haven murders — Connecticut (1976-78)

Between 1976 and 1978, an unidentified killer stalked New Haven, Connecticut, selecting black women as victims, preying chiefly on prostitutes working in the neighborhood of Chapel Street, a short walk from Yale University. Police are hesitant to speculate on connections in the several crimes, but four of the known victims had records of arrests for prostitution, and three were killed within a single month, thus reducing the odds of coincidence or separate killers at large in the college community. Following the death of victim Terry Williams, 23, found nude and shot in a motel room, frightened blacks established "soul patrols," with men escorting hookers to their "jobs" and standing by to watch for clues. At this writing, neither homicide detectives nor private patrols have succeeded in naming the killer.

New Orleans murders — Louisiana (1987-88)

In the space of a year, between December 1987 and December 1988, five women in their 20s were strangled or asphyxiated in New Orleans by persons unknown, prompting authorities to speculate — however cautiously — on the possibility of a serial killer at large. The first victim, 27-year-old Ruth Peart, was found in the Hollygrove neighborhood, her nude body hidden in the crawlspace beneath a house. On January 2, 1988, 24-year-old Corinne Morgan was strangled in Hollygrove, six blocks away, her corpse found fully clothed. Number three, 24-year-old Carol Bissitt, was discovered in her home on June 13, strangled like the others, a telephone cord and the sash from a robe still wrapped around her neck. A black "Jane Doe" — excluded from the series in some published articles — was found in a New Orleans park on November 30, choked to death by wads of paper shoved down her throat. The last to die, one week later, was Krystal Burroughs, found nude and strangled in a condemned dwelling frequented by homeless squatters.

At this writing, no suspects in the Crescent City strangulation murders have been publicly identified. The case remains unsolved — and unconnected, say police, to another series of 24 murders that plagued New Orleans between 1991 and 1995.

"Occult" murders — California (1972-75)

In February 1975, California's Department of Justice issued a confidential report stating that 14 unsolved murders in the past three years had been committed by a single man. Six victims had been found near Santa Rosa, in Sonoma County; five were found in San Francisco, with one each in Redding, Marysville, and Monterey. The murders were distinguished from a host of other unsolved homicides by similar disposal of the bodies and the killer's fondness for retaining souvenirs.

The chain of homicides began on February 4, 1972, when Maureen Strong and Yvonne Weber, both 12 years old, vanished on their way home from a Santa Rosa skating rink. Their skeletons were found December 28, on an embankment near a rural road in eastern Sonoma County. The killer had removed the clothing and a single gold earring from each victim.

On March 4, 1972, Kim Allen, a 19-year-old coed, vanished while hitchhiking in Santa Rosa. Her nude body, strangled with clothesline, was found in a creek bed; there were superficial cuts on her chest, rope burns on her wrists and ankles. Once again, the clothing and one gold earring were missing.

On November 21, 1972, 13-year-old Lori Jursa vanished from a Santa Rosa market. She was nude upon discovery, three weeks later, and the cause of death was listed as a broken neck. She still had wire loops in her ear lobes, but her earrings had been removed.

The killer shifted to San Francisco with spring, strangling Rosa Vasquez and dumping her nude body on May 29, 1973. Fifteen-year-old Yvonne Quilintang received similar treatment on June 9. Angela Thomas was found naked and dead July 2, but she had been smothered. On July 13, Nancy Gidley was snatched from a local motel and strangled, her nude body dumped in a high school parking lot.

The "occult" angle surfaced that same month, after Caroline Davis was kidnapped on July 15. A runaway from Shasta County, she was last seen thumbing for rides on Highway 101, near Santa Rosa. Poisoned with strychnine, she was found on July 31, at the precise spot where the first two victims were discovered seven months earlier. On the bank above her body, searchers found a strange design arranged from twigs, laid out to form two interlocking squares. An unnamed source described the sculpture as a witchy symbol understood to designate "the carrier of spirits."

On July 22, 1973, the nearly nude body of Nancy Feusi was found near Redding, California, the cause of death obscured by decomposition. On November 4, the scene shifted back to San Francisco with discovery of Laura O'Dell's nude, strangled body. Therese Walsh, age 22, was hitching rides from Malibu to Garberville when she met her killer on December 22, 1973. Raped, hog-tied and strangled, she was dumped near the spot where Kim Allen was found in March 1972.

According to police, the same man murdered Brenda Merchant, at Marysville, by stabbing her to death on February 1, 1974, discarding her semi-nude corpse beside a rural road. On September 29, 14-year-old Donna Braun, nude and strangled, was found floating in the Salinas River near Monterey. And so, presumably, the murders ceased.

A 15th victim, inadvertently omitted from the government's report, was Jeannette Kamahele, age 20, a coed who disappeared on April 25, 1972, while hitchhiking near Santa Rosa. Her skeletal remains were finally unearthed on July 6, 1979, hog-tied in a shallow grave within 100 yards of Lori Jursa's final resting place.

The "occult" theory's chief proponent was Sergeant Erwin Carlstedt, of Sonoma County. Impressed by the sticks found at one murder scene, he also found significance in victims being dumped along the east side of a road. In passing, Carlstedt told associates that seven women killed in Washington, between January and July 1974, had been abducted in the waning ("sacrificial") phase of the moon. The 1975 report suggested that the killer was "familiar with witchcraft or the occult, because of a witchcraft symbol found during the Caroline Davis case and the possible occult involvement in the missing females in the states of Oregon and Washington."

Unfortunately for the Carlstedt thesis, all the victims killed in Washington were ultimately credited to serial killer Ted Bundy, while research into Bundy's movements has cleared him of any involvement in the California murders. Likewise, the reputed "witchcraft symbol" proved to be a piece of childish art, constructed by a small boy on vacation as a likeness of the family's car and trailer.

Slayer Harvey Carignan has also been suggested as a suspect in the unsolved murders, based upon a traffic ticket he collected in Solano County, east of Santa Rosa, on June 20, 1973. Again, no solid evidence exists, and one week later Carignan was claiming victims in the state of Minnesota, leading to his ultimate arrest in September 1974. He was in jail when Donna Braun was murdered, and the other bodies showed no evidence of Carignan's traditional resort to beating with a hammer.

An intriguing theory published during 1986, by author Robert Graysmith, credits the elusive **Zodiac** killer with these and many other unsolved homicides. The point is moot, until such time as a solution is discovered. In the meantime, we can only say that one or more sadistic killers may be still at large within the Golden State.

"Operation Enigma" —
See: **Prostitute murders — England**

"Orange Coast Killer" — California (1977-79)

The latter 1970s were witness to a sudden rash of random, homicidal violence in America, alerting criminologists to a disturbing increase in the incidence of serial murders. Some regions of the country — Texas, Florida, New York — seemed bent on hogging headlines for their local maniacs, but none could hold a candle to the killing fields of southern California, where the "Hillside Strangler," "Freeway Killer," "Sunset Slayer," "Skid Row Slasher," and a host of others plied their trade. One such — the "Orange Coast Killer" — went his ghoulish counterparts one better, slipping out of newsprint into legend as the one who got away.

In retrospect, detectives would agree the terror dated back to August 2, 1977, when Jane Bennington was slain in Corona Del Mar. Attacked in her home, the 29-year-old was raped, then beaten to death with a blunt instrument. Her killer left no clues for the police, and in the gap of 18 months before his next appearance, other homicides took precedence, demanding the attention of investigators.

The killer returned with a vengeance on April Fool's Day 1979, raping Kimberly Rawlines in her Costa Mesa home before beating her to death. On May 14, Savannah Anderson, age 22, was assaulted and bludgeoned in Irvine. Ten days later, Kim Whitecotton, 20, survived an attack in her apartment, in Santa Ana Heights, her graphic description of the incident spreading panic among her neighbors.

Overnight, there was a run on guns and guard dogs in the neighborhoods that seemed to mark the killer's chosen hunting ground. Publicity alerted women to the danger of an unlocked door or window, while composite sketches of the suspect — featuring a dark mustache and pock-marked cheeks — told women who to look for. Still, it seemed the slayer was invisible to everyone except his victims, free to come and go at will.

Jane Pettengill, age 24, was chosen on July 19, assaulted in her Costa Mesa home. She would survive, unlike her neighbor, 30-year-old Marolyn Carleton, who was raped and bludgeoned on September 14. The killer moved to Tustin on September 30, administering a near-fatal beating to Diana Green.

A week later, he killed 24-year-old Debra Jean Kennedy in Tustin. On December 21, the slayer claimed his only teenage victim, battering Debra Lynn Senior in Costa Mesa, afterward raping her corpse.

A special task force stalked the killer through a maze of clues and useless "tips" from frightened members of the public, all in vain. As summer faded into autumn, slowly giving way to winter, it became apparent that their man was gone. This time, the disappearance was no ruse, no holiday. The Orange Coast Killer, for whatever reason, had retired. As far as homicide detectives know, their man is still at large.

Perm' murders — Russia (1996)

Authorities have released few details in the case of a serial murderer active in Perm', a hundred miles west of the Ural Mountains in central Russia. On August 29, 1996, Perm's police chief, Andrei Kamenev, grudgingly told reporters, "It is true that we are looking for a killer who has already killed seven people. His latest victim was a woman who was raped and stabbed in an elevator."

Even more alarming, for local residents, was the fact that their local predator had run up his seven-victim body count in a mere three months. Unfortunately, tight-lipped officials have had nothing more to say about the case. Unless captured, tried, and executed in secret, their stalker is presumably still at large.

Perth murders — Australia (1996-97)

Authorities in Perth, Western Australia, describe the elusive serial killer blamed for slaying three local women as a "verbal, intelligent man who has been able to get the trust of his victims." The first to die, 18-year-old Sarah Spiers, vanished in

January 1996, after visiting friends at the Continental Hotel, and was never seen again. Jane Rimmer, 23, disappeared from the same affluent suburb six months later, in July 1996, buried 25 miles from Perth. The third and last (so far) to die, 28-year-old Ciara Glennon, was last seen alive when she left the Continental on March 17, 1997, her body found three weeks later, in a shallow grave some 40 miles outside of town. Evidence found at the gravesites led police to speculate that the killer washes his car after planting each corpse, presumably in an effort to remove trace evidence.

Detective Paul Ferguson, in charge of the manhunt, has suggested to reporters that the killer may be someone in authority, perhaps a policeman or security guard.

"These are not random attacks," Ferguson declared. "The person or persons responsible are very organized. The age and type of women targeted show these attacks don't just happen anywhere, to anyone."

Another theory, popular with some investigators, pegs the killer as a taxi driver, and while investigation of Perth's 3,000 licensed cabbies has yet to produce a suspect, announcement of the theory cut night-time taxi trade by 40 percent in Western Australia's largest city.

Petworth murders — Washington, D.C. (1996-97)

Residents of the nation's capital are no strangers to violent death — or to unsolved serial killings, for that matter. The most recent string of homicides reported (at this writing) involves the murders of six women in the Petworth and Park View neighborhoods of Washington, D.C. Police believe they have solved at least two of the murders, with the arrest of a suspect in January 1998. And yet...

No cause of death has been determined for the first quartet of Petworth victims, a circumstance which understandably hampers the filing of criminal charges. Number one, Priscilla Mosley, was found on November 17, 1996, on Newton Place. The next to die, Lateashia Blocker, was discovered on May 8, 1997, hauled up from beneath the floorboards of an abandoned house on Princeton Place, three miles from Capitol Hill. Emile Davis was another crawlspace victim, found beneath a Princeton Place dwelling on August 9, 1997. Two months later, on October 13, an unidentified woman's torso was discovered in the 1400 block of Meridian Place, DNA tests still in progress at this writing to determine whether it belongs to 41-year-old Jessica Cole, a former resident of Princeton Place reported missing three days earlier.

The geographic pattern was readily apparent, with one victim a known Princeton Place resident, while two others were dumped there, in close proximity to one another. That pattern continued on November 18, 1997, when 39-year-old Jacqueline Birch was found strangled to death inside another Princeton Place building. Nearly two weeks later, on December 1, another strangulation victim — 34-year-old Dana Hill, a Princeton Place native, still frequently seen in the district — was dumped behind a fast-food restaurant, a mile and a half from the Capitol.

Petworth residents had been living in fear for 12 months, before the *Washington Post* called attention to the deaths in November 1997 and a Princeton Place Task Force was created to investigate the crimes. Even then, authorities refused to speculate on the possibility of a serial killer at large, pursuing what the *Post* called "great lengths" to find alternate scenarios. Hill's case, despite her lifelong links to Princeton Place, was initially severed from the others by task force investigators, reconsidered only once they had a suspect in their sights.

That suspect, arrested on January 29, 1998, was 34-year-old Darryl Donnell Turner, an unemployed Princeton Place resident who lived on the same block once occupied by Debra Hill and *next door* to the building where Jacqueline Birch was found strangled. Police charged Turner with two counts of first-degree murder in those cases, and while they "have not ruled out" a connection to the other four deaths, Homicide Commander Alfred Broadbent told reporters, "He is not the only target of our investigation."

Indeed, while neighbors lined up to describe Turner as a "quiet gentleman" who never "ran his mouth," court records unearthed by the *Post* revealed at least one other suspect in the slayings, questioned three times by the task force and presently jailed without bond on unrelated charges.

Acting Police Chief Sonya Procter told the press, "We do expect to make more arrests. The only thing I can say definitely is that we believe we have strong cases in these two murders. There will be other developments."

And pending those developments, at least four of the Petworth slayings will remain officially unsolved, the killer(s) still at large.

"Pomona Strangler" — California (1993-95)

Black prostitutes were the chosen prey of an apparent serial killer who struck at least seven times around Pomona, in eastern Los Angeles County. The first four victims, killed in 1993, were all known streetwalkers who frequented "The Strip" — Holt Avenue — and police assume they met their killer on the job. Three more women were slain in near-identical circumstances, during 1994 and '95, while authorities remained clueless in the case. FBI agents visited Pomona in April 1994 to review the evidence and sketch a psychological profile of the elusive killer, but their efforts were in vain. To date, authorities still have no suspect in the case; the seven homicides are "open" and unsolved.

Portland murders — Oregon (1983-84)

While the search for Seattle's "**Green River killer**" was under way, police were distracted by a series of unsolved murders in Portland, Oregon, 170 miles to the south. No link was ever demonstrated to the Portland murderer who claimed at least four victims — all black women, all known prostitutes — between March 1983 and April 1984, but like his more prolific soul-mate in Seattle, Portland's maniac remains at large.

The first to die, on March 23, 1983, was 24-year-old Essie Jackson, strangled to death by an unknown assailant, her nude body dumped on an embankment near Overlook Park. Four months later, on July 9, 20-year-old Tonja Harry was fished out of the Columbia River Slough, the cause of death recorded as asphyxiation. Angela Anderson, strangled to death at 16, was found three days before Christmas in a vacant house. Nineteen-year-old Vickie Williams, stabbed repeatedly, was found in shrubbery near a Portland shopping mall, on April 23, 1984.

One published source reports 11 victims in the Portland series, without naming names, and feminists were outraged when a police lieutenant described murder as "an occupational hazard" for hookers. Additional reports claim that Portland authorities refused to cooperate with members of the "Green River" task force, stubbornly withholding the names of two local murder suspects. Without a solid lead to date, authorities can only guess at the killer's identity, his motives, and the circumstances that compelled him to "retire."

Priest murders — United States (1982-89)

Francis Leslie Craven was a second-grade student at St. Mary's Catholic School, in Lynn, Massachusetts, when he first voiced his desire to be a priest. Ordained two decades later, in 1963, he served first in Kokomo, Indiana, then spent six years as a chaplain in the United States Navy. Returning to civilian life in 1974, Father Craven was assigned to Holy Spirits Church in Tuscaloosa, Alabama. Twelve years later, he transferred to St. William's parish in Guntersville, northeast of Birmingham, where he served as chaplain for the Marshall County Hospice and the Cursillo Ministry, a spiritual retreat serving 29 Alabama counties. By all accounts, Craven was well-liked and respected by all who knew him, untainted by the financial and sexual scandals that have tarred so many clerics during recent years. In short, he seemed to be the proverbial man "without an enemy in the world."

On January 2, 1989, Father Craven flew from Birmingham to spend a week with friends in Fort Myers, Florida. He returned on Saturday, January 7, phoning ahead from a stopover in Atlanta to have a friend drop his van off at the Birmingham airport. Craven's flight was on time, and he found the van waiting for him, loaded with expensive electronics gear that included a cellular phone, CB radio, and stereo system, along with two cameras. Shortly after 10:00 A.M., he called from the airport to thank his friend for delivering the van, along with a prayer book left in the van as a gift. Craven announced that he was driving back to Guntersville, and hoped to arrive in time for Mass, at 11:00 A.M.

He never made it.

At the time he should have been in church, one of his friends in Florida received a call from Craven's mobile telephone. They had arranged a "one-ring" signal to confirm his safe arrival, and Craven's friend was understandably confused when the caller stayed on the line to chat. In retrospect, she would describe the call as "strange" — a man whose voice she did not recognize, introducing himself with unprecedented formality as "Father Craven," mispronouncing her name as he reported, "I got back to Birmingham without a hitch." Police would later speculate that Craven was speaking in code, perhaps alerting his friend to the presence of an armed hitchhiker in the van, but the prospect seemed unlikely, since Craven was known to avoid picking up strangers.

In any case, the call to Florida was Craven's last known contact with a living soul. At 4:00 P.M. that Saturday, a motorist near Tuscaloosa — 60 miles southwest of Birmingham, in the opposite direction from Guntersville — noted a trash dump burning off Highway 69. A closer look revealed a human body on the smoking pyre, and police were summoned to investigate. By that time, 30 hours overdue at home, Father Craven had been listed as a missing person, and his body was identified from dental charts on Sunday, January 8. An autopsy revealed brain damage and broken bones consistent with a brutal beating, but the medical examiner could not be certain whether Craven was dead or alive when his killer had set him on fire.

Investigators found a service station, roughly two miles from the burn site, where a clerk recalled a shaggy-haired white man, aged 20 to 30 years, arriving on foot to purchase a gallon of gasoline on Saturday afternoon. The man was in a hurry, walking off without his change, in the direction of the dump where Father Craven's corpse was found an hour later. Craven's burned out van was found a week after the murder at Windam Springs, some 12 miles north of the spot where his body was burned. Robbery was discounted as a motive in the slaying, after detectives found Craven's cameras and electronics gear inside the vehicle, all melted by the blaze. Devoid of clues or suspects, homicide detectives ran a check for similar crimes through the FBI's computer system in Washington, D.C., and were surprised to learn of three other Catholic priests murdered in similar circumstances, since 1982.

Father Reynaldo Riviera, pastor of St. Francis Church in Santa Fe, New Mexico, had received a telephone call on August 7, 1982, asking him to perform last rights for a parishioner in tiny Waldo, near the eastern border of the San Felipe Indian Reservation. The caller, never publicly identified, offered to meet Father Riviera at a rest stop on Highway 301, guiding him on from there to the home in question. An intensive search was launched when Riviera failed to return from his mission of mercy, and he was found on August 9, shot to death in the desert, three miles from the highway rest stop. His car was subsequently found abandoned, four miles from the murder scene, investigators noting that they found no evidence of robbery or sexual activity that would explain the crime.

Two years later, in August 1984, a certain Father Carrigan, newly assigned to Sacred Heart Church in Ronan, Montana, had vanished soon after arriving in town. After two days on the missing roster, Carrigan was found near Flathead Lake, some 10 miles north of Ronan, strangled with a wire coat hanger. Once again, robbery was ruled out as a motive, when police found $12,000 untouched in Carrigan's pocket. As in the other priestly homicides, the victim's car was dumped nearby — in this case, five miles from the murder scene. Authorities declared that Father Carrigan had not been in Montana long enough to make a mortal enemy, and nothing in his background helped explain the crime.

Another 28 months elapsed before the third murder, in Oklahoma City. Father Richard Dolan, age 66, was the founder of a local halfway house for alcoholics, funding the project through sale of his art work and social events that had earned him a reputation as the "Bingo King" of Oklahoma City. The victim of a savage beating in his own apartment, Dolan had been dead two days before his landlord found the body. His Oldsmobile station wagon was missing, found stripped of tires and wheels, beneath a nearby bridge. Police suspected that the theft occurred after the killer dumped the car, since nothing had been stolen from the victim's flat, and murder for a set of well-worn tires was dubious, at best.

Only the death of Father Craven, with its vague description of a suspect, offered any realistic prospect for solution, after so much time had passed.

As one detective told the press in Tuscaloosa, "What we need to know is where he was and what he was doing in the four hours from when he left the airport in Birmingham and when his body was burned on the trash pile. Someone someplace has the answer to that question. Someday we will learn who it is."

Perhaps, but as the 10-year anniversary of Father Craven's death approaches, homicide investigators are no closer to an answer than they were in January 1989. As for the other brutal homicides of Catholic priests, while no official designation of a murder series has been made, authorities have speculated publicly on links between the several crimes. At present, all remain unsolved, the killer(s) still at large.

Prince Georges County murders — Maryland (1986-87)

Between December 1986 and January 1987, five black women from the District of Columbia were murdered and their bodies dumped near Suitland, in Prince Georges County, Maryland. By September 1987, at least four more women were murdered in Washington, but the conviction of a suspect in one case has brought authorities no closer to solution of the other crimes.

The first victim, 20-year-old Dorothy Miller, was found in the woods near Suitland's Bradbury Recreation Center on December 13, 1986. Killed by an apparent drug overdose, Miller had also been violently sodomized, a fact that linked her death with those of four other victims discovered a month later.

On January 11, 1987, young patrons of the recreation center noticed women's clothing hanging in a tree nearby. Investigating, they discovered the body of 25-year-old Pamela Malcolm, missing from her Suitland home since October 22. An autopsy revealed she had been sodomized and stabbed to death.

On January 12, a team of 50 police recruits swept through the forest north of the U.S. Census Bureau's headquarters, seeking more clues in the two homicides. Instead of evidence, they found two more corpses, identified as 22-year-old Cynthia Westbury and 26-year-old Juanita Walls. Both had been reported missing from the District of Columbia and both were sodomized, before or after they were stabbed to death.

Number five, 22-year-old Angela Wilkerson, was found near Suitland on January 13, and authorities reported that four of the victims had lived within a one-mile radius of each other, in Southeast Washington. All four of the D.C. victims were unemployed, and at least two had frequented the same restaurant, on Good Hope Road.

On January 15, another "profile" victim, 20-year-old Janice Morton, was found naked, beaten and strangled to death in a Northeast Washington alley. That investigation was still under way on April 5, when a nude "Jane Doe" was discovered near Euclid and 13th Street, Northwest, her body dumped in a secluded driveway. A 31-year-old suspect, Alton Alonzo Best, was indicted for Norton's slaying on April 7, and he confessed to the crime on June 9. Authorities say Best knew two of the

Maryland victims, but the fact remains that his conviction did not stop the killing.

On April 10, with Best in jail, an unknown suspect in a van attempted to abduct a 25-year-old woman one block from the home of Suitland victim Pamela Malcolm. Police were still checking the facts of that case five days later, when another black victim, Donna Nichols, was beaten to death in a Washington alley. On June 24, 21-year-old Cheryl Henderson was found in a wooded area of Southeast Washington, less than two miles from Suitland, with her throat slashed from ear to ear. Another female victim was discovered on September 21, at a Southeast Washington apartment complex, authorities refusing to discuss the cause of death or possible connection to their other "open" cases.

At this writing, the Maryland-Washington series of murders remains unsolved, the killer(s) unidentified. His preference for blacks has led to speculation that the **"Freeway Phantom"** may have surfaced, after 15 years of inactivity, but homicide detectives have revealed no evidence of a connection to the early unsolved crimes.

Prince Georges Hospital — Maryland (1984-85)

Jane Bolding was employed as a nurse at Prince Georges Hospital, in a Maryland suburb of Washington, D.C., for nine years before authorities became suspicious of her conduct on the job. For much of that time, she worked the intensive care unit, tending patients in the direst extreme. Death is a daily fact of life in ICU, but during 1984 and early 1985, Jane Bolding's patients seemed to die like flies, a startling number suffering from cardiac arrest. On March 9, 1985, she was relieved of duty pending an administrative probe of what officials called "a pattern of unsubstantiated but suspicious information relating to incidents in the intensive care unit."

The investigation yielded grim results. According to statistical analysis, performed by the Centers for Disease Control in Atlanta, Georgia, Bolding had been the attending nurse in 40 percent of all ICU deaths between January 1984 and March 1985. In concrete terms, she had witnessed the deaths of 57 patients; her closest competitor on staff had lost only five patients during the same period, and none of the hospital's remaining 93 nurses had lost more than four. Additionally, Bolding was the Prince Georges nurse attending 65 percent of all the patients who experienced cardiac arrest in ICU during the night shift.

On March 20, 1985, Bolding was charged with first-degree murder in the death of Elinor Dickerson, age 70, who died in ICU at 12:05 A.M., September 29, 1984. According to police, their suspect confessed to injecting the patient with potassium, inducing cardiac arrest in the name of "mercy." While Bolding was released on bond to stay with relatives, authorities announced that they were checking into other recent deaths. It was suggested that the final body count might run as high as 17.

Dismissed from her job on March 26, Bolding was encouraged when the prosecution's case appeared to crumble two days later. The state's attorney for Prince Georges County scolded police for arresting the nurse against his wishes, branding her confession insufficient to support a case at trial. Bolding's charges were dropped in mid-May, but detectives returned to the search with a vengeance, seizing 200 boxes of hospital records on May 31, scouring the files for information on 22 "suspicious" deaths.

On December 16, 1986, a Maryland grand jury indicted Jane Bolding on three counts of murder and seven counts of assault with intent to kill. Elinor Dickerson was back on the list as a victim, joined by patients Isadore Scheiber and Martha Moore. Scheiber allegedly survived two potassium injections, on October 2 and 11, 1984, before a third injection killed him on October 12. Martha Moore was less hardy, surviving only one attack — on October 27 — before a second injection finished her off the next day. Patient Mary Morbeto reportedly survived a single injection, in March 1984, while Gary Dodson weathered three consecutive attacks a year later, in the week before Bolding's suspension from duty.

After various delays, Jane Bolding's murder trial began in May of 1988, with prosecutors dubbing her a "killing angel." Bolding waived her right to trial by jury, placing her fate in the hands of a judge who promptly declared her confession — obtained after 33 hours of grilling without an attorney — inadmissible as evidence. Deprived of the confession, lacking any witnesses, the prosecution had no case. On June 20, 1988, Bolding was acquitted on all counts. The case of the Prince Georges Hospital murders remains officially unsolved.

Princeton murders — New Jersey (1989)

On September 24, 1989, the *New York Times* announced that authorities in Mercer County, New Jersey, were seeking a possible serial killer, blamed for the recent murders of two women in Princeton. According to the *Times* report, both unnamed victims died from multiple stab wounds, one killed on the campus of Princeton's Hun School, the other in a public parking lot. A third female victim had survived near-fatal stab wounds, presumably inflicted by the same assailant, with all three attacks occurring "in less than six months." Police had no suspects at the time, and have repeatedly declined to answer any correspondence dealing with the case. From all appearances, the Princeton homicides remain unsolved today.

"Prostitute Hunter" — Portugal (1992-93)

While police in the Portuguese capital city were stalking the elusive "**Lisbon Ripper**," yet another murderer of drug-addicted prostitutes appeared to complicate their work. Still unidentified today, Lisbon's second serial killer — dubbed the "Prostitute Hunter" — claimed at least two victims between November 1982 and March 1993, both junkie hookers in their 20s, tortured with cigarette burns before they were beaten and strangled to death, their bodies stuffed contemptuously into trash cans.

At first, authorities believed the killings might have been committed by their local "Ripper" trying out a new technique, but they soon decided that the trash-can murders were the work of a distinct and separate predator.

As explained by psychiatrist Alves Gomes, involved in both manhunts, "The methods are different, but both killers enjoy torturing and killing, and feel aggrandized by the terror they see in the eyes of their victims."

Sadly, that psychological insight fell short of fingering a suspect, and the brutal crimes remain unpunished.

Prostitute murders — Canada (1985-87)

From April 1985 through summer 1987, five suspected prostitutes were murdered in the western provinces of Canada, their killer unidentified. Authorities are still divided on the question of responsibility, and they are even known to disagree about the final body count. In August 1987, the *CBS Evening News* made passing reference to a dozen hookers slain in British Columbia, but the record of related cases seems to stand at five, with one of those killed in the neighboring province of Alberta.

The first confirmed victim, on April Fool's Day 1985, was Pauline Johnson, a former prostitute found murdered at Coquitlam, B.C. Twenty months later, in December 1986, two strippers and suspected prostitutes were killed in North Vancouver, their bodies dumped together near Indian River Road. Coquitlam police admitted they were "certainly interested" in apparent connections between the murders, but comparison brought them no closer to a solution. In January 1987, officers of the Royal Canadian Mounted Police visited Seattle, Washington, comparing notes on their murders with detectives from the "**Green River**" task force, but again the search led nowhere.

On June 4, 1987, officers in Calgary, Alberta, found the naked, decomposed remains of Annette Leger, a 21-year-old local prostitute, stuffed in a highway culvert. Three weeks later, on June 27, another working girl — 23-year-old Carol Davis — was murdered and dumped in a brushy area outside of Burnaby, B.C. Again, police acknowledged "similarities," while stopping short of making definite connections in the case. As in the troubling "**highway murders**" some years earlier, these crimes remain unsolved today.

Prostitute murders — Canada (1996)

On May 23, 1996, authorities in Toronto publicly linked the deaths of three local prostitutes, shot and killed on city streets within a span of three hours. According to Detective Sergeant Jim McDermott, ballistics and autopsy tests confirmed that the three women "all died of gunshot wounds to the head, and they were all killed with the same gun."

McDermott told reporters that police were "quite concerned" for the safety of Toronto hookers. While violence remains an occupational hazard for ladies of the evening, Toronto's quick-trigger gunman appears to have retired for the time being — or, perhaps, changed his method — since no further slayings have been perpetrated with the elusive pistol. Police remain without suspects in the case at this writing.

Prostitute murders — District of Columbia (1989)

In August 1989, police in the nation's capital grudgingly admitted there was "some resemblance" between the April 2 murder of 20-year-old prostitute Mary Ellen Sullenberger (found naked and shot in the chest) and the August 12 slaying of another local hooker, 29-year-old Cori Louise Jones.

According to detectives, Jones had been abducted by her killer within a block of the Sullenberger death scene, after which she was shot several times in the chest, then dumped from the killer's automobile. Further possible evidence of a pattern in the slayings came from the description of the victims themselves, both described by police as "overweight" Caucasians. Robbery has been suggested as a motive in the crimes, but police still have no suspects in the case, and no murder weapon to compare with bullets taken from the corpses during autopsy.

Prostitute murders — England (1987-94)

The probable existence of a new serial killer in London was revealed on May 26, 1996, when British authorities announced the formation of a special task force — code-named "Operation Enigma" — to review files on the unsolved murders of 200 women spanning the past decade. Specifically at issue were the deaths of nine women, nearly all prostitutes, who were strangled or beaten to death between 1987 and 1994, their nude or semi-nude bodies found discarded on open ground in or around London. Unspecified "common features" in the nine slayings suggested to police (and to journalists) that the crimes might have been perpetrated by a single individual.

The murders date back to January 1987, when 27-year-old Marina Monti, a known prostitute and junkie, was found strangled and beaten to death near Wormwood Scrubs Prison in west London. The next "official" victim in the series, from February 1991, was another known prostitute, 22-year-old Janine Downs, her choked and battered body found beneath a hedge along the Telford-to-Wolverhampton Road. Seven more victims would follow in similar style, over the next three years, the murders still unsolved by early 1996, when "Operation Enigma" was conceived.

As part of their effort to catch the elusive strangler, British authorities consulted "mindhunters" from the FBI's Behavioral Science Unit, at Quantico, Virginia. One member of the team, Agent Richard Ault (now retired), told authorities that "From the general information, such an individual is likely to be personable and not stand out. He is able to blend in because he can approach and solicit victims."

Ault and company pegged the British stalker as an "organized" serial killer — meaning that he plans crimes in advance and cleans up afterward, to eradicate clues — but their insight brought London detectives no closer to an arrest. Two years and counting since the first announcement of "Enigma," British police still have no suspect in hand, and some spokesmen are reluctant even to link the nine murders. James Dickinson, assistant chief constable from Essex and coordinator of the task force, is on record as saying — despite the touted similarities — investigators "do not feel that there were sufficient grounds to link the nine inquiries." The killer (or killers), meanwhile, remains at large.

Prostitute murders — Massachusetts: See "Highway Killer" (1988)

Prostitute murders — Michigan (1990-97)

On February 3, 1998, Michigan state police announced the formation of a task force to investigate "at least 20" murders of known prostitutes across the Wolverine State, dating back to 1990. No details were provided on the cases, as officers from various local jurisdictions prepared for the first task force meeting, in Livonia. Press reports noted that the task force would also "focus on attempted murders and missing person reports throughout southeastern Michigan," suggesting that the final body count may well exceed the initial reference to 20 victims.

Spokesmen for the task force noted that their job was further complicated by the lifestyle of the women who had fallen prey to one or more unknown predators over the years. As Macomb County sheriff's Lieutenant Cal Eschenburg told reporters, "It's hard enough for a detective to do their job [sic] when they're dealing with people who abide by the legal system. But when you involve someone who may be dealing in [a] criminal enterprise like drugs and prostitution, it really takes the investigator into a whole subculture."

Lieutenant Brian Krutell, with three unsolved murders on his plate in Mt. Clemens, told the press, "We have nothing concrete on any of the cases. A task force can't hurt." But, thus far, neither has it helped, apparently, as all the homicides remain unsolved, the killer(s) still at large.

Prostitute murders — Minnesota (1996)

The grisly case of an apparent serial killer who beat and stabbed known prostitutes to death, before setting their bodies on fire, plagued Minneapolis authorities in June and July 1996. Two of the three murders occurred in heavily wooded Theodore Wirth Park, with the third not far away, suggesting a territorial killer with some fixation on the park, or the people it attracts.

The stalker's first victim, 42-year-old Deborah LaVoie, was found inside the park near Bassett Creek on June 3, 1996. Her body had been doused with gasoline and set afire, apparently after she was killed by other means. While LaVoie was identified, autopsy results were unable to disclose the cause of death.

Just more than two weeks later, on June 16, 36-year-old Avis Warfield was found 12 blocks east of Wirth Park, on Elwood Avenue North. She had been stabbed to death before her body, like LaVoie's, was set on fire with gasoline.

Half a dozen children saw the killer on Saturday night, July 19, when he returned to Wirth Park with victim number three. Attracted by the light of his blazing fire, they saw a balding black man, roughly six feet tall, standing beside the pyre with a gasoline can in one hand. The kids scattered when he ordered them to "Get the hell outta here," but two or three of them recalled distinctive facial hair — a goatee, or perhaps a Fu Manchu mustache. At least one of them also glimpsed his car — a full-size sedan, maroon in color, with distinctive "star wheel" hubcaps. The license plate allegedly included numerals 7 and 2, a circumstance which — if correct — still left Minnesota authorities with 175,000 suspect vehicles.

The latest victim was burned so badly that determination of race and gender were stalled for several days, but he was finally identified as 21-year-old Keooudorn Phothisane, a 21-year-old Laotian transvestite. (Recent hormone therapy, resulting in the growth of breasts, further delayed identification of the corpse.) According to police, Phothisane was beaten to death, then transported to Wirth Park, where his body was set afire, the cremation interrupted by arrival of unexpected witnesses.

Minneapolis authorities report that all three victims had records of arrests for prostitution and drug violations, suggesting that they may have met their killer on West Broadway, between Girard and Penn Avenues, where many hookers spend each evening "on the stroll." All three reportedly suffered mutilations which police refuse to describe, and investigators believe the bodies were burned to destroy evidence, rather than as part of some compulsive ritual. At this writing, there have been no further slayings in the Wirth Park series, and the case remains unsolved.

Prostitute murders — Mississippi (1994-95)

Mishandling of critical evidence by the FBI crime lab in Washington, D.C., is blamed by local authorities for their failure to solve the murders of four alleged prostitutes in Jackson, Mississippi. All four women were strangled after sex, with the latest victim, Cheryl Garcia, killed in January 1995. Nine months later, in September, Jackson police packed up DNA samples from all four crime scenes, plus samples taken from a suspect, and shipped the lot off to Washington, for examination by federal experts. By late August 1996, there were still no results from the Bureau, and Garcia's mother, Virginia Swann, was informed by police that the suspect in her daughter's slaying "had been turned loose because there wasn't enough evidence." Disgusted by the news, Swann told reporters, "I just don't understand it. I don't feel good about this at all."

Neither did Jackson Police Detective Ned Garner, admitting that the case was stalled, their best suspect at liberty. Until the DNA results came back, he told reporters, "we have nothing to show he committed all those" murders. As far as the delay, police spokesman Lee Vance reported, "The only explanation I've ever been given is that they have a lot of cases." Back in Washington, the word from Jay Miller, chief of the FBI's forensic science lab, was not encouraging. "We can't service all the requests that we get," he told *USA Today,* and delays of a year or more are not unusual. At this writing, there has *still* been no report of a solution in the Jackson homicides.

Prostitute murders — New York (1989-92)

Grim memories of serial killer Arthur Shawcross were revived around Rochester, New York, in autumn 1992, when four women with criminal records for drug abuse and prostitution were found murdered in northwestern Monroe County, the bodies discarded within a few miles of one another. A November 1992 report in the *New York Times* advised that the corpses of 10 more women with similar backgrounds had been found "elsewhere," since 1989 (the year of Shawcross's arrest), and that police were also searching for two unnamed hookers listed as missing persons.

Despite the eerie parallels with Shawcross and the apparent geographic link in at least four cases, Rochester police were understandably reluctant to admit the presence of a second serial killer in town.

"We know what the public thinks out there," Monroe County Sheriff Andrew Meloni told reporters, quickly adding that it would be "irresponsible" to speculate on any links between the crimes.

Undersheriff Patrick O'Flynn, for his part, told the press, "We're definitely not working with one person [sic]. There are many similarities, but there are also many dissimilarities."

And on that vague note, the story ends. One killer or several, Rochester lawmen are apparently no closer to an arrest at this writing than they were in November 1992. The case (or cases) of Rochester's murdered prostitutes remains unsolved.

Prostitute murders — Rhode Island (1990-91)

Suspects remain elusive in this case of three Woonsocket women, found strangled between December 1990 and March 1991. Local police report that 32-year-old Dianne Goulet, 18-year-old Christine Miller, and 23-year-old Wendy Madden all died in similar fashion, all with records of arrest on drug and prostitution charges. As of March 22, 1991, authorities were examining certain unspecified links in the series of murders, but no further leads have been announced in the past seven years, and the case remains officially unsolved.

Prostitute murders — Scotland (1997-98)

A late-breaking case from Glasgow, Scotland, involves the murder of seven prostitutes, apparently by the same killer, between September 1997 and March 1998. Glasgow police announced their hunt for a possible serial killer on March 2, after 27-year-old Margaret Lafferty was found beaten to death in a downtown alley. A previous victim, 21-year-old Tracy Wylde, was found dead in a Glasgow council flat in November 1997. Authorities have questioned some 1,500 persons in that case, completing DNA tests on Wylde's friends, relatives, and several former "johns," without result. Published photographs of Wylde and an unknown man, walking together on the night she died, have likewise failed to identify a suspect in the case.

"El Psicópata" — Costa Rica (1987-??)

Costa Rican authorities announced, in 1997 that some 31 victims may have been murdered over the course of a decade, by an elusive slayer aptly dubbed "The Psychopath." Previous estimates had been more modest, pegging the stalker's body count at 19 (including several victims who have not been found), but frustrated manhunters have added another dozen names to the list, all young men and women who vanished without a trace during 1996. Despite a recent plea for FBI assistance in tracking the killer, police in this Central American republic are no closer to their man today, than when the string of grisly crimes began.

El Psicópata does his hunting, for the most part, in a rural area lately dubbed the "Triangle of Death," stretching from the southwestern quarter of Alajuela to the eastern part of Cartago, a few miles east of the nation's capital, at San Jose. Taking a cue from Italy's "**Monster of Florence**," the killer preys on young lovers, creeping up on couples as they make love and shooting them to death with a large-caliber weapon, afterward mutilating the female's breasts and genitals. Occasional diversions from the pattern involve young women murdered on their own, crime scenes including evidence of postmortem sexual assault.

Local authorities have drawn up several "profiles" of their unknown subject, all in vain. One theory blames the murders on a deranged ex-soldier or policeman, while another brands the killer as a child of wealthy stock — perhaps a politician's son, or offspring of a mighty landlord. Duration of the crime spree indicates a killer in his 30s, possibly his 40s, and police believe he "could be" quite intelligent (presumably because they haven't caught him yet). It is believed by some investigators that *El Psicópata* follows and observes his chosen prey for several days, before killing, yet one fact shines above all others in the case: whoever or whatever he turns out to be, at this writing The Psychopath is still at large.

Railway murders — Sweden (1948)

An interesting case of serial murder was reported from Sweden during 1948, wherein victims, selected apparently at random, were pushed from speeding trains at different points along the country's southern railroad network. According to police reports, released on November 29, there had been five such incidents — all on weekends — within the past five weeks. Four victims had died from injuries sustained in their falls, bodies recovered from trackside hours later; a fifth, prizefighter Carl Nilsson, managed to survive, but could remember no details of the attack. After ruling out accidental falls, police declared that they were searching for "a sadist." His — or her — identity may only be surmised, since no suspect was ever identified or brought to trial.

"Redhead" murders — United States (1984-92?)

On April 24, 1985, FBI agents met with local detectives from various jurisdictions at a special conference held in Nashville, Tennessee. Their purpose: to coordinate investigations into homicides of female victims in a five-state area, committed between mid-September 1984 and early April 1985. Although the victims were reported to have certain traits in common, leading homicide detectives to suspect their deaths may be related, none have been identified so far. In law enforcement parlance, they are all "Jane Does."

While one account refers to *eight* established victims, murdered since October 1983, the only published list is limited to six. In age, they range from roughly 18 years to 40; their hair color ranged from strawberry blond to deep auburn, with every shading of red in between, suggesting a killer fascinated by redheads. All were strangled or suffocated, their bodies discarded near interstate highways forming a corridor of murder between Arkansas in the southwest and Pennsylvania in the northeast.

The first "Jane Doe" was found near Shereville, Arkansas, on September 16, 1984. Two days before Christmas, a second corpse was found in Comru Township, Pennsylvania. New Year's Day found number three near Jellico, Tennessee, and a fourth victim was retrieved near Hernando, Mississippi, on January 24, 1985. On March 31, Ashland City, Tennessee, was the site of another gruesome discovery. The last "official" victim cited by the media was found on April 1, 1985, along Interstate 75, near Corbin, Kentucky.

Prior to the Nashville conference, a list of potential victims had included 12 "Jane Does." With the meeting behind them, lawmen felt secure in dropping four women killed in **Fort Worth**, Texas, between September 1984 and February 1985; another found beside I-81, near Greenville, Tennessee, on April 14, 1985; and yet another, found in Ohio on April 24.

In March of 1985, detectives had been prematurely optimistic, pinning hopes upon the testimony of a living victim. Linda Schacke had been choked unconscious with her own torn shirt outside Cleveland, Tennessee, and left for dead in a culvert beside Interstate 40. The crime seemed to fit, and Schacke was able to pick her assailant from a police lineup. Truck driver Jerry Leon Johns was arrested on March 6, 1985, charged with felonious assault and aggravated kidnapping in Knox County, Tennessee, but he possessed airtight alibis for every other date in question from the murder spree.

At this writing, neither the "Jane Doe" redheads nor their slayer have been publicly identified. A presumed seventh victim, and the first one identified — 45-year-old Delia Trauernicht, found in Giles County, Tennessee, on April 30, 1990 — was added to the list five years after the conference in Nashville, but her addition brought detectives no closer to solution of the case.

Another 26 months passed before Tennessee investigators announced that ex-nun Vickie Sue Metzger, found strangled near Monteagle on June 11, 1992, was being listed as a victim in the "redhead" series. Police Lieutenant Jerry Mayes, coordinator of the "Crime Stoppers" program in Nashville, told journalists he had compiled a list of 12 related murders in the case, but without viable suspects, police can only speculate on the killer's identity and whereabouts.

Richland murders — Georgia (1981-82)

On the night of March 28, 1982, 16-year-old Wanda Faye Reddick was dragged screaming from her bed by a kidnapper who had first crept through the family home in Richland, Georgia, removing light bulbs from their sockets in an effort to delay pursuit. Her lifeless body was recovered six days later, outside town, in rural Stewart County. According to press reports, Reddick's abduction and murder marked the third similar incident targeting local teenagers in less than a year. Tanya Nix, 14, and 17-year-old Marie Sellers had been slain in 1981, their killer still unknown at this writing.

"River Monster" — South Africa (1997)

Police in Transkei, South Africa, blame a serial killer on the loose for at least seven deaths, attributed by local natives to a "river monster" described as "half-fish, half-horse." Victims of the "monster" were reportedly attacked while crossing the Mzintlava River, near Rubaleko village, but locals are well familiar with crocodiles, and police are understandably reluctant to credit reports of an unknown hybrid predator at large. Still, the victims *were* slaughtered by something — or some-*one* — and South African police, lately plagued with a nationwide rash of serial murders, suspect a human hand in the slayings. With no solid clues in the case, Inspector Maphelo Ngame could only tell journalists, "The matter has been reported to the police by several people in Mount Ayliff, and while the monster is said to have struck on different occasions, the affected families have given similar accounts of how the victims were attacked." Thus far, no suspects — human or otherwise — have been identified.

Riverdell Hospital — New Jersey (1965-66)

In 1966, Bergen County authorities launched a probe of nine suspicious deaths at Riverdell Hospital, a small osteopathic facility located in Oradell, New Jersey. In each case, patients were admitted to the hospital for surgery and died of unrelated causes, before or after routine procedures. Despite the identification and trial of a suspect on murder charges, this intriguing case is still unsolved.

Carl Rohrbeck, age 73, was the first to die, admitted for hernia surgery on December 12, 1965, and lost to a diagnosed "coronary occlusion" the next day. Four-year-old Nancy Savino was signed in for an appendectomy on March 19, 1966, her death on March 21 attributed to some "undetermined physiological reaction." Margaret Henderson, 26, was admitted to Riverdell on April 22; she died the following day, after successful exploratory surgery. On May 15, 62-year-old Edith Post was booked in for surgery, lost two days later to undetermined causes. Ira Holster, 64, entered Riverdell for gall bladder surgery on July 12, dying without apparent cause on the 29th. Frank Biggs was complaining of an ulcer when he checked in on August 20; a week later, the 59-year-old patient was dead. Eighty-year-old Mary Muentener died on September 1, seven days after she was admitted for gall bladder surgery. Emma Arzt, age 70, was another gall bladder patient, admitted on September 18, dead by September 23. Eileen Shaw, 36, also lasted five days at Riverdell, dying on October 23, after a successful Cesarean section.

Hospital administrators launched their investigation on November 1, 1966, after a Riverdell surgeon found 18 vials of curare — most nearly empty — in the locker assigned to Dr. Mario Jascalevich. An Argentine immigrant, Jascalevich — initially dubbed "Dr. X" by the press — moved to the United States in 1955, setting up his practice in New Jersey. Confronted with the vials of poison, he explained that he had been engaged in personal experiments with dogs. No motive could be ascertained for homicide, and 10 years passed before the state charged Dr. Jascalevich with five counts of murder, in May 1976. Formally accused of slaying patients Savino, Henderson, Rohrbeck, Biggs and Arzt, the 39-year-old physician surrendered his medical license pending resolution of the case.

At trial, in 1978, two of the murder counts were dismissed for lack of evidence. After thirty-four weeks of testimony, Dr. Jascalevich was acquitted by jurors on October 24, returning to his native Argentina a short time later. He died there, of a cerebral hemorrhage, in September 1984. The case of the curare deaths at Riverdell remains officially unsolved today.

Rodeo murders — Wyoming (1974)

The Rawlins, Wyoming, "rodeo murders" occurred in July and August 1974, claiming four lives in the span of seven weeks. Unsolved despite intensive work by local law enforcement agencies, the crimes were similar enough in execution to deserve inclusion here, although three of the victims are still missing, precluding establishment of a homicidal "signature" in the case.

The first two victims, Carlene Brown, of Rawlins, and her good friend Christy Gross, of Bowdle, South Dakota, disappeared on Independence Day, while visiting the Little Britches Rodeo in Rawlins. Officers had found no trace of the two 19-year-olds by August 4, when Debra Meyers, 15, was added to the local missing list. On August 23, 10-year-old Jaylene Banker was separated from friends at the Rawlins fairgrounds, while watching the Carbon County rodeo, and she immediately disappeared.

Nine years elapsed before the skeleton of Christy Gross was found, three miles south of Sinclair, Wyoming, on October 27, 1983. Killed by two blows to the skull, Gross was identified by means of dental charts and a ring found with her bones. Despite a lame attempt to link Ted Bundy with the case, no solid evidence exists connecting him — or any other identifiable suspect — with the homicides in Rawlins.

St. Louis child murders — Missouri (1993)

On the afternoon of November 18, 1993, 9-year-old Angie Housman vanished on the one-block stroll between her school bus stop and home, in the St. Louis suburb of St. Ann. A neighbor told police that she recalled seeing the little girl pass by, alone and seemingly untroubled, but the rest was silence, until a quail hunter found Angie's body nine days later and some 20 miles away in a wooded section of the August A. Bush Wildlife Area. The child was nude when found, and while police have sealed her autopsy report, official spokesmen grant that her death was "extremely violent."

One day less than two weeks later, on December 1, 10-year-old Cassidy Senter was reported missing from suburban Hazelwood, four miles due north of St. Ann. The child had gone to string Christmas lights at a friend's house, again within a block or so of home, but she never arrived. Her body, swaddled in a quilt and bedspread, was discovered in a St. Louis alley on December 9, postmortem examination revealing that Cassidy had been beaten to death by persons unknown.

Police determined they were looking for a man — or men, although the likelihood of two child killers roaming north St. Louis in such close proximity seemed minimal — but they had nothing in the way of a description or I.D. to help them in their search. Known pedophiles and sex offenders were interrogated, but the registered molesters all appeared to have firm alibis, leaving investigators at a loss for suspects.

Speaking to the press, FBI Agent James Nelson could only say, "We know we have a child killer. The community is very frightened, and they should be." On the basis of "extraordinary similarities" between the two murders and two failed abduction attempts, Nelson confirmed an official belief that the crimes were "the work of one person."

A further element of confusion was introduced with reports that police were seeking links between the two child murders and the beating death of 20-year-old Amy Bohn eight weeks before the Senter homicide. A waitress in Chesterfield, 10 miles west of St. Louis, Bohn had vanished after leaving work, around 10:30 P.M. on October 4. Her half-naked body was found the next day in a Montgomery County cornfield, north of Hermann, Missouri, head and hands wrapped tightly with electrician's tape. If any link was found between Bohn's murder and the two child-slayings, though, police have kept it to themselves, and all three cases remain unsolved at this writing.

St. Louis kidnap-murders — Missouri (1974)

In the fall of 1974, St. Louis authorities were baffled by two double murders in the space of 13 days, committed under nearly identical circumstances, defying the best efforts of local homicide detectives. On October 28, manager Frederick Gent and clerk Todd Friedman were abducted from a local electronics store, their absence reported when a customer found the shop empty that morning. A small amount of cash was evidently missing, but a larger sum was left behind, and valuable items in the shop were not disturbed. At last report, the missing men had not been found.

On November 10, pharmacist Bernard Grossman and his sales clerk, 18-year-old Susan Psaris, were snatched from Grossman's drugstore, shot to death execution-style on a nearby football field. Once more, aside from an apparent petty theft of cash — with larger sums ignored — there seemed to be no evidence of robbery, and Grossman's stock of drugs was left untouched. Police referred to "common threads" between the double murder and the previous abduction, but they hesitate to link the cases publicly. The case remains unsolved today, at least one killer still at large.

Salem murders — Oregon (1981-83)

The Pacific Northwest has produced a disproportionate number of serial killers in recent years, and several have managed to escape detection, remaining at large despite the best efforts of state and local law enforcement. One such predator was active in the area of Salem, Oregon, from February 1981 through March 1983, claiming at least six lives in a two-year period.

The first known victim was 21-year-old Terry Monroe, reported missing on February 13, 1981, after she left a Salem tavern "to get some air" and never returned. Her body was discarded in the nearby Willamette River, recovered by searchers more than a month later.

Sherry Eyerly, 18, was delivering pizzas in Salem on July 4, 1982, when she vanished en route to a caller's fictitious address. Her delivery van was found abandoned, but her body has not been recovered. A suspect in the case committed suicide after preliminary interrogation, but police are now uncertain of his guilt.

Four weeks later, on July 31, 9-year-old Danielle Good disappeared from her bedroom, at home, without signs of a struggle. Her skeleton was found, along with some of her clothes, by a farmer near Scio, Oregon, on February 14, 1983.

On November 22, 1982, 27-year-old Patricia Loganbill was shot and killed at the Salem veterinary clinic where she worked. An autopsy revealed that Loganbill was pregnant when she died. Some 15 weeks elapsed before the final outrage, on March 8, 1983, when 32-year-old Laurel Wilson and her nine-year-old daughter, Erika, were shot to death in their beds, at home, by an unknown intruder.

Without a suspect, the authorities refuse to speculate on positive connections in the series, but investigators from Seattle have ruled out involvement by the elusive "Green River killer," since none of the Salem victims were prostitutes. Likewise, Salem's open cases have been pronounced unconnected to serial slayer William Smith, convicted of other local murders during the same period.

San Diego murders — California (1931-36)

Forty years before another psycho-slayer terrorized the city, residents of San Diego were traumatized by a five-year series of murders claiming female victims between the ages of 10 and 22. Details are vague and hard to come by at the present time. Newspaper articles published in early 1947 remarked on a "striking similarity" between San Diego's murders and the slaying of "Black Dahlia" Elizabeth Short (whose nude and mutilated body, neatly severed at the waist, was dumped on Norton Avenue, in Los Angeles, on January 15, 1947). San Diego newsmen speculated that Short — who once lived briefly in their city — "could well have been the latest victim of a sadist who has terrorized the city for 15 years," but the claim seems doubly exaggerated, since San Diego's slasher had apparently killed no one after 1936, and none of his victims were dissected in "Black Dahlia" style.

The first apparent victim of the San Diego stalker, in February 1931, was 10-year-old Virginia Brooks, "attacked and murdered" (no details available) after she was lured into a stranger's car. "A few months later," victim Dolly Bibbens — described in press reports as an "attractive and well-to-do widow," was beaten to death in her own apartment. Two weeks after that, 22-year-old Hazel Bradshaw made the victims list, stabbed 17 times by an unknown assailant, her body dumped in Balboa Park.

The killer(s) took a three-year break after Bradshaw, resurfacing in March 1934 to perpetrate a vaguely described "similar crime" against Mrs. Wesley Adams. A month later, in April, the nude body of 17-year-old Louise Teuber was found hanging from a tree, police convinced that she was raped and murdered elsewhere. Before that fateful summer ended, 16-year-old Celia Cota was "attacked, tortured and strangled" on her way home from a local movie theater. The final victim, killed by unspecified means in 1936, was Riverside YWCA secretary Ruth Muir, the daughter of a wealthy Arizona banker.

On balance, there seems to be sufficient cause for doubting a lone killer's role in all seven crimes, but San Diego police and reporters were seemingly convinced of a single hand at work. Whether that conclusion amounts to sound detective work or wishful thinking, the end result is still the same. To date, none of the San Diego cases have been solved.

San Diego murders — California (1985-88)

In August 1988, authorities from Washington and California issued an announcement that at least ten unsolved murders, logged in San Diego since June of 1985, were "definitely" linked with other homicides committed near Seattle and Tacoma by the elusive "**Green River killer**." One detective referred to the connection as "common knowledge," and some investigators placed the body count a good deal higher. Lieutenant Bill Baxter, head of the San Diego County sheriff's homicide department, declared that at least 10 — and no more than 12 — women had been murdered by one man over the past three years. Detective Tom Streed, leading the investigation, was inclined to think the killer's death toll might have reached 18. Whatever their differences of opinion, all concerned agreed upon 10 victims in the case.

The first to die had been 22-year-old Donna Gentile, last seen alive on June 22, 1985. Her naked, strangled body was recovered three days later, in the neighborhood of Mount Laguna, rocks and gravel packed inside her mouth and throat.

The second victim was a young "Jane Doe," her body badly decomposed when hikers found it near a rural creek, head wedged beneath a tree limb, on July 22, 1986. Nearby, authorities found clothing and a wedding ring believed to be the victim's, but the evidence has not provided any clue to her identity.

Theresa Brewer, 26 years old, was next to face the killer's wrath. Bound in a fetal position and "probably strangled," her body was found on August 3, 1986, identified three days later from a comparison of dental records.

On April 23, 1987, a group of illegal immigrants discovered the nude, decomposing remains of Rosemarie Ritter, age 29. Despite a ruling of death due to methamphetamine poisoning, she is listed as one of the murderer's "definite" victims. Two months later, on June 22, 32-year-old Anna Varela was found in Pine Valley, by joggers who nearly stumbled over her naked, strangled corpse.

Sally Moorman-Field, a 19-year-old prostitute and drug user, joined the list on September 20, 1987, stripped and strangled prior to her discovery by bicyclists. The cause of death was undetermined five days later, when the decomposed remains of Sara Gedalicia, a 36-year-old transient, were discovered at Alpine. Likewise, on October 19, authorities could list no cause of death for 24-year-old Diana Moffitt, but dismemberment of her skeleton placed her on the victims list.

Another "Jane Doe" victim, found at Rancho Bernardo, on April 13, 1988, had been dead for a week when her body was discovered, the cause of death once again undetermined. Melissa Sandoval, a 20-year-old junkie prostitute, was last seen alive on May 21, climbing into the car of an unidentified "trick." Her strangled body was recovered eight days later, within 30 yards of the previous dumpsite at Rancho Bernardo.

Solutions remain as elusive as a definitive body count in the San Diego murders, but as with the Green River slayings in Washington State, there has been no shortage of publicized suspects. One such, 41-year-old ex-convict Ronald Elliott Porter, was arrested in October 1988 for beating and raping a San Diego woman. Porter initially denied the charges, but he cut a deal with prosecutors six months later, pleading guilty in return for a four-year sentence on reduced charges of sexual battery and assault with a deadly weapon. One week before his scheduled parole, in September 1991, Porter was indicted for the murders of 26-year-old Carol Gushrowski (slain in June 1986) and 43-year-old Sandra Cwik (found dead in July 1988), plus five counts of attempted murder pertaining to rape victims who survived his attacks. The Gushrowski case was dismissed for lack of evidence when Porter's trial began, in August 1992, but the defendant was convicted of second-degree murder (on Cwik), plus two counts of rape with a foreign object and one count of assault resulting in great bodily injury. Sentenced to a maximum of 15 years in December 1992, Porter is eligible for parole in 1999.

Another San Diego killer, tattooed biker Alan Michael Stevens (a.k.a. "Buzzard"), was 46 years old at the time of his December 1988 arrest on charges of murdering 26-year-old Cynthia McVey, found hog-tied and strangled three weeks earlier. Fingerprints linked Stevens to the corpse, and he was convicted of first-degree murder in October 1990, sentenced to a prison term of 25 years to life. San Diego authorities call Stevens their prime suspect in at least three more murders, but no further charges have been filed to date.

A final suspect, Richard Allen Sanders, has been linked in media reports to both the San Diego *and* Green River homicides. No charges have been filed, however, since Sanders was dead — killed outside Yacolt, Washington in March 1989 by two close-range shotgun blasts to the back — before he was named as a suspect in the notorious murder sprees. A one-time bouncer and saloon proprietor, Sanders was posthumously named by authorities as a suspected narcotics manufacturer and alleged producer of "snuff" films featuring murders of certain unnamed prostitutes. The latter information was reportedly provided by police informants. One of them, Joel Hansen, identified Sanders's killer as a friend, 30-year-old Clifford Brethour, convicted of the slaying and sentenced to a 15-year jail term in September 1989. (Hansen, convicted as an accomplice, drew a sentence of 11 to 14 years.) Authorities in

Washington agree that Sanders was "once" a suspect in the Green River case, but neither series of murders is treated as closed with his death.

San Mateo County murders — California (1976)

An "ancient" case by police standards, the 1976 stabbing deaths of five young women in San Mateo County, California, is probably unsolvable today, although police involved in the original investigation still debate the case from time to time. All five victims were young brunettes, who — like most of the women slain by Ted Bundy — wore their hair parted in the middle. The killer, apparently, also left hairs of his own on at least two of the bodies, and police took samples from 256 suspects before obtaining a tentative match.

The owner of the suspect hairs — never publicly identified — was later convicted of raping a teenage girl in a neighboring county, but he was never charged with murder, since hairs — unlike fingerprints — cannot be linked to one exclusive source. FBI crime lab reports told California authorities that fewer than one person in every 4,000 possessed the same type of hair, but in a state with more than 30 *million* residents, that still did not reduce the odds enough to rate indictment or conviction. Serial slayer Henry Lee Lucas toured California murder sites in early 1985, confessing to several slayings over the past decade, but San Mateo detectives dismissed him as a suspect in their string of unsolved stabbings. The *other* suspect, meanwhile, was released on parole and moved to southern California in 1981, where he presumably remains at large.

Shoreline murders — Washington (1995)

On April 2, 1995, police in Shoreline, Washington, publicly blamed a serial killer for the recent murders of two health care workers, both found gagged, bound, and stabbed to death in their own apartments, after which the flats were set on fire. Barbara Walsh, age 54, was killed in February, while 43-year-old Renee Powell died in near-identical circumstances, in the last week of March. Recognition of the problem did nothing to produce a suspect, however, and at last report, the Shoreline homicides remained open, no solution in sight.

"Sidney Sniper" — Virginia (1960s)

Nicknamed for the Richmond, Virginia, neighborhood that he terrorized during the early 1960s, the "Sidney sniper" killed five persons and wounded seven others in a series of hit-and-run attacks. Never identified, the gunman "retired" as suddenly and mysteriously as he had launched his campaign, leaving police baffled in his wake. Ironically, the random shootings had a beneficial side effect on Richmond's high-crime district, with streets deserted and the local crime rate dropping sharply during the sniper's year of peak activity.

"Soda Pop Slasher" — New York (?-?)

Verifiable facts are as elusive as the killer in this case of an unindicted fiend who (allegedly) killed and mutilated his victims with broken soft-drink bottles. The case was first revealed in *Fatal Analysis* (1997), billed as "a harrowing real-life story of professional privilege and serial murder." Problems arise with a prefatory note, however, explaining that "the authors have changed, added, or altered some events as well as locations, names, and identifying characteristics. The chronology of events has likewise been altered. The book also makes use of composite secondary characters."

Thus rendered unidentifiable, for all intents and purposes, the case has proved impossible to verify. Cover copy on the paperback edition tells us that "[t]he New York newspapers dubbed the gruesome killer the Soda Pop Slasher," yet no such nickname appears in any available newspaper index for the past two decades. Likewise, with names, dates, locations and other "identifying characteristics" — including, presumably, the slayer's method of operation — altered to protect all concerned, a random search of murder cases listed in the *New York Times Index* presents researchers with a hopeless task. Still, because the book's publishers list it as nonfiction, the case is included here, for what it may be worth.

The putative author of *Fatal Analysis* — assisted, if not "ghosted," by veteran *New York Times* reporter Thomas Clavin — is Dr. Martin Obler, Ph.D. Like his subject, however, Dr. Obler emerges from the book as a man of mystery, self-described in his own epilogue as "a well-respected psychologist, widely published and a full professor at a leading university." (The book's flyleaf lists Obler as a professor of psychology at Brooklyn College, in New York.) And yet, while researching this entry in January 1998, I was informed (by reference librarians at Indiana University, in Bloomington), that Dr. Obler was not listed in the *National Faculty Directory*, nor were any academic publications with his by-line readily identified. He *was* listed on the Internet web site of Brooklyn College, in the Educational Services Department, and a phone call to that institution (on January 26, 1998) identified Obler as an *associate* professor of psychology. According to the secretary with whom I spoke, Obler, while tenured, was not then a full professor. "The difference," she told me, "is the paycheck."

Academic details notwithstanding, "the core" of Obler's tale, as described in the author's note, is drawn from an alleged experience in private practice, where Dr. Obler identified one of his clients — pseudonymous "Devon Cardou" — as the serial mangler of at least 13 victims around Greenwich Village. Obler describes Devon as a twisted genius (I.Q. 154), referred to him for counseling over problems "of a sexual nature" at an unnamed "major university" in New York. Traumatized in childhood by watching his father sodomize his mother, Devon works out his private demons with a broken pop bottle, mutilating the rectums of victims male and female, ranging in age from their teens to late 30s. In a climax redolent of Hollywood, NYPD Detective Callahan (shades of Dirty Harry!) gets wise to Obler's link with the killer, but Obler stands fast on professional ethics, refusing to identify the slasher. (This in itself is peculiar, since physicians and therapists in all 50 states are absolved of confidentiality — in fact, they are *required* to turn their patients in — when human lives are threatened by ongoing crimes.)

In the *film noir* finale of *Fatal Analysis*, Devon kidnaps Obler's girlfriend, "Rachel," but Obler manages to save her in an unarmed confrontation with his patient, using sheer force of will to persuade the Soda Pop Slasher that "You want to stop killing." Devon is free to get on with his life, Obler stipulates, as long as he keeps his nose clean in the future. "Remember I'll be checking, listening," Obler warns his patient. "I am the guardian of the gate, Devon, and I'm watching..." Obler and Rachel (or Robyn, in the book's acknowledgements) live happily ever after, while Devon — not unlike Brett Easton Ellis's fictional *American Psycho* — moves on to join a prominent law firm, rubbing shoulders with Congressmen at TV press conferences. Through it all, Obler tells his readers, "I *was* still the guardian of the gate. And I had to remain there. My watch was not over."

Fact or fiction? There is no way to be absolutely sure, but some of the events — including Obler's private pursuit of a serial killer, avoiding police even after his lover is kidnapped — are so unusual that doubts arise, unbidden, in a cautious reader's mind, inviting comparison with the murky plot lines of such cinematic psycho-thrillers as *Dressed to Kill, Jagged Edge,* and *Final Analysis.* (N.B.: A review of *Fatal Analysis,* posted on the Internet at amazon.com, adds further confusion to the case. It reads, in part: "I should start by saying that I am the author's son and wrote part of the original text. The original text was completely based in fact with some dramatic license mostly in the dialogue. The murders were real, although some anachronisms were present. However, the book was basically rewritten by the publisher without the consent of the author and greatly fictionalized. Even worse, the publisher did a poor job of this, hence the comments that the kidnapping did not ring true.") Barring the discovery of details that would make the case susceptible to proof, I leave the final verdict to my readers, and wish them well.

Southside Slayer — California (1983-87)

Unidentified at this writing, the "Southside Slayer" of Los Angeles is credited with at least 14 homicides between September 1983 and May 1987. At least three other victims are considered possible additions to the list, and three more managed to survive encounters with the stalker, offering police descriptions of a black man in his early 30s, sporting a mustache and baseball cap. The killer's chosen victims have been women, mostly black and mainly prostitutes, tortured with superficial cuts before they were strangled or stabbed to death in a grisly "pattern of overkill," their bodies dumped on residential streets, in alleyways and schoolyards.

Loletha Prevot was the killer's first known victim, found dead in Los Angeles on September 4, 1983. Four months passed before the killer struck again, on New Year's Day, dumping the corpse of Patricia Coleman in Inglewood. Another 10 months slipped away before discovery of a third victim, Sheila Burton — alias Burris — on November 18, 1984.

The elusive slayer adopted a regular schedule in 1985, beginning with the murder of Frankie Bell on January 1. Patricia Dennis was the next to fall, her mutilated body recovered on February 11. The first victim for March was Sheily Wilson, murdered in Inglewood on the 20th. Three days later, the stalker claimed Lillian Stoval in Los Angeles. Number eight was Patsy Webb, murdered on April 15, with Cathy Gustavson joining the list on July 28.

Thus far, the killer had missed only once, leaving one victim comatose after a savage beating. On August 6, his next intended target managed to escape by leaping from his moving car. She offered homicide detectives a description and assisted in the preparation of a widely published sketch, but officers appeared no closer to their suspect than they were in 1983.

Rebounding from his recent failure with another kill, the slayer dumped Gail Ficklin's body in Los Angeles on August 15. A 12-week lull was broken on November 6, with Gayle Rouselle's murder in Gardena, and the killer returned the next day to slaughter Myrtle Collier in L.A. Nesia McElrath, 23, was found slain on December 19, and Elizabeth Landcraft's mutilated corpse was found on December 22, 1985. The day after Christmas, Gidget Castro's body was discarded in the City of Commerce.

The new year was five days old when Tammy Scretchings met her killer in Los Angeles, becoming number 14 on the Southside Slayer's hit parade. On January 10, a 27-year-old prostitute was beaten and a male acquaintance stabbed when he attempted to restrain her violent customer. Their physical descriptions of the suspect tallied with reports from the survivor who escaped in August 1985.

The killer chalked up number 16, Lorna Reed, on February 11, 1986, discarding her corpse at San Dimas, 25 miles east of his usual hunting ground. Prostitute Verna Williams was found on May 26, her body slumped in the stairwell of a Los Angeles elementary school, and Trina Chaney joined the list November 3, in Watts. In January 1988, police announced that Carolyn Barney — killed May 29, 1987 — was being added to the Southside list.

Three other victims have been unofficially connected to the Southside Slayer, though detectives hesitate to make a positive I.D. Loretta Jones, a 22-year-old coed with no criminal record, was murdered and dumped in a Los Angeles alley on April 15, 1986. A white "Jane Doe," age 25 to 30, was discovered strangled in a garbage dumpster three weeks later. Finally, Canoscha Griffin, 22, was stabbed to death on the grounds of a local high school, her body discovered on July 24.

By early 1988, police were backing off their initial body count, noting that defendant Charles Mosley had been convicted in one of the 1986 murders. While five more cases — involving victims Barney, Burris, Castro, Ficklin and McElrath — were considered "closed" with the arrest of two other serial slayers, Louis Craine and Daniel Siebert. Los Angeles police were less fortunate with their hasty arrest of a black L.A. County sheriff's deputy, Rickey Ross, as a suspect in the Southside case, when ballistics tests on the officer's pistol cleared him of involvement in the crimes. The case remains unsolved today.

Spokane murders — Washington (1984-97)

Police raised specters of the dreaded **"Green River Killer's"** return in January 1998, when they publicly suggested that four recent murders of women around Spokane, Washington, might be linked to deaths of 14 other victims in the area since 1984. (The year in which Seattle's "Green River" bogeyman "retired" and disappeared without a trace). The latest victim — like many of the Green River dead — all shared histories of prostitution, drug abuse, or both, but these were shot, presenting authorities with a stark deviation from the previous predator's pattern.

Homicide detectives were anxious to avoid the label of "prostitute murders" in their latest manhunt, while admitting the "extreme likelihood" that their four most recent victims were all shot to death by the same killer(s). At the same time, Spokane police captain Chuck Bown told reporters, "We are confident that not all of the 18 are connected. We are also confident that four are. Then there are those in the middle, which we are still evaluating."

"Those in the middle" were three women found murdered around Spokane between late August and mid-October 1997. Two victims, both shot in the head — 20-year-old Heather Hernandez and 16-year-old Jennifer Joseph — were found separately on August 26, while October's victim was fished out of the Spokane River. The four "definitely" linked victims — Darla Scott, Shawn Johnson, Laurie Wason, and Shawn McClenahan — were found around Spokane, each shot in the head, between November 5 and December 26. On Friday, January 30, 1998, police added another victim to the list: 24-year-old Melinda Mercer, found dead in Tacoma on December 7, shot in the head, her death bearing "striking similarities" to the murders of victims Scott, Johnson, Wason, and McClenahan.

The task force assigned to these murders is also examining homicides of three women killed within as many months, in 1990, plus four more murders dating back to 1984. In addition to the dead, it was reported that four more women have disappeared from Spokane since mid-October 1997, their fate and whereabouts unknown at this writing. As police spokesman Dick Cottam told the press, "The deaths involve women whose life styles placed them at some risk. Because of their circumstances, in some cases a victim might have been missing for several weeks before her absence was reported." As for a solution in the case, Captain Bown can only say that he expects the manhunt to be "a long, arduous task."

As if in response to that announcement, yet another woman's corpse was found on Sunday, February 8, 1998, in western Spokane County. Although the victim is publicly unidentified at this writing, police declared that she fit the elusive killer's pattern in "all three categories" — i.e., a victim involved with drugs and/or prostitution, shot to death and dumped in a rural area.

Spotsylvania child murders — Virginia (1996-97)

Authorities in this small Virginia town, some 30 miles north of Richmond, announced in August 1997 that the recent murders of three adolescent girls were probably the work of an unidentified serial killer still prowling the streets. The stalker's victims were identified as 16-year-old Sofia Silva, 15-year-old Kristin Lisk, and Kristin's 12-year-old sister, Kati Lisk. Silva was the first to die, in September 1996, her body dredged from a creek in rural Spotsylvania County. The Lisk sisters vanished together, on May 1, 1997, their bodies found floating in a nearby river five days later.

In blaming the deaths on one unknown predator, detectives cited striking similarities between the cases. The victims were all of a comparable age, all slender, athletic brunettes. The Lisk and Silva families lived within 10 miles of each other, and all three victims were snatched from their homes after school, with no sign of a struggle. Again, in each case, the fully-clothed corpses were left in water, within 40 miles of their homes, none bearing any obvious signs of trauma. The announcement of a child-killer at large elicited predictable anxiety from parents in the neighborhood, but no new slayings have occurred to date, and a task force organized to solve the crimes — including local, state, and federal officers — still has no suspects in the case.

"State Fair" murders — Oklahoma (1981)

On September 26, 1981, Charlotte Kinsey and Cinda Pallett, both 13, phoned home to tell their parents that they had been offered work, unloading stuffed animals for a midway arcade at the Oklahoma City fairgrounds. Neither girl came home that evening, and police assigned to track them down discovered witnesses who saw them with an unknown man that afternoon, before they disappeared.

The search was still in progress three days later, when two more girls were reported missing. Sheryl Vaughn, 16, of Newalla, Oklahoma, and Susan Thompson, 16, promptly vanished. Their car was found on Interstate 40, east of town, keys still in the ignition, but no trace of the girls could be discovered.

On October 9, police in Greenville, Alabama, arrested a traveling carnival worker, 36-year-old Donald Michael Corey, on charges of kidnapping Charlotte Kinsey and Cinda Pallett. Returned to Oklahoma on October 13, Corey was cleared of all charges six days later, when police verified that he had been in Texas on September 26. Embarrassed by the error, officers would only say their suspect bore a "striking" resemblance to the innocent Corey. At this writing, the four girls remain missing and presumed dead, their abductor still unnamed.

Strangulation murders — New York (1982)

Investigators cautiously refused to speculate on possible connections in the deaths of five women, strangled in Manhattan and Brooklyn between March and August 1982, but spokesmen of NYPD told the press that a link in the series of crimes was "not discounted." Evidence in at least one of the cases reportedly pointed toward multiple killers, but police declined to specify their reasons for believing that at least one death was unrelated to the others.

The series of murders — if series it was — began with the strangulation of Sheryl Guida, 22, found at Coney Island on March 18. Rita Nixon, a 21-year-old visitor from Portsmouth, Virginia, was strangled and dumped behind a school in Chinatown, on July 15. Gloria DeLeon, 31, of Bergen County, New Jersey, was the third victim, her lifeless body discarded in Manhattan. Patricia Shea, a 40-year-old physician's assistant from Queens, was discovered in Brooklyn's Prospect Park, on July 26. The fifth victim, a "Jane Doe," was found floating in the Narrows, off Bay Ridge in Brooklyn, on August 3; she had been beaten, raped, and strangled with an electric cord, still wrapped around her neck.

To date, no solid leads have been discovered in these crimes, no suspects brought to trial. If any further stranglings are connected to the original five, police and journalists have kept the public in the dark.

Taxi cab murders — Belarus (1996-97)

Taxi drivers in Brest, near the Belarussian border with Poland, were terrorized in the winter of 1996-97, by a serial killer blamed for the brutal murders of three cabbies and a gas station attendant over four months' time. After the final slaying, reported in January 1997, angry drivers staged a protest demonstration, surrounding the latest murder scene with their taxis and honking their horns nonstop for half an hour. Despite the public outcry, at last report, police still had no suspect in the murders and the case remains unsolved.

Taxi cab murders — Indiana (1993)

Cab drivers in Indianapolis, like their colleagues in any other city, face predicable risks on the job from armed robbers and random psychopaths. They suffer fewer casualties per year than cabbies in New York, Chicago, or Los Angeles, but there is no safe-conduct pass from danger, even when they travel armed.

On February 5, 1993, 57-year-old Samuel Smith was found dead in his taxi, parked in an alley near the 400 block of North Concord Street. He had been shot several times in the back of the head and apparently robbed. Police still had no suspect in that case five months later, on July 12, when 50-year-old Charles Nixon drove his cab up to a fire station on East 34th Street, then staggered out and collapsed on the floor, dying from a gunshot in the back that pierced his heart.

Authorities could only speculate about the killer's motive, since Nixon still carried his wallet and cash, but the presumption was attempted robbery. Dispatchers for the Yellow Cab Company report that Nixon had been sent to the 3700 block of North Bancroft Street around 1:15 A.M., to pick up a fare known only as "John." Company records show that Nixon turned his meter on three minutes later, bound for some unknown destination. His shooting was reported to dispatchers, by police, at 1:30 A.M. Ironically, Nixon had carried a pistol for self-defense on the job until the previous week, when it was confiscated by authorities for lack of a legal permit.

Armed or not, however, Nixon's girlfriend told reporters that "He wasn't going to give up nothing without a fight."

At last report, local homicide detectives were "looking at the possibility that Nixon and Smith were killed by the same person," but no suspects have been named in either case. Unless jailed in the meantime on unrelated charges, the killer (or killers) remains at large.

Taxi cab murders — New York (1980)

In October 1980, residents of Buffalo, New York, were stunned and horrified by the murders of two black cab drivers on successive nights, details of the crimes suggesting grisly human sacrifice. The first victim, 71-year-old Parker Edwards, was found in the trunk of his cab on October 8, skull crushed with a blunt instrument, his heart cut out and missing from the murder scene. The next day, 40-year-old Ernest Jones was found beside the Niagara River in Tonawanda, bludgeoned to death, the heart ripped from his chest. His blood-spattered taxi was retrieved by police in Buffalo, three miles away. Erie County District Attorney Edward Cosgrove told reporters, "This is the most bizarre thing I have ever seen in my life. Any word I reach for to describe it is inadequate."

Worse yet, from the standpoint of racial harmony, four other Buffalo blacks had been killed in the past 18 days, all gunned down with the same .22-caliber weapon. Then, barely 24 hours after the murder of cabbie Ernest Jones, 37-year-old Colin Cole was assaulted in his Buffalo hospital room by a white man snarling, "I hate niggers." A nurse's arrival saved Cole from death by strangulation, but his condition was listed as serious, with severe damage done to his throat. Descriptions of the would-be strangler roughly matched eyewitness reports of the elusive ".22-caliber killer."

Some authorities believed the mystery was solved three months later, with the arrest of army private Joseph Christopher at Fort Benning, Georgia, charged with stabbing a black fellow soldier. A search of Christopher's former residence, near Buffalo, turned up quantities of .22-caliber ammunition, a gun barrel, and two sawed-off rifle stocks. More to the point, authorities learned that Christopher had joined the army on November 13, arriving at Fort Benning six days later. He was absent on leave from December 19 to January 4, with a bus ticket recording his arrival in Manhattan on December 20 — two days before five blacks and one Hispanic victim were stabbed in the city, four of them fatally.

Hospitalized following a May 6, 1981 suicide attempt, Christopher bragged to a nurse of his involvement in the September shootings around Buffalo. Four days later, he was charged with three of the ".22-caliber" slayings, a fourth murder charge added to the list on June 29, plus further counts related to nonfatal Buffalo stabbings in December 1980 and January 1981. In New York City, indictments were returned in two of the December 1980 stabbings.

Joseph Christopher was ruled incompetent for trial in December 1981, but that judgment was reversed in April 1982. On April 27 of that year, after 12 days of testimony, Christopher was convicted on three counts of first-degree murder in Buffalo, drawing a prison term of 60 years to life. Seventeen months later, in September 1983, he sat for an interview with Buffalo journalists, estimating that his murder spree had claimed a minimum of 13 lives. Reporters noted that "he did not deny" the grisly "heart murders" of October 1980, but neither did he confess to the crimes, and no charges have ever been filed in those cases. In July 1985, Christopher's Buffalo conviction was overturned on grounds that the judge improperly barred testimony pointing toward mental incompetence. Three months later, in Manhattan, a jury rejected the killer's insanity plea, convicting him on one count of murder and another of attempted murder. At this writing, the mutilation slayings of Parker Edwards and Ernest Jones remain officially unsolved.

Taxi cab murders — New York (1990)

Driving a cab in New York City is dirty, dangerous work. In 1990 alone, 35 New York cabbies were murdered on the job, while police arrested suspects in only 10 of those cases, for a solution rate of 29 percent. As if the threat from junkies, teenage gang-bangers and random stickup artists was not bad enough, the spring of 1990 also saw at least four cabbies — some say seven — gunned down by a serial killer who, in the words of one police spokesman, "is getting into cabs and all he wants to do is shoot the driver."

The first known victim in the murder series, 37-year-old Anton Jones, was found dead in his cab at 6:40 A.M. on March 7, shot once in the head. Jones had picked up his last, nameless fare on Eastchester Road, bound for the junction of 241st Street and White Plains Road, but he never made it, his cab found at Wilder and Stouen Avenues, in the borough's Wakefield section.

Seven days later, at 5:00 A.M. on March 14, 43-year-old Elliott Whitaker radioed his dispatcher a report that he had just picked up a fare on Boston Road, in the Bronx, and was headed for the train station on White Plains Road. A few minutes later, the same dispatcher received a telephone call, reporting that Whitaker's cab had struck a parked car on East 214th Street. Police responding to the accident call found

Whitaker dead in the driver's seat, killed by multiple close-range shots to the head.

The killer struck again on April 10. Paul Burghard was a 25-year-old college student, driving cabs at night to make ends meet. At 2:25 that morning, he picked up a passenger outside Montefiore Hospital, in the Bronx. Fifteen minutes later, another cabbie reported sighting Burghard's cab on Wilson Avenue, in the Williamsburg section of the Bronx, its driver slumped over the wheel. Patrolmen found him dead, shot twice in the head at close range, an estimated sixty dollars missing from the cab.

Thus far, all three victims had been killed with the same .22-caliber pistol. A witness to one shooting described the killer as a black man with a thin mustache, assisting artists in the preparation of a sketch that was distributed on posters, coupled with a $20,000 reward for information leading to the gunman's arrest. Predictably, the offer brought in many calls, but none led homicide investigators to a viable suspect.

The suspect sketch was still in preparation on April 11, when Jamaican native Dennis Forbes, age 41, was shot in his taxi at the corner of East 169th Street and Sheridan Avenue, in the Bronx. He clung to life for 24 hours at Lincoln Hospital, then died without regaining consciousness. Eyewitnesses reported two black teenagers fleeing his cab, and a .25-caliber pistol was found on the seat near his body, prompting authorities to speculate that Forbes's death was unrelated to the trio of murders already under investigation.

Three days later, at 10:30 P.M. on April 14, 38-year-old Rafael Montes de Oca was dispatched to pick up a fare on East 188th Street, in the Bronx. He had been specially requested by a frequent customer, known only as "George," but this time the ride ended in death. It was 11:55 P.M. before another cabbie saw de Oca's taxi parked at the corner of East 188th and Webster Avenue, its driver slumped over the wheel.

As in the other series murders, Rafael de Oca had been shot in the head at close range with a .22-caliber pistol.

A special NYPD task force organized to solve the taxi murders now had 30 officers engaged in the pursuit of one elusive suspect, but they were no closer to their man than they had been when Anton Jones was killed, in early March. On the afternoon of April 21, while a 300-car funeral procession rolled across the Triborough Bridge, conveying Rafael de Oca to his final resting place, news reports announced the death of taxi driver Bakary Simpara, comatose since he was shot in the Bronx district of Clasons Point, back on March 21. Authorities specifically denied a link between his murder and the random gunman they were after, calling common robbery "a good bet" in Simpara's slaying.

There were no such doubts on Sunday, April 22, when cabbie Muhammad Salim, a 48-year-old Pakistani national, was found dead in his taxi, shot once behind the left ear, in the West Bronx district of Tremond. Death had come suddenly for the latest victim, with food half-chewed in his mouth, his wallet empty on the seat beside him. Police acknowledged Salim's murder as "part of the same pattern" including victims Jones, Whitaker, and Burghard.

Mayor David Dinkins held a press conference in the wake of Salim's murder, announcing expansion of the taxi-murders task force to include another 20 officers. "These killings represent more than a brutal attack on the drivers who have fallen victim," Dinkins told his television audience. "They have also become an assault on the vital link in our transportation system."

It was a dramatic step, but all in vain. As we approach the new millennium, the brutal deaths of four (or maybe seven) New York taxi drivers still remain unsolved.

Taxi cab murders — Texas (1984-85)

In 1984 and '85, San Antonio taxi drivers were terrorized by the murder of one cabbie and the disappearance of two others over an eight-month period. Driver Pete Lozano was killed in his cab during November 1984, and the unknown assailant was still at large when 68-year-old Julio Villanueva was reported missing on June 17, 1985. His privately owned cab was found in a Brooksville, Florida, parking lot on July 4, and two days later, searchers acting on a self-styled psychic's tip recovered Villanueva's missing briefcase. In the meantime, cab driver Luis Salazar, age 32, had last been seen in San Antonio on the night of July 5, reported missing by his girlfriend two days later. At this writing, no trace of the missing cabbies has been found, and the identity of their assailant remains a mystery.

Texas child murders — (1977-93)

On Saturday afternoon, September 4, 1993, seven-year-old Ashley Estell accompanied her parents to Carpenter Park, in Plano, Texas, five miles north of Dallas. They had gone to watch her older brother play soccer, joining a crowd of some 2,000 spectators, but Ashley soon tired of the game and went to visit the nearby children's playground. By the time the soccer game was finished, she had disappeared, no trace of her discovered in a search that lasted until 9:00 P.M. The next morning, bright and early, the hunt resumed, and it was straight-up noon when searchers found her body sprawled beside a country road, some six miles from the park. Postmortem tests attributed her death to ligature strangulation, and Ashley's death was logged as the ninth unsolved murder of a Dallas-area child in the past 16 years.

The first to die, back in September 1977 had been 12-year-old Susie Mages, kidnapped from a Denton laundromat on the 25th of the month. Nine days later, on October 4, her corpse had been recovered from an Oak Cliff gravel pit. Two years and one month later, on October 23, 1979, seven-year-old Elizabeth Barclay was kidnapped on the short walk from her home to a neighborhood grocery store, found dead in Van Zandt County five days before Christmas. Another 42 months elapsed before 11-year-old Julie Fuller vanished, on June 27, 1983, while taking out the garbage at an Arlington motel where her mother was employed; her body was found the next day, at a trash dump in Fort Worth. Amber Crum, age two, went missing on December 26, 1983, snatched from a vehicle parked outside a Pleasant Grove grocery store, her body never found. (A suspect, charged with murder in that case, was later released, all charges against him dismissed.) On January 19, 1985, five-year-old Christi Meeks had been kidnapped from her mother's apartment, in Mesquite, found dead at Lake Texhoma, on the Texas-Oklahoma border, three months later. Fourteen-year-old Jennifer Day was kidnapped from her job at a Dallas doughnut shop on June 23, 1985, her body found at a Plano construction site the next morning. On November 3, 1987, four-year-old Roxann Reyes was snatched from her parents' apartment in Garland, found dead in a field near Murphy, Texas, on May 22, 1988.

The most recent child slaying, before Ashley Estell's, had occurred on July 18, 1993, when eight-year-old Kim Nguyen disappeared from his neighborhood in Garland. A victim of autism (and the only male victim thus far), Kim had wandered away from home around 7:00 A.M., with a massive search beginning some four hours later. His shirt was found on a nearby street, two days after Kim vanished, but it was July 29 before searchers discovered his corpse, in a field near Mesquite. The cause of death was officially undetermined, and police refused to say if Kim had been molested by his murderer. They also refused to speculate on any links in the series of murders, although Garland detective Lana Kirkham granted it was "very rare" for two young children to be kidnapped and killed in such close proximity.

Criminologists were re-examining the Estell murder scene on September 23, 1993, when 23-year-old Michael Blair drove up to the site, parked his car, and approached them with various questions concerning the manhunt. Blair's behavior was curious enough to rate a trip downtown, for questioning, and he seemed happy to accommodate police, granting permission for a search of his car that turned up fibers similar to some found on Ashley's corpse. A hasty background check identified Blair as a convicted burglar and pedophile, sentenced to a 10-year prison term in 1989 for breaking into a house and molesting an 11-year-old occupant. Paroled in April 1990, after serving barely 18 months of his sentence, Blair had been jailed for burglary again in February 1991, but the grand jury refused to indict him, thus avoiding revocation of parole. The fibers from his car got Blair indicted for capital murder, in Ashley Estell's case, but authorities deny any link between their suspect and the previous murders of eight Dallas-area children. Those other crimes remain unsolved today.

"3X" murders — New York (1930)

Before the 1970s and "Son of Sam," the residents of Queens, in New York City, were familiar with another phantom gunman stalking human targets in their midst. Like "Sam," he kept up running correspondence with the press, explaining his attacks in terms that only he could fully comprehend. Unlike his imitator though, the original Queens killer managed to escape detection, and his case remains unsolved today.

On June 11, 1930, grocer Joe Mozynski parked with 19-year-old Catherine May along an isolated lover's lane in College Point, a neighborhood of Queens. They wanted privacy, and they were startled by a stranger who approached their car, produced a gun, and shot the grocer dead without a word of warning. Catherine May was ordered from the car and raped by the assailant; afterward, he searched her purse and burned some letters she was carrying. That done, he walked her to the nearest trolley stop and put her on a homebound car, first handing her a note that had been printed with a rubber stamp, in crimson ink. It read:

Joseph Mozynski
3X3-X-097

Suspicious homicide detectives were still holding May as a material witness when the killer's first letter reached a local newspaper, on June 13. Despite its brevity, it seemed to make no sense at all.

> Kindly print this letter in your paper for Mozynski's friends: "CC-NY ADCM-Y16a-DQR-PA ...241 PM6 Queens." By doing this you may save their lives. We do not want any more shooting unless we have to.

A second letter arrived on June 14, branding Mozynski "a dirty rat," declaring that the killer accosted his victim "to get certain documents but unfortunately they were not in his possession at that time." Providing a concise description of the murder gun and ammunition, for purposes of verification, the letter closed with a warning that "14 more of Mozynski's friends will join him" if the crucial documents were not delivered.

On June 16, Noel Sowley and Elizabeth Ring were parked near Creedmore, Queens, when a gunman approached their car, demanding Sowley's driver's license. Turning toward the outer darkness, he appeared to flash a coded signal with his flashlight, finally turning back to Sowley. "You're the one we want, all right," he said. "You're going to get what Joe got."

With that, the gunman executed Sowley, rifling his pockets before he turned on the woman. Avoiding rape with the display of a religious medal, Elizabeth Ring was left with a note similar to the one Catherine May had received on June 11.

Next morning, the killer mailed a new letter, with two spent cartridges enclosed. The note described "V-5 Sowley" as "one more of Mozynski's friends," adding that "thirteen more men and one woman will go if they do not make peace with us and stop bleeding us to death."

A massive search of New York City failed to turn a suspect, even with descriptions from the two eyewitnesses. On June 21, the killer surfaced in Philadelphia, mailing threats to Joe Mozynski's brother in an effort to secure "those papers." While the manhunt shifted into Pennsylvania, New York police received another long and rambling letter from the gunman. Describing himself as an agent of an anti-communist group, "the Red Diamond of Russia," the killer proclaimed: "The last document, N.J. 4-3-44 returned to us the 19 at 9 P.M. My mission is ended. There is no further cause for worry."

True to his word, the "3X" killer disappeared without another note or crime to mark his passing. Six years later, during June of 1936, a suspect in New Jersey signed confessions to the murders, but his story was discredited by homicide detectives and he was dispatched to an asylum. Memories of phantom gunmen were revived by the October 1937 "lipstick murders," so called after high-school sweethearts Lewis Weiss and Frances Hajek were shot in their car, circles drawn on the forehead of each victim with Hajek's lipstick, but that case, too, remained unsolved.

The "3X" legend grew with time and distance, swiftly losing contact with reality. As World War II approached, the homicides were blamed by sundry pamphleteers on Axis spies. A generation later, writing of the case in *Open Files,* author Jay Robert Nash described "3X" as "a maniac bomber [who] plagued New York City in the early 1930s by planting various homemade bombs throughout Manhattan, particularly at the sites of major landmarks." In retrospect, there is no need to make the phantom more or less than what he was. The truth is grim enough.

"Toledo Clubber" — Ohio (1925-26)

A classic bogeyman, the "Clubber" terrorized Toledo's population during 1925 and '26, assaulting women, beating some of them to death and leaving others gravely wounded in the wake of his attacks. Before the madness ran its course, the faceless suspect also stood accused of lighting fires and planting bombs in a bizarre and motiveless campaign of terror aimed at random targets.

The war of nerves began in 1925, when several lumber yards were torched within a period of hours. Guards were posted, and the unknown arsonist — or someone else — then started bombing homes and tenements. The FBI was called in when explosives wrecked the mailbox of a Catholic priest, and suddenly the bombings ended, as mysteriously as they had begun.

The madman was not finished with his game, however. As contemporary newsmen put their case, "the alleged fiend then turned to attacks upon women," killing three or four (reports vary) and wounding at least five others in a series of brutal rapes, invariably ending with the victims clubbed insensate. Rewards totaling $12,000 were raised for the maniac's capture, with no takers, when suddenly the violence ceased.

It started up afresh in late October 1926, with two more slayings added to the Clubber's tally in a single day. The first victim was schoolteacher Lily Croy, age 26, bludgeoned and raped within sight of her classroom in the early morning hours of October 26. The second victim, 47-year-old Mary Allen, was discovered in her home that afternoon. Police initially attributed her death to gunshot wounds, but later changed their story to report that Croy and Allen had been murdered with the same blunt instrument, the evidence recalling other Clubber homicides.

Around Toledo, lapsed rewards were dusted off and boosted by another rash of contributions, while police swept up a crop of local "odd-balls," finding several who has slipped away from mental institutions. Another rash of arson fires erupted on November 23, inflicting $200,000 damage at a single lumber yard, sweeping on from there to damage an ice company ($10,000), two other businesses, the city street department's stable, an apartment building, and a railroad freight car.

Officers got nowhere in their search for the Toledo Clubber, but again, as during 1925, the crime spree ended of its own accord. Was one demented individual to blame for all the rapes and beatings, fires and bombings? Did police create a monster in their bid to "clear the books" on unsolved local crimes? Whatever else he may have been, the Clubber stands reliably accused of half a dozen homicides, together with an equal number of assaults in which his victims lived to tell the tale. He remains unidentified at this writing, another of the ones who got away.

Toronto rape-murders — Canada (1982)

Between May and July of 1982, Toronto citizens were stunned by a series of brutal rape-assaults that left four young women dead and a fifth gravely injured. An editorial in the *Toronto Star* described the victims as "a cheerleader, a nanny, a mother and a bride-to-be."

While angry women's groups attacked the notion that rape victims are invariably young and attractive, thus somehow "inviting" assault, local residents cringed from the published accounts of the crimes: pantyhose tied around one victim's neck; another's skull crushed with a brick; a third naked and floating face-down in the river.

The first to die, on May 28, was 19-year-old Jennifer Isford, battered and discarded on a lawn close by her parents' home. Four other attacks would follow in the next six weeks, climaxing with the July strangulation of 38-year-old Judy DeLisle. Police described the crimes as "apparently unconnected," but locals remain unconvinced of the "coincidence." At this writing, the case remains unsolved.

"Torso" murders — California (1990-91)

In May 1991, police in Oakland, California, announced the possibility that an unknown serial killer might be responsible for the murders of two "Jane Doe" victims, murdered and dismembered in their city over the past seven months. Victim number one, a black woman, was found October 17, 1990, floating in the Oakland Estuary, off the 4000 block of Seventh Street. The headless, limbless torso had been stuffed inside a burlap bag, together with a gray knit long-sleeved shirt. No "obvious cause" of death was discovered — i.e., no stab or gunshot wounds apparent on the torso — and the mystery was not resolved when one of the victim's legs washed ashore, three weeks later. No trace of the victim's head, arms, or missing leg was ever found.

Seven months elapsed before the second "torso" victim, a red-haired Caucasian female, was found by a fisherman on May 15, 1991. The second torso occupied another burlap sack and was hauled from the estuary within 100 yards of the spot where her predecessor was found in October. A blue-and-red sunburst tattoo on the victim's left shoulder led to her identification as 43-year-old Leslie Deneveu, variously described in media reports as "a Berkeley transient" and a resident of nearby Richmond, California.

Acknowledged similarities in the two homicides included "cleanly severed" heads and limbs, the placement of both torsos inside burlap bags, discovery of both victims within close proximity to one another, placement of each body in the water a short time before it was found, and the absence of "definitive" fatal wounds on either corpse. A sharp knife or a fine-toothed saw was suspected as the instrument of dissection in both cases. Authorities further speculated that the Oakland crimes might be connected to the discovery of a woman's severed leg in the Sacramento Delta, on March 11, 1991, but no positive link has been proved to date. Seven years after the fact, the Oakland "torso" murders remain unsolved, their perpetrator theoretically at large.

"Torso" murders — Ohio:
See "Mad Butcher of Kingsbury Run"

Torture murders — USA/Canada (19??-91)

This intriguing, but sadly under-reported case, involves the torture slayings of at least nine victims, scattered across the breadth of the United States, with one murder reported from Canada. Nationally publicized for the first (and only) time in November 1991, the series of "particularly brutal" homicides is said to include victims slain in Ohio, California, Virginia, Maryland, Pennsylvania, and Ontario, Canada. No dates or specific locations were provided, although homicide detective Bruce Van Horn, from Columbus, Ohio, spoke briefly to journalists on November 24, telling them, "What is unique about all these cases is the amount of pain the killer inflicts."

According to Van Horn, the unidentified victims were variously beaten, raped, and stabbed before they burned to death, "many" of them placed alive in cars, which were then set afire. No updates on the manhunt have been published since that first, sketchy press release, suggesting that the savage crimes are still unsolved — if not ongoing — and the predator responsible is still at large.

Town Hospital — France (1944-47)

From 1944 to 1947, doctors and police alike were baffled by a string of homicides committed at the Town Hospital in Macon, France, north of Lyons. Seventeen patients in the hospital's gynecology ward died mysteriously following successful surgery, autopsies revealing that each in turn was killed by an injection of poison. On June 13, 1947, helpless detectives proclaimed that the killer was growing more cautious, allowing six months to pass between the murders of his last two victims. With public exposure, the killings apparently ceased, and the case remains unsolved today.

Transient murders — California (1987-88)

This intriguing, unsolved case involved the shooting deaths of five homeless transients, all white men in their 50s or 60s, killed around Bell, California (southeast of Los Angeles) between December 1987 and April 1988. Authorities acknowledged ongoing investigation of "a possible relationship" among the slayings, but no suspect was ever identified.

The first known victim of Bell's phantom gunman, 52-year-old James Stout, was killed four days before Christmas 1987, along a local railroad right of way. The next to die, 66-year-old Eric Ford, was found in front of the town's public library on March 14, 1988. Number three, 66-year-old Dennis Lynch, was discovered inside an abandoned building, on April 7. Three days elapsed before the last two victims were found, some 80 feet apart, on the same railroad right of way where James Stout had been slain, 16 weeks earlier. One of the latest victims was Jack Horn, age 62; his companion in death was described as a 57-year-old man, but his name was withheld by police. To date, more than a decade since the last reported shooting in the series, no solution to the case has been revealed.

"Trash bag" murders — New York (1989)

Between July and October 1989, four Hispanic men were robbed and brutally beaten to death in New York City's borough of Queens, their bodies left to rot in bags, discovered by pedestrians. To date, only one of the four battered victims has been identified by police, and their killer remains at large.

The first "Juan Doe" victim was found on July 31, 1989, discarded in a plastic trash bag on a vacant lot, at 135-40 155th Street in Queens. Hands bound behind his back, he had been clubbed to death with a hammer or other blunt instrument, stripped of his wallet, any jewelry he may have worn, and any documents that would have helped police identify the corpse. Four days later, a second unknown victim was found in identical condition, dumped on another vacant lot, this time at 167-20 120th Avenue. The third to die — identified as Fernando Suarez, a 32-year-old deliveryman from Garfield, New Jersey — turned up in a green canvas bag on August 25, left like so much rubbish at the corner of 172nd Street and 126th Avenue. (Unlike the other victims, Suarez had a quarter in his pocket.) Number four, still unidentified, was found October 4 on Cranston Avenue, when a pedestrian noticed one leg protruding from a trash bag left on a vacant lot between 134th and 135th Streets.

Detectives did their best, presumably, with what they had, but it came down to nothing in the end, and while no more attacks have been reported in the series, neither has the killer been identified or brought to book in four sadistic homicides.

Tri-county murders — Texas (1971-75)

A mystifying case from southeast Texas, still unsolved, involves the death or disappearance of girls and young women in a tri-county region on the Gulf of Mexico. Conflicting stories from investigators and the media have so confounded matters that to date, the body count has variously ranged from 16 victims to an estimated maximum of 40. After more than 20 years, one thing — and one thing only — may be said with certainty: the killer is unknown, presumably at large.

On April 5, 1981, a UPI dispatch quoted Lieutenant Nat Wingo, of the Brazoria County Sheriff's Department, as stating that 21 girls had been kidnapped and killed during a four-year span in the early 1970s. Wingo seemed to consider his roster an incomplete list, speculating that as many as 40 victims may have been slaughtered during the same general period. (When pressed for details by this author, Wingo indicated that the press "got that all wrong," but he refused to specify the errors or release a list of victims.) On April 7, the Associated Press announced that bodies of 21 victims had been recovered in Brazoria, Harris, and Galveston Counties since females began disappearing in 1971. At least eight of the deaths in Brazoria County were "similar," but police stopped short of blaming a serial killer. (Lieutenant Wingo, by contrast, was "certain" of one killer's responsibility in "most" of the crimes.)

Based upon available reports, the victims killed or kidnapped in Brazoria and southern Harris Counties ranged in age from 12 to 21, with most aged 14 or 15. All where white and fair, described as slender, with long brown hair parted in the middle. Eight of the dead, recovered over a 10-year period, were reportedly found near bodies of water. At least three Brazoria County victims were shot, while two others were beaten to death.

The only victims publicly identified — 12-year-old Brooks Bracewell and 14-year-old Georgia Greer — vanished from Dickinson, Texas, on September 6, 1974. Their skulls were found by an oil rig worker near Alvin, in 1976, but they were not identified until April 4, 1981, thereby reopening a stagnant investigation. Authorities from the affected areas convened that month to share their meager evidence, declaring that a list of 18 victims had been sorted out for special study. Two of the cases had already resulted in convictions, but they were left with the others "for purposes of comparison." All but one of the victims were murdered between 1971 and 1975, with 11 killed in the first year alone. At this writing, the case remains open, with no end in sight.

"Truckstop Killer" — United States (19??-19??)

A bogeyman tailor-made for America's mobile freeway culture, the elusive "Truckstop Killer" has haunted police from coast to coast, over the past two decades. His crimes smack of fiction — a rootless killer traveling where his mood takes him, claiming untold numbers of victims, in the mold of pulse-pounding movies like *Duel* and *Road Games.* Drawn primarily to hitchhikers, stranded female motorists, and "lot lizards" — prostitutes who work the parking lots of truck-stops, the faceless killing machine is said to abduct his victims, and often rape and torture them before he grants them the release of death, then dumps their corpses on the shoulder of some interstate highway, miles away from the crime scene. Various published reports on the case credit the Truckstop Killer with body counts ranging from a dozen victims to 100 or more. Some claim to trace his murder spree across a quarter-century.

The problem, simply stated, is that "he" may not exist.

Each state has unsolved homicides on file, and some of them, inevitably, involve women abducted from truckstops, from their cars, or while hitchhiking. Some of those victims disappear without a trace, while others are discarded like trash on the roadside, their bodies found days, weeks — even years — after they were first reported missing. In a fair number of cases, typically involving prostitutes who travel widely under varied names, there may be no police reports at all. Some of these homicides resemble one another: cause of death, description of the victims or the unknown suspect and his vehicle. In others, where remains are found at all, advanced decomposition may disguise the cause of death, even the victim's name.

Public discussion of a single "Truckstop Killer" began sometime in the mid-1980s, around the time the FBI computerized its files on unsolved homicides, and has continued unabated to the present day. No homicide investigator worth his salt believes that *every* murder in this category is committed by a single roving maniac. On the other hand, they often speak in terms of certain similarities or evidence (unspecified, of course) that seems to link a string of deaths, particularly in the eastern half of the United States.

Two statements from police in January 1992 suggest the scope and complexity of the problem. On January 23, authorities in Muncie, Indiana, announced that the recent murder of 20-year-old prostitute Crystal Sedam, found January 4 beside Interstate 69, was "similar" to several other homicides since 1989. Detective Robert Pyle compared the case to that of 37-year-old Georgia Shreve, found in August 1991 along I-74, in Montgomery County, and told reporters, "We are looking into the possibility this murder is connected to other murders in Indiana and other parts of the country."

Three days later, Pennsylvania state police told the press that a serial killer might be responsible for "several" of 17 unsolved murders committed along Keystone State highways since 1976. The similarities: Many of the victims were hookers known to work truckstops, and the killer(s) apparently took items of personal ID as souvenirs of the hunt.

A classic "Truckstop" case, and the only one to date with a description of the suspect or his rig, is the August 1992 murder of 21-year-old Tammy Zywicki. Tammy was en route to Grinnell College, in Iowa, after dropping her brother off at Northwestern University, in Evanston, Illinois, when she vanished on August 23. By the time a missing person report was issued, Tammy's car had already been found by Illinois state police, parked on the shoulder of Interstate 80, two miles west of Utica, with the hood raised as if to signal engine failure. No trace of the young blonde remained, and reports of her disappearance brought telephone calls from several witnesses. Two had seen her car around 3:25 P.M. on the day she vanished, parked behind an eighteen-wheeler that was painted white, with a brown diagonal stripe on the side of its trailer. The apparent driver of the rig had been a white man with dark, shoulder-length hair. He and his truck were gone before another witness passed the site, near 4:00 P.M., and saw Tammy's car parked with the hood up. A highway patrolman arrived on the scene at 5:15 P.M. and logged his discovery for the record.

Ten days later, on September 2, a truck driver in Lawrence County, Missouri, stopped along I-44 to investigate something wrapped in a red blanket, lying in a roadside ditch. He found a woman's decomposing body swaddled in the blanket, and used his CB radio to call police. Dental records confirmed it was Tammy Zywicki, an autopsy counting 75 knife wounds on her hands, arms and body. She had been murdered elsewhere — perhaps in the slayer's truck — and then transported to the point where her body was found, a full 160 miles from her abandoned car. To date, despite the anonymous donation of a $100,000 reward, the case remains unsolved.

Zywicki's murder was one of the first discussed in June 1993, when 100 police officers and FBI agents from seven states gathered in Springfield, Missouri, for a conference dubbed SHARE (Solving Homicides and Reviewing Evidence). Each participant in the gathering brought at least one unsolved case to discuss, but the main focus narrowed down to 27 murders dating back to 1969, including female victims found in Arkansas, Illinois, Kansas, Louisiana, Missouri, and Nebraska. Not all of them were "truckstop" victims — one, for example, was found drowned in her own bathtub — but at least five were transported some distance before their bodies were dumped, and ten of the 27 are still missing.

Perhaps the most disturbing aspect of the "Truckstop Killer" case has been the revelation of *how many* long-haul truckers seem to get their kicks from raping, torturing and killing helpless victims as they cruise our nation's highways. Indeed, smart money now suggests that there never was a single killer in the case, but rather a ghoulish subculture of truckers who kill as they travel, discarding victims like litter on the roadside. A partial list from recent years includes the following predators, all of whom may be considered suspects in some portion of the murders here considered:

- Scotty William Cox – Committed to mental institutions a stunning 115 times since 1979, this trucker was arrested by Washington state authorities in 1991, on charges of forging IDs. By year's end, Cox was publicly identified as a prime suspect in "at least 20 killings" committed in Washington, Oregon, and British Columbia.
- John Joseph Fautenberry – A long-haul trucker from 1982 through early 1991, Fautenberry seems to have committed his first murder in Oregon during 1984. Charged with five slayings that spanned the continent from Alaska to New Jersey, Fautenberry broke the normal pattern here by apparently killing more men than women, typically gunning his victims down for their money. A guilty plea to murder in Ohio earned him a death sentence in September 1992.
- Alvin Wilson – Convicted in 1984 for trying to rape a Virginia woman, whose car he rammed with his truck, Wilson was sentenced to six years in prison, paroled in June 1986. Next accused of trying to strangle a woman in Ohio, he was "cleared" by his travel log, although the victim had memorized the number on his truck's North Carolina license plate. Jailed by Florida police in 1991, on charges of rape and attempted murder, Wilson was publicly named as a suspect in 11 murders ranging from Ohio to Alabama

and the Carolinas. In June 1991, Ohio authorities officially cleared Wilson of suspicion in six of the Buckeye State's 12 "truckstop" cases, without commenting on the other six. Four months later, he was convicted in Florida, on three counts of sexual battery, burglary, and kidnapping.

- Benjamin Herbert Boyle – Suspected of a 1979 Colorado rape and a 1985 California slaying, this trucker was convicted in October 1986 for the year-old Texas murder of Gail Smith, age 20. Boyle was executed for that crime in 1997.
- James Cruz – A trucker since 1984, Cruz was arrested in September 1993 for the murder of 17-year-old hitchhiker Dawn Birnbaum, dumped along I-80 in Pennsylvania six months earlier. Convicted of that crime in 1994 and sentenced to life without parole, Cruz was also examined as a suspect in five Missouri homicides, reportedly cleared on the basis of fuel receipts and travel logs.
- Oscar Ray Bolin, Jr. – An Indiana native, this long-haul driver was sentenced to death in 1991 for three Florida murders committed five years earlier. Additional murder and rape charges were filed in Texas, while media reports describe Bolin as "a suspect in dozens of other slayings across the country."
- Robert Ben Rhoades – A sexual sadist who traveled with his own custom-designed torture kit, Rhoades was sentenced to life in September 1992, for the Ohio murder of a 14-year-old girl he abducted from Texas. Photographs seized from his apartment document the girl's sexual abuse and torture spanning days of captivity. Suspected of additional homicides, Rhoades has yet to be charged in any other cases.
- Sean Goble – A trucker since 1992, arrested in April 1995 for a February murder in North Carolina, this bearded hulk soon pled guilty to that and two other homicides, the "bo-

nus" victims discarded in Tennessee and Virginia. Detectives from 10 other states were reportedly lined up to question the talkative killer, but no further charges have been filed against him at this writing.

Truman Memorial Veterans Hospital — Missouri (1992)

In the eight months between January 1 and August 22, 48 patients died in Ward 4 East at the Truman Memorial Veterans Hospital in Columbia, Missouri. The numbers were startling, since Ward 4 East was a 27-bed facility for patients with non-surgical ailments, and while many of the dead had suffered from chronic diseases, VA physicians had given them no hints that death was imminent. On August 27, the hospital's quality assurance manager approached Dr. Gordon Christensen, associate chief of staff for research and development, with the suggestion that "a problem" might exist on Ward 4 East. That very day, according to his later testimony, Dr. Christensen began to work "around the clock" on a statistical analysis of recent deaths at Truman, which he finished on September 2.

One nurse — initially dubbed "Nurse H" — was found to be on duty when 45 of the deaths occurred, and Dr. Christensen subsequently told Congressional investigators, "The probability of it occurring by accident was so infinitely small that I couldn't calculate the number."

Pressed for a figure, he said that the odds against "Nurse H" being present at so many deaths by mere chance was "less than one in a million."

With those disturbing numbers in hand, Christensen called an emergency meeting at Truman on September 2, 1992, presenting his data to hospital director Joseph Kurzejeski. Dr. Christensen urged that police or FBI agents be notified, but

Kurzejeski flatly refused to involve any local authorities. Five days later, he likewise rejected Christensen's request to consult an independent biostatistician and confirm his findings.

On September 8, a second plea to inform police or federal agents was denied. Instead, on September 14, an internal Peer Review Board was appointed to review the five most recent deaths, *without* being informed that one nurse was a suspect in the case. The board's report was "inconclusive," and when a later board of inquiry convened, specifically to investigate a Truman intern's charges against "Nurse H," Christensen was forbidden by Kurzejeski from presenting his statistics to the board.

The story broke on September 25, 1992, after an anonymous caller tipped local TV and newspaper reporters to the rash of deaths on Ward 4 East. Ten days later, Missouri Congressman Ken Jacobs met with lower-level hospital employees to discuss the case, afterward sharing their concerns with the FBI. On October 7, Director Kurzejeski responded by warning Truman staffers that any disclosure of "confidential and privileged quality assurance information" was a criminal offense, punishable by fines ranging from $5,000 to $20,000. Undeterred by the not-so-subtle threat, Dr. Christensen took his stats to the Inspector General's office, a November 1992 report from the House Committee on Government Operations charging that the Veterans Administration routinely discourages reporting of substandard medical care by harassing or dismissing whistle blowers.

In February and March 1993, FBI agents exhumed the corpses of 13 patients who had died in 1992, on Ward 4 East. Christensen, meanwhile, was pressing the Inspector General's office for a full investigation of the deaths and apparent cover-up, but the response would be a year in coming.

For his part, Director Kurzejeski, in a March 16 report to the VA, complained that "Several clinical service chiefs who are not committed to the goals of this facility and the Department of Veterans Affairs (and their practice of involving others at a higher organizational level) continue to cause management to devote a considerable amount of time to this unprofessional conduct."

"Nurse H," meanwhile — formally "cleared of suspicion" by Director Kurzejeski in September 1992 — had found himself a second part-time job at a private nursing home in Ashland, when it opened in June 1993. Six months later, publicly identified for the first time as one Richard Williams, he resigned from Truman Memorial. In July 1994, following criticism of the Ashland facility by state inspectors, Williams left from that position as well. Director Kurzejeski had already retired by that time, leaving Truman Memorial with an "outstanding" performance rating and an $8,000 bonus for his fine work between October 1992 and September 1993. It was October 1995 before the House of Representatives reported its vague findings on the case, citing Kurzejeski and two subordinates for a "management breakdown" that presented an appearance of subterfuge at Truman Memorial.

Christensen, for his part, was unconvinced. "If it looks like a cover-up, sounds like a cover-up, acts like a cover-up...," he told reporters. "The report is full of half-truths, incomplete statements and inconsistencies."

At this writing, no charges have been filed in the Truman Memorial case, and FBI agents have yet to release their findings on the 13 corpses exhumed in 1993. In the absence of indictment and conviction at trial Nurse Williams must, of course, be presumed innocent of any criminal acts. A civil lawsuit filed on June 1, 1995, accused Truman Memorial of wrongful death in the case of Elzie Havrum, one of those exhumed in 1993, but the case has yet to be resolved.

Tuscaloosa murders — Alabama (1989-90)

Investigators in this Alabama college town (and former Ku Klux Klan headquarters) believe they have a local serial killer on their hands, based on evidence from ballistics tests concluded in March 1991. Those tests revealed that the weapon used to kill Robert and Kathryn McRae in 1989 also fired the bullets that killed A.C. and Carolyn Worthy, found in their fire-gutted home on October 15, 1990. Beyond linking the murders, however, ballistics evidence was useless in pointing police toward a suspect, or telling them where the murder gun could be found. At last report, investigation of the murders was continuing, with no prediction of arrests.

".22-caliber murders" — Georgia (1993)

Waycross, Georgia, is a modest, generally peaceable community of 19,000 souls, the seat of Ware County, located some 10 miles north of the brooding Okefenokee Swamp. Many — if not most — of the town's population are churchgoers. Nineteen-year-old Jason Hampton fit that mold, teaching Sunday school at the Brooks United Methŏdist Church with his girlfriend, 17-year-old Charlye Dixon, on May 31, 1993. After church, the couple changed out of their Sunday best and took a ride in Jason's pickup, off to do some fishing on the nearby Satilla River, north of town. Their respective parents were worried when the teens failed to return by 10:00 P.M., and because Charlye's father was a Waycross police sergeant, authorities dispensed with the normal red tape to begin an immediate search.

Even so, it was 12 hours later — near 10:00 A.M. on Monday, before a motorist spotted Jason's pickup and found him slumped dead in the seat, shot several times at close range with a .22-caliber weapon. Charlye Dixon's corpse was found a short time later 10 miles away, near the small community of Pebble Hill. Like Hampton, she had been shot several times with the same .22, her fatal wound a point-blank round to the back of the head. She was found fully clothed, with no evidence of sexual assault... but why, then, had the killer driven her so far away from the original murder scene?

Police were still puzzling over that question at 3:45 P.M. on Monday, when Gail Taylor, a 40-year-old nurse, was found shot to death in the carport of her home, in nearby Jamestown. Ware County sheriff's deputies publicly discounted any link between her slaying and the Hampton-Dixon murders, while admitting that the Taylor murder weapon was a .22, the fatal shot administered from close range, to the back of the victim's head.

A $20,000 reward for information on the crimes brought no takers, and police staked their slender hopes on a psychological profile of the killer. As sketched by a Georgia psychologist, the shooter was a white man, aged 23 to 30, probably a high-school dropout who had never married, a chronic underachiever employed at some manual trade. He was a thief propelled by lust, the armchair "mindhunter" explained, perhaps unable to achieve erections with a partner. Finally, the analyst guessed that the killer might have an accomplice, who now feared for his life and could be vulnerable under questioning.

Of course, detectives had to *find* him, first, and that turned out to be impossible. In November 1993, police thought they might have caught a break, following a minor traffic accident in Waycross. One of the drivers involved was 23-year-old Jimmy Holbrook, a nervous type who shot himself in the head when patrolmen asked for his driver's license. Holbrook used a .22 to do the deed, his suicide initially regarded by investigators as a sign of guilt, but subsequent ballistics tests proved that his pistol was not used on any of the victims killed in

May. Thus far, the $20,000 reward is still unclaimed in Waycross, the town's ".22-caliber killer" still at large.

"Tylenol murders" — United States (1982)

The unsolved "Tylenol murders" are unique among serial killings, in that the slayer never actually saw his victims, and had no idea of their identity or number until he (or she) was advised of the deaths by media reports. Perhaps predictably, by its very nature, the case has also had a greater impact on American society — and beyond — than any other case of serial murder in history.

The terror began on September 29, 1982, when 12-year-old Mary Kellerman, a resident of suburban Elks Grove Village, near Chicago, complained to her parents of a scratchy throat and sniffles. Treated with an Extra-Strength Tylenol capsule, Mary was found unconscious on the bathroom floor at 7:00 A.M. the next morning. She died three hours later, at a local hospital. Autopsy results determined that the capsule Mary Kellerman ingested had contained a lethal mix of normal Tylenol and deadly cyanide.

Those results had yet to be reported on the afternoon of September 29, when three members of the Janus family, residing in another Chicago suburb, swallowed Extra-Strength Tylenol capsules and shortly collapsed. None of the three was saved, despite the best efforts of physicians working on their case around the clock.

With the body count at four and holding for the moment, a local firefighter, Lieutenant Phillip Cappitelli, began putting two and two together in his mind. He was aware of Mary Kellerman's death from conversations with a relative; now, with reports of the Janus triple poisoning on his police scanner, he huddled with co-workers, soon making the link between Extra-Strength Tylenol and the four victims to date. Warnings were issued throughout greater Chicago on September 30, but three more victims had already been poisoned in the meantime, none of whom would manage to survive.

On October 1, 1982, the manufacturers of Extra-Strength Tylenol recalled some 264,000 bottles of their product from stores in Chicago and environs, while the U.S. Food and Drug Administration broadcast warnings for consumers to avoid the drug, until such time as an investigation was completed. Four days later, the recall went nationwide, after police in Oroville, California, blamed Tylenol laced with strychnine for the near-fatal convulsions suffered by victim Greg Blagg. By October 6, authorities in Canada, Great Britain, Norway, Italy, the Philippines, and South Korea were also taking steps to clear the suspect bottles from their shelves. The following day, authorities in Philadelphia retracted their suicide verdict in the April 3 death of a student, William Pascual, deciding the incident "might have been connected" to poisoned Tylenol capsules. A fresh examination of Extra-Strength Tylenol capsules found in Pascual's apartment found them contaminated with cyanide.

Back in Chicago, meanwhile, investigators traced the deadly capsules to the stores where they were purchased. On October 4, it was announced that one additional tainted bottle of Extra-Strength Tylenol had been found at each of five stores examined. Because of the small number found citywide, police concluded that the Tylenol was bought or stolen, "spiked" with poison by a lurking killer, then surreptitiously returned to store shelves. That judgment was buttressed on October 5, after medical examiners toured the Tylenol plant in Fort Washington, Pennsylvania. Cyanide *was* used at the plant, but security measures were tight, and the odds against in-house contamination were pegged at "a million to one."

The immediate result of the scare was a call for new and stricter safety features in the packaging of patent medicines. In Illinois, Cook County's board of supervisors passed an ordinance on October 4, 1982, requiring that all such containers sold within the county must have "tamper-proof" seals. The very next day, a federal task force convened to address the problem on a national basis. By October 6, Secretary of Health and Human Services Richard Schweiker had issued executive orders requiring tamper-resistant seals on all patent medicines and similar items designed for human consumption. Another step toward safety from random poisoning followed with invention of the "caplet" — i.e., capsule-shaped (but solid) tablets that cannot be opened and contaminated.

Still, prevention was easier than punishment in this troubling case, where the lurking killer (or killers) left no clues behind. It is a testament to human nature that, with the Tylenol scare at its height, certain opportunistic felons tried to jump on the bandwagon, demanding cash to avert future poisonings, but while they went to prison on extortion charges, none were ever linked to the actual murders. There was also a brief rash of "copycat" crimes, with victims in Colorado and Florida injured, respectively, by eye drops and mouthwash tainted with acid. In the final analysis, homicide investigators in Illinois, California and Pennsylvania could never decide if their poisoning cases were linked. Officially, the unknown "Tylenol killer" faces seven counts of murder for the crimes around Chicago, if and when police are able to identify a suspect. But at 16 years and counting since the crimes, it seems unlikely that the case will ever actually be solved.

"Valley Killer" — New Hampshire/Vermont (1978-88)

The scenic Connecticut River Valley forms a natural border between the states of New Hampshire and Vermont — a generally quiet, peaceful place to live. And yet, since 1978, the region has been terrorized by two vicious serial killers. One was captured and incarcerated for his crimes in 1983; the other — and more lethal of the two — remains at large today.

The first known victim of the faceless stalker known to locals as the "Valley Killer" was 26-year-old Cathy Millican, an enthusiastic birdwatcher, last seen alive on September 24, 1978, when she drove to a wetlands preserve at New London, New Hampshire, to practice her hobby. She failed to return home that night, and her body was found the next day, sprawled near a path through the wetlands, her clothing disarranged, belongings scattered along the trail as if she had been dragged for some distance. Millican was killed by stab wounds to the throat, after which her slayer drove the knife repeatedly into her lower body, clearly a sadistic sexual attack.

Police were still puzzling over that case a year later, when 13-year-old Sherry Nastasia was reported missing in Springfield, Vermont. Skeletal remains, found on December 13, included a broken leg and fractured ribs, but the cause of death was tentatively fixed as strangulation. Twelve-year-old Theresa Fenton was abducted while riding her bike in Springfield, on August 29, 1981; found alive the next day, but hopelessly injured by a savage beating, she died on August 31. The next victim, 11-year-old Caty Richards, was kidnapped on April 9, 1983, found beaten to death the next day, but this time a witness was able to describe the killer and his car. Suspect Gary Schaefer was quickly arrested, and later confessed to the murders of Fenton and Richards, plus the abduction of a female hitchhiker who managed to escape his clutches in November 1982. In December 1983, he pled no contest to one murder count (Caty Richards) and one charge of kidnapping (the survivor). Schaefer never admitted involvement in Sherry Nastasia's death, but most investigators think he is responsible for that crime, as well.

The "Valley Killer," meanwhile, seems to have gone on hiatus while Schaefer was playing his cat-and-mouse game with police around Springfield. His next presumed victim was 17-year-old Bernice Courtemanche, last seen alive on May 30, 1984, when she left her job as a nurse's aide at the Sullivan County Nursing Home, in Beauregard Village, New Hampshire. A co-worker drove Bernice to nearby Claremont, where she announced her intention of hitchhiking to Newport, for a visit with her boyfriend. Bernice never arrived, authorities fearing that she may have drowned in the flood tide of a nearby river. Their hopes for a "natural" solution to the mystery were dashed on April 19, 1986, when skeletal remains were found by two fishermen near Kellyville, New Hampshire. Bernice was identified from dental records three days later, knife marks on her cervical vertebrae indicating she was stabbed to death.

In the two years between Bernice's disappearance and the discovery of her remains, the Valley Killer had already claimed three more victims. Ellen Fried, a 26-year-old nurse, was last seen alive on the night of July 10, 1984, reported missing after she missed two days of work at Valley Regional Hospital, in Claremont. Her car was found soon after, parked on a narrow forest lane nearby, but it was September 19, 1985, before her skeleton was found at Newport, New Hampshire. Fried was identified on October 1, and while the first autopsy failed to note a cause of death, subsequent reexamination found apparent knife wounds, listing her death as a homicide by stabbing.

Eva Morse, a single mother with one 10-year-old daughter, arrived at her regular job in Charlestown, New Hampshire, at 7:00 A.M. on July 10, 1985, but never punched in. Instead, she lingered barely long enough to make a telephone call, then told her supervisor that she was going home sick. A co-worker who spoke with her before she left would later tell police that Eva was bound for Claremont, hitchhiking to visit her one-time lesbian lover. As word of her disappearance spread, a motorist reported giving Morse a lift to the Charlestown-Claremont line, and there she vanished — until loggers found her skeleton on April 25, 1986, the skull nearly severed by stab wounds.

Lynda Moore was the next to die, found stabbed to death in the kitchen of her home at Saxtons River, Vermont — south of Springfield — when her husband came home from work on April 15, 1986. The medical examiner counted more than two dozen stab wounds to her throat and abdomen, plus defensive cuts on both hands and arms. Moore's husband was initially suspected by police, as every spouse is suspect in such cases, but investigation swiftly cleared him of involvement in the crime.

The Valley Killer's apparent medical fetish resurfaced in January 1987, when he chose another nurse as his next victim. Barbara Agnew, 36, lived in Norwich, Vermont, and worked part-time at Mary Hitchcock Memorial Hospital, across the river in Hanover, New Hampshire. She was last seen alive on January 10, after a day of skiing with a friend near Winhall, Vermont. Three days later, her wallet and a woman's blood-stained clothing were found in the dumpster at a gas station south of White River Junction, Vermont, and a call to Agnew's workplace confirmed that she was missing. Her car was found abandoned on January 14, at a highway rest stop in Hartford, Vermont; police noted that her skis were missing, although her poles and boots were left behind. Agnew's remains, preserved intact by frigid weather, were found by hikers near Hartland, Vermont, on March 28. An autopsy revealed multiple stab wounds to the neck, apparently inflicted from behind, plus gashes to the lower abdomen that had become the Valley Killer's signature.

By this time, homicide investigators had their eyes on two more unsolved murders from the area, one dating back to June 11, 1968, when 15-year-old Jo Anne Dunham vanished from Claremont, New Hampshire. Found strangled the next day, her death bore no resemblance to the unknown slasher's crimes, but police noted that her corpse was found within a mile of the point where Eva Morse was last seen alive.

Another victim, 25-year-old Elizabeth Critchley, had disappeared on July 25, 1981, while hitchhiking from Massachusetts to her home in Vermont. Found two weeks later at Unity, New Hampshire, she had not been stabbed, but neither could the coroner determine any other cause of death. Her body had been found three miles from Gary Schaefer's home, and while authorities had questioned him about the case, he was never positively linked to Critchley's death. In fact, police now saw, her body had been dumped within two miles of the point where Eva Morse and Jo Anne Dunham were slain.

To this day, authorities cannot agree if victims Dunham and Critchley belong on the Valley Killer's hit list. They feel more confidence concerning Jane Boroski, a pregnant 22-year-old who was attacked at a country store on Route 9, south of Keene, New Hampshire, on the night of August 6, 1988. An unknown man approached Boroski in the parking lot, dragging her out of her car, and pulled a knife when she fought back. At one point in their scuffle, when she asked why he had chosen her, the man replied, "You beat up my girlfriend." Boroski denied it, and the man appeared confused. "Isn't this a Massachusetts car?" he asked. Boroski pointed out New Hampshire license plates, and the stranger hesitated, began to turn away, then rushed her with the knife again. Boroski was stabbed before approaching headlights caused her attacker to flee, but she survived her wounds and gave birth to a healthy daughter, two months later.

Boroski also described her assailant for police, assisting in the preparation of a sketch that was widely published throughout the Connecticut River Valley. In 1991, the crime was reenacted — and the sketch displayed for a national audience — on TV's *Unsolved Mysteries,* hosted by Robert Stack. The program had a history of clearing unsolved crimes, but there were no leads generated in Boroski's case. The Valley Killer, though apparently "retired" since August 1988, is unidentified and still at large today.

"Vampire" murders — Colombia (1963-64)

Between October 1963 and February 1964, at least 10 boys between the ages of 10 and 18 were found dead in the city of Cali, Colombia, their bodies discarded on vacant lots around town. Medical examiners blamed the deaths on deliberate extraction of blood, and police declared that they were searching for a black-market "blood ring," members of which were believed to be slaughtering children and selling their blood for $25 a quart.

Commercial vampires had been suspect in the slayings since December 1963, when 12-year-old twins mysteriously vanished, then turned up four days later in weakened condition. The boys told police they had been kidnapped, taken to a house where other boys were being held, and given shots to make them sleep. From that point, speculation took control, with officers assuming blood had been extracted and, presumably, put up for sale.

In truth, the city's modern hospital attracted sufferers from all around Colombia, creating a brisk market in blood required for surgery, transfusions, and the like. Despite top-level prices and police suspicions, though, the Cali "vampire" slayings have remained unsolved, without a shred of solid evidence to build a case in court.

"Warsaw Slasher" — Poland (1922)

On March 4, 1922, police in Warsaw, Poland, publicly announced discovery of 11 mutilated women in a wooded region of the city's suburbs. At the time their report was filed, no trace had been found of the slayer who left his young female victims with torn hair, fractured skulls, and "similar terrible wounds" to their torsos. No solution to the case was ever made public, and the crimes remain, apparently, unsolved.

Washington County murders — Pennsylvania (1976-77)

In a period of seven months, between November 1976 and June 1977, five young women were raped and murdered within a 25-mile radius of Washington, Pennsylvania, their killer striking with impunity and leaving homicide investigators at a loss for clues. Despite a fair description of the suspect, published in the form of artist's sketches, there were no arrests, and none are now anticipated in a case that terrorized the peaceful border region, holding women prisoners of fear inside their homes.

The stalker's first victim was 21-year-old Susan Rush, a native of Washington County, found strangled and locked in the trunk of her car on November 25, 1976. Detectives noted that her body had been "hastily clothed," her bra and panties left on the front seat, and a postmortem examination confirmed that the victim was raped prior to death.

On February 13, 1977, 16-year-old Mary Gency was reported missing from her home in North Charleroi. She had gone out for a walk after supper and never returned, her body recovered three days later from the woods at Fallowfield Township. Gency was beaten to death with a blunt instrument, raped before death by an assailant whom the county coroner described as "a mad animal."

Debra Capiola, seventeen, was last seen alive on March 17, walking to meet her school bus in nearby Imperial, in Allegheny County. She never arrived at school, and searchers found her body in a wooded section of southwestern Washington County on March 22. Capiola had been raped before she was strangled with her own blue jeans, the pants left wrapped around her neck.

Two months later, on the afternoon of May 19, 18-year-old Brenda Ritter was found dead at South Strabane Township, in Washington County. Nude except for shoes and stockings, she had been raped, then strangled with a piece of her own clothing, tightened around her neck with a stick.

In June, the killer strayed from Pennsylvania, but he did not travel far. His final victim was Roberta Elam, 26, a novice at Mount St. Joseph Mother House, in Oglebay Park, West Virginia, near Wheeling. Preparing to take her vows as a nun, Elam's religious career was cut short by the savage who raped and strangled her on June 13, dumping her corpse within 75 yards of the convent.

On the afternoon of June 15, authorities released a sketch of a long-haired suspect seen near the Ritter homicide scene, but none of the resultant tips proved fruitful. When the murder series ended, as mysteriously as it had begun, police could only speculate about the strangler's identity and whereabouts. Unless deceased or jailed on other, unrelated charges, he is still at large today.

Washington, D.C. murders — 1988

In a three-month period, between mid-August and October 1988, three women were killed and a fourth gravely injured in Washington, D.C., by an unknown assailant who savagely beat and strangled them. Twenty-one-year-old Lawanda Scott was the first victim, found beaten to death on August 12. Victim number two, a "Jane Doe" in her 20s, found dead and apparently raped on September 6; autopsy reports attributed her death to a combination of blunt-force trauma and strangulation. Another three weeks passed before a third woman (left anonymous in media reports) was beaten and shot several times by an unidentified attacker, but she survived her wounds, despite serious injury. October's victim was 21-year-old Gloria Carter, beaten and strangled to death in the pattern of Lawanda Scott and "Jane Doe."

Despite apparent similarities in at least three of the cases — attacks by violent manual assault, occurring at rough three-week intervals — Washington police hesitated to suggest they had a serial killer on the prowl. They were, of course, "looking into" possible links between the crimes, but there was no evidence "conclusively linking" the cases, which led detectives to call them "unrelated," siting any reference to a possible serial killer as "inappropriate." However many perpetrators were at large in Washington, the crimes are still unsolved after a decade of investigation, and seem likely to remain so for all time.

"West Side Rapist" — California (1974-75)

Within a single year, between November 1974 and October 1975, a vicious prowler terrorized the west side of Los Angeles, raping 33 women and killing at least 10. While all of his victims were elderly, ranging in age from 63 to 92 years, the incessant attacks spread an aura of fear city-wide, boosting gun sales, turning neighbor against neighbor as dark suspicions flourished. In the end, he slipped away without a trace and left police to search in vain for clues to his identity.

The first to die, on November 7, 1974, was 72-year-old Mary Scialese, followed the next day by Lucy Grant, age 92. On November 14, the slayer claimed Lillian Kramer, 67, rebounding on the night of December 4 to kill 74-year-old Ramona Gartner. A new year brought no respite from the violence, with 71-year-old Sylvia Vogal murdered on March 22, 1975. Una Cartwright, age 78, was slaughtered on April 8, with 75-year-old Olga Harper killed two weeks later. Murdered on May 22, 86-year-old Effie Martin was the eighth fatality in 23 attacks. Her death was followed by the September homicide of Cora Perry, 79, and the slaying of 63-year-old Leah Leshefsky on October 28.

By New Year's Day, two months had passed without a new assault, and residents of West L.A. began to breathe a little easier. In time, they would forget, but homicide detectives would continue searching for their man across a decade, covering the same ground endlessly, without result. A possible solution to the case has been suggested in the person of Brandon Tholmer, confined for three years to a state mental hospital after raping a 79-year-old woman in October 1975. Eleven years later, in 1986, Tholmer — then 37 — was sentenced to life in prison for the rape-slayings of four elderly women since 1981. To date, no evidence has been produced connecting

Tholmer with the earlier series of murders, and the West Side Rapist remains officially unidentified.

Wiltshire murders — England (1986)

On December 21, 1986, detectives in Wiltshire, England, announced their search for connections in the recent slayings of two women, killed within hours of each other at Salisbury. In the early morning hours of December 19, victim Ruth Perrett, age 25, was found naked and dead in her room at a halfway hostel for recovering mental patients. Last seen alive at a party the previous evening, she had been raped and strangled by her assailant. The following day, police at Ringwood, near Southampton, were following up a missing-person report when they found 45-year-old Beryl Deacon dead in her car, another victim of sexual assault.

A third fatality was added to the list when homicide investigators voiced concerns about a possible link between the two latest murders and that of Linda Cooke, age 24, a one-time barmaid raped and murdered in the town of Portsmouth, on December 10. Cooke's death was seen as possibly related to a string of unsolved rapes, mostly targeting nurses and female doctors at area hospitals over the past year. Police arrested several suspects in the case, but none was ultimately prosecuted. The most recent, described in press reports as a sailor, was released in January 1987 with no charges filed against him. At this writing, the case remains unsolved.

Yakima reservation murders — Washington (1980-92)

Authorities are divided in their opinions as to whether a serial killer is responsible for the murders of at least 13 women, committed since 1980 on the 1.3 million-acre Yakima Indian Reservation, in Washington state. Eleven of the 13 victims were Native American, most of them born and raised on the reservation, many with histories of alcohol abuse. Most of the victims were in their 20s; at least eight left children behind. Some were stabbed to death, while others were beaten, shot, or strangled; two were apparently drowned, and one was run down by a car. The bodies have typically been dumped in remote, wooded areas, where decomposition and exposure to the elements or scavengers erases evidence, leaving the cause of death unknown in several cases. At least two other Indian women — Karen Louise Johnly and Daisey May Tallman, both in their 20s — were also reported missing between 1987 and 1992, but their names have not been added to the "official" Yakima victims list.

One lawman who believes a serial killer *is* responsible for the murders, Melford Hall, retired in 1989 after 22 years as a criminal investigator for the Bureau of Indian Affairs, cited the homicides as part of his reason for leaving the job.

As Hall told reporters in January 1993, "They'll probably say, He doesn't know what he's talking about. But then you look at all these names."

Hall links the murders to rampant alcoholism, so prominent at Yakima and other reservations. "My own opinion," he explains, "is this guy sits at a tavern someplace and waits for an intoxicated woman and grabs her."

Yakima's Tribal Police Department, meanwhile, refuses all requests for interviews on the murders, but agents from the FBI's Seattle field office fulfilled Hall's prediction, calling it "extremely unlikely" that one killer was responsible for all 13 of the Yakima murders. FBI spokesman William Gore referred to "significant evidence" and "logical suspects" in three of the cases, although no charges were filed. On January 27, 1993, the FBI declared that 12 of the Yakima murders "are closed, though they could be reopened if new information surfaced."

But the question remains: Is anybody looking? Hall, for one, was bitter toward the FBI. "A lot of times we would call them," he told reporters, "and they'd say, 'Just send over a report.' They spent millions of dollars over there [i.e., on the **Green River** murders], and wouldn't spend anything here."

It is a further point of bitter irony, Hall noted, that the FBI has direct responsibility for all murders committed on Indian reservations, but none at all in local murders, like Seattle's infamous "Green River" case.

Another lawman who compared the two unsolved cases was Yakima County Sheriff's Deputy Dave Johnson, who complained that murder investigations are hampered by the tendency of some tribal members to leave the reservation without informing friends or family. "It's kind of like the Green River victims, many of whom were prostitutes," Johnson said. "You have individuals with no permanent address."

One who resented the comparison was Johnnie Wyman, whose sister — 44-year-old JoAnne Betty Wyman John — was found dead on the reservation in 1991, three years after she disappeared.

"The authorities take the attitude that it's just a bunch of drunken Indian women," Wyman told the press. "It's just another slap in the face. I can't candy-coat it for anybody. She was my sister, and she meant something to me."

The most recent slaying — and that which finally brought national publicity to the murders — was that of Shari Dee Sampson Ewell, found strangled and sexually mutilated on December 30, 1992, in a section of the reservation closed to non-Indians. Sufficient media attention was generated by Ewell's death that the Yakima Indian Nation offered a $1,000 reward for information leading to the killer's arrest, the fund increased by $5,000 from the FBI on May 14, 1993. Thus far, the money has not helped. The murders on the Yakima reservation remain unsolved.

Zephyrhills murders — Florida (1973-77)

Despite the relative antiquity of this case, authorities and journalists in Zephyrhills, Florida — the seat of Pasco County, northeast of Tampa — declined to answer my requests for information on a series of murders spanning the years from 1973 to 1977. Vague press reports allude to eight female victims — mostly nude dancers or hookers — with long blond or light-brown hair. Skeletal remains of the eighth presumed victim, apparently unidentified, were found in December 1977, some 500 yards from the place where 49-year-old Wilma Wood was discovered in 1973, and barely 100 yards from the spot where 38-year-old Emily Grieve was found dead on October 21, 1977. The rest is mystery, like the identity of the killer (or killers) who slaughtered eight women and dumped them around Zephyrhills. It *can* be said with certainty that the last known murder in the series occurred at least a week *before* Ted Bundy made his way to Florida, and roughly seven years before Bobby Joe Long began stalking topless dancers in Tampa, committing 10 known homicides and fifty-odd rapes. As for the rest, the case remains unsolved, the Pasco County stalker unidentified.

"Zodiac" — California (1966-??)

California's most elusive serial killer claimed his first victim on October 30, 1966, in Riverside. That evening, Cheri Jo Bates, an 18-year-old freshman at Riverside City College, emerged from the campus library to find her car disabled, the distributor coil disconnected. Police theorize that her killer approached with an offer of help, then dragged her behind some nearby shrubbery, where a furious struggle ended with Cheri stabbed in the chest and back, her throat slashed so deeply that she was nearly decapitated.

In November 1966, a letter to the local press declared that Cheri "is not the first and she will not be the last." Following publication of an article about the case, on April 30, 1967, identical letters were posted to the newspaper, police, and to the victim's father. They read: "Bates had to die. There will be more."

On December 20, 1968, 17-year-old David Faraday was parked with his date, 16-year-old Betty Lou Jensen, on a rural road east of the Vallejo city limits, in northern California. A night-stalking gunman found them there and killed both teenagers, shooting Faraday in the head as he sat behind the wheel of his car. Betty Lou ran 30 feet before she was cut down by a tight group of five shots in the back, fired from a .22-caliber automatic pistol.

July 4, 1969. Michael Mageau, 19, picked up his date, 22-year-old Darlene Ferrin, for a night on the town. At one point, Mageau believed they were being followed, but Darlene seemed to recognize the other motorist, telling Mageau, "Don't worry about it." By midnight, they were parked at Blue Rock Springs Park, when a familiar vehicle pulled alongside and the driver shined a bright light in their eyes, opening fire with a 9mm pistol. Hit four times, Mageau survived; Darlene, with nine wounds, was dead on arrival at a local hospital.

Forty minutes after the shooting, Vallejo police received an anonymous call, directing officers to the murder scene. Before hanging up, the male caller declared, "I also killed those kids last year."

In retrospect, friends and relatives recalled that Darlene Ferrin had been suffering harassment through anonymous phone calls and intimidating visits by a heavyset stranger in the weeks before her death. She called the strange man "Paul," and told one girlfriend that he wished to silence her because she had seen him commit a murder. Police searched for "Paul" in the wake of Darlene's slaying, but he was never located or identified.

On July 31, 1969, the killer mailed letters to three Bay Area newspapers, each containing one-third of a cryptic cipher. Ultimately broken by a local high-school teacher, the message began: "I like killing people because it is so much fun." The author explained that he was killing in an effort to "collect slaves," who would serve him in the afterlife. Another correspondence, mailed on August 7, introduced the "Zodiac" trade name and provided details of the latest murder, leaving police in no doubt that its author was the killer.

On September 27, 20-year-old Bryan Hartnell and Cecilia Shepherd, 22, were enjoying a picnic at Lake Berryessa, near Vallejo, when they were accosted by a hooded gunman. Covering them with a pistol, the stranger described himself as an escaped convict who needed their car "to go to Mexico." Producing a coil of clothesline, he bound both victims before drawing a long knife, stabbing Hartnell five times in the back. Cecilia Shepherd was stabbed 14 times, including four in the chest as she twisted away from the plunging blade.

Departing the scene, their assailant paused at Hartnell's car, to scribble on the door with a felt-tipped pen. He wrote:

Vallejo
12-20-68
7-4-69
Sept 27-69-6:30
by knife

A phone call to police reported the crime, but by that time, a fisherman had already discovered the victims. Brian Hartnell would survive his wounds, but Cecilia Shepherd was doomed, another victim for the man who called himself the Zodiac.

On October 11, San Francisco cab driver Paul Stine was shot in the head and killed with a 9mm automatic pistol. Witnesses saw the gunman escape on foot, toward the Presidio, and police descended on the neighborhood in force. At one point in the search, two patrolmen stopped a heavyset pedestrian and were directed in pursuit of their elusive prey, not realizing that the "tip" had been provided by the very man they sought.

In the wake of Stine's murder, the Zodiac launched a new barrage of letters, some containing swatches of the cabbie's bloodstained shirt. Successive messages claimed seven victims, instead of the established five, as the killer threatened to "wipe out a school bus some morning." He also vowed to change his method of "collecting souls;" "They shall look like routing robberies, killings of anger, & a few fake suicides, etc." Five days before Christmas, he wrote to prominent attorney Melvin Belli, pleading for help with the chilling remark that "I cannot remain in control for much longer."

On March 22, 1970, Kathleen Johns was driving with her infant daughter, near Modesto, California, when another motorist pulled her over, flashing his headlights and beeping his horn. The man informed her that a rear tire on her car seemed dangerously loose; he worked on it briefly, with a lug wrench, but when she tried to drive away, the wheel fell off. Her benefactor offered a lift to the nearest garage, then took Kathleen on an aimless drive through the countryside, threatening her life and that of her child before she managed to escape from the car, hiding in a roadside irrigation ditch. Reporting the abduction at a local police station, Johns noticed a wanted poster bearing sketches of the Zodiac, and she identified the man as her attacker.

Nine more letters were received from Zodiac between April 1970 and March 1971, but police were unable to trace further crimes in the series. On January 30, 1974, a San Francisco newspaper received the first authentic Zodiac letter in nearly three years, signing off with the notation: "Me-37; SFPD-0."

One officer who took the estimated body count seriously was Sheriff Don Striepke, of Sonoma County. In a 1975 report, Striepke referred to a series of 40 unsolved murders in four western states, which seemed to form a giant "Z" when plotted on the map. While tantalizing, Striepke's theory seemed to fall apart with the identification of Theodore Bundy as a prime suspect in several of the homicides.

On April 24, 1978, the Zodiac mailed his 21st letter, chilling Bay Area residents with the news that "I am back with you." No traceable crimes were committed, however, and Homicide Inspector Dave Toschi was later removed from the Zodiac detail on suspicion of writing the letter himself. In fact, while Toschi confessed to writing several anonymous letters to the press, praising his own performance on the case, expert analysts agree that the April note was, in fact, written by the killer.

Theories abound in the Zodiac case. One was aired by author "George Oakes" (a pseudonym) in the November 1981 issue of *California* magazine, based on a presumption of the killer's obsession with water, clocks, binary mathematics, and the writings of Lewis Carroll. Oakes claimed to know the Zodiac's identity and says the killer telephoned him several times, at home. He blames the Zodiac for an arson fire that ravaged 25,000 acres near Lake Berryessa in June 1981, but *California* editors acknowledged that FBI agents "weren't very impressed" with the theory. Spokesmen for the California State Attorney General's office went further, describing the tale as "a lot of bull."

Author Robert Graysmith also claims to know the Zodiac by name, calling his suspect "Robert Hall Starr" in a book published during 1986. A resident of Vallejo, "Starr" is described as a gun buff and suspected child molester, confirmed as a prime Zodiac suspect by several detectives (and flatly rejected by others). Graysmith credits Zodiac with a total of 49 "possible" victims between October 1966 and May 1981, three of whom survived his attacks. In addition to the six known dead and three confirmed survivors, Graysmith included 15 **"occult" murders** linked to one unidentified slayer in northern California and 15 other **"astrological" murder** victims killed in close proximity to a solstice or equinox — nine confirmed by police as the work of a single man. Of 40 "possible" victims listed by Graysmith, 39 were female, variously shot, stabbed, beaten, strangled, drowned and poisoned... perhaps in accordance with Zodiac's promise to alter his method of "collecting slaves."

A copycat "Zodiac" killer (Heriberto Seda) was convicted in New York in June 1998, but the original killer is still unidentified.

Bibliography

Baldwin, James. "Atlanta: the evidence of things not seen." *Playboy*, December 1981.

Barry, Steven. "For five years, Philly's freaky fish cutter filleted females!" *Official Detective,* August 1992.

Beaubien, Roxanne. "Tips sought in unsolved killings." *Toronto Free Press,* February 5, 1998.

Beaufait, Howard. "Kingsbury Run murders." *Homespun,* November 1955.

Beaupre, Becky. "Key evidence in 4 Miss. slayings untested after year." *USA Today,* August 20, 1996.

Benedict, Barry. "Was the snuff moviemaker the Green River killer?" *Master Detective,* July 1992.

Boardman, Krist. "Is the northeast stalker still on the prowl?" *Detective Files,* July 1991.

Browne, Andrew. "A serial killer stalks a Chinese city." Reuters, May 21, 1992.

Busch, Alva. *Roadside Prey.* New York: Pinnacle Books, 1996.

Cameron, Jackie. "Serial killing of young girls feared." *The Independent,* February 4, 1998.

Codrescu, Andrei. "Terror stalks the Big Easy." *Playboy,* March 1996.

Cooper, Pam. "No cover-up at VA." *Missourian,* October 1, 1995.

Corsaletti, Louis. "More than one body found at Bothell site." *Seattle Times,* February 13, 1998.

Cox, Bill. "The Texas child killers." *Detective Cases,* June 1994.

D'Ambro, Gia. "8 women butchered in the shocking case of the Philadelphia slasher." He*adquarters Detective,* September 1993

Davidson, Bill. "The town that lives in terror." *Good Housekeeping,* September 1977.

Dettlinger, Cher, and Jeff Prugh. *The List.* Atlanta, GA: Philmay, 1983.

Escobar, Gabriel, and Maria Fernandez. "Arrest made in cluster of D.C. killings." *Washington Post,* January 30, 1998.

Fimrite, Peter. "Police identify Oakland torso." *San Francisco Chronicle,* May 17, 1991.

Fischer, Mary. "Was Wayne Williams framed?" *GQ,* April 1991.

Fonseca, Teresa. "Can you help solve the blue light murders?" *True Police,* April 1996.

Franklin, Erica. "Wounded taxi driver made it to fire station before dying." *Indianapolis Star,* July 13, 1993.

Furillo, Andy. "Police fear serial killer in Oakland." *San Francisco Examiner,* May 17, 1991.

Furillo, Andy. "Torsos in bay suggest a serial killer." *San Francisco Examiner,* May 16, 1991.

Ginsburg, Philip. *The Shadow of Death.* New York: Jove Books, 1993.

Godwin, John. *Murder USA*. New York: Ballantine, 1978.

Graysmith, Robert. *Zodiac.* New York: St. Martin's Press, 1986.

Griggs, John. "Highway of strangled whores." *Detective Dragnet,* December 1995.

Hamilton, Steve. "12-month manhunt for Kansas City's Gilham Park strangler." *True Detective,* January 1993.

Harris, Harry. "Oakland police seek serial killer." *Oakland Tribune,* May 16, 1991.

Heise, Jack. "Mystery slayer of the Okefenokee swamp." *Detective Files,* May 1994.

Heise, Jack. "Who's killing the Roman Catholic Priests!" *Headquarters Detective,* November 1989.

Heise, Jack. "Who's strangling the turnpike hookers?" *True Police,* December 1991.

Hornbeck, Mark. "Police suspect serial killer is loose: Grand Rapids killings may be work of one person." *Detroit News,* October 16, 1996.

Howard, Clark. *Zebra.* New York: Berkley, 1980.

Johnson, Angella. "'Dead' children found alive." *Mail & Guardian,* January 23, 1988.

Kanhema, Newton. "South African police fear ritual killings of children." Pan African News Agency, January 20, 1998.

Kelly, Bill. "The mystery of Laura Bradbury." *Headquarters Detective,* May 1994.

Kelly, Bill. "Tattooed biker drove women to the grave." *Headquarters Detective,* July 1991.

King, Gary. "Who snuffed the snuff moviemaker?" *True Detective,* January 1994.

Koenig, Joseph. "Atlanta's phantom lovers' lane slayer." *Front Page Detective,* August 1979.

Kohut, John. "Canton Ripper's grisly record remains a secret." *The Times,* June 14, 1992.

Kornblut, Anne. "Probe of Springfield slayings criticized." *Boston Globe,* March 20, 1998.

Labalme, Jenny. "4 men identified from Hamilton County bones." *Indianapolis Star,* September 13, 1996.

Labalme, Jenny. "Handcuffs, more bones found in woods." *Indianapolis Star,* July 3, 1996.

Lamb, Michael. "Torso murders: 40 years unsolved." *Sunday Plain Dealer Magazine,* October 12, 1975.

Lane, Brian, and Wilfred Gregg. *The Encyclopedia of Serial Killers.* New York: Diamond Books, 1992.

Langlois, Janet. Belle Gunness: *The Lady Bluebeard.* Bloomington, IN: Indiana University Press, 1985.

Latner, Ken. "Houston's house of horror." *True Police,* February 1997.

Leavy, Walter. "The mystery of the disappearing blacks." *Ebony,* December 1980.

Lopez, Robert. "Police baffled by woman's savage murder." *Oakland Tribune,* May 18, 1991.

Lynn, Adam. "Detectives link Tacoma killing to Spokane's." *Spokesman-Review,* January 31, 1998.

Martin, John. *Butcher's Dozen.* New York: Harper & Brothers, 1950.

Mauder, Jack. "The 3X murders." *American Mercury,* June 1940.

Mauro, Larry. "Long-haul serial killer." *True Police,* June 1993.

Mauro, Larry. "Missouri sex strangler claims 72nd victim!" *True Police,* October 1990.

Mauro, Larry. "27 missing, murdered and mutilated women." *Headquarters Detective,* January 1994.

McAlary, Mike. "He's the 'Last Call Killer.'" *Daily News,* August 9, 1993.

McConnell, Brian. *Found Naked and Dead.* London: New English Library, 1974.

McDowell, Rider. "On the trail of the Zodiac." *This World,* May 8 and May 15, 1994.

McInnes, Jon. "The skulking sex monster who preys on young lovers!" *Official Detective,* February 1988.

McNeill, Robert. "Stop 'Bible John' before he kills again!" *Detective Files,* January 1997.

Michaud, Stephen, and Hugh Aynesworth. *Murderers Among Us.* New York: Signet, 1991.

Miley, Scott. "Body found in Ohio identified as city man." *Indianapolis Star,* September 19, 1990.

Morgan, Kevin. "Ohio sheriff urges IPD to focus on gay killings." *Indianapolis Star,* October 11, 1990.

Morgan, Kevin, and Kyle Niederpruem. "Complexities compound slaying cases." *Indianapolis Star,* September 20, 1990.

Morrison, Blake. "Children offered details on suspect in 3 killings." *St. Paul Pioneer Press,* July 23, 1996.

Murphy, Brian. "Italians pack courtroom to see 'Monster of Florence.'" *Seattle World,* May 8, 1994.

Myers, Laura. "Authorities discount idea of serial killer preying on women." Associated Press, November 28, 1990.

Nasser, Haya El. "Fear stalks L.A. streets." *USA Today,* June 3, 1993.

Newton, Michael. *Hunting Humans.* Port Townsend, WA: Loompanics Unlimited, 1990.

Newton, Michael. *Raising Hell.* New York: Avon, 1993.

Newton, Michael. *Serial Slaughter.* Port Townsend, WA: Loompanics Unlimited, 1992.

Nickel, Steven. Torso: *The Story of Eliot Ness and the Search for a Psychopathic Killer.* Winston-Salem, NC: J.F. Blair, 1989.

Niekirk, Philip von. *"A time to kill."* Maxim, Summer 1997.

Oakes, George. "Portrait of the artist as a mass murderer." *California,* November 1981.

O'Brien, John. "9 women split from throat to abdomen!" *Detective Dragnet,* February 1994.

Oke, Iasiah. *Blood Secrets.* Buffalo, NY: Prometheus Books, 1989.

Pardo, Steve. "Police team to solve prostitute killings." *Detroit News,* February 4, 1998.

Patterson, James J. "Gays tell IPD to heighten protection." *Indianapolis Star,* March 18, 1992.

Patterson, James J. "Link to 10 gay slayings sought." *Indianapolis Star,* March 17, 1992.

Philpin, John. *Stalemate.* New York: Bantam, 1997.

Ponzani, Michael. "Trucker nailed as interstate strangler." *Headquarters Detective,* January 1995.

Pron, Nick. "Science could solve murders." *Toronto Star,* February 5, 1998.

Radner, Henry. "'Child cannibal' loose in St. Louis." *Detective Dragnet,* October 1994.

Radner, Henry "Did the fish cutter practice on whores?" *Headquarters Detective,* September 1989.

Radner, Henry "Serial killer went on a 41-whore orgy." *Detective Cases,* April 1990.

Radner, Henry "Sex-crazed strangler who preyed on hitchhikers." S*tartling Detective,* September 1993.

Radner, Henry "Top cop linked to black hooker murders." *Headquarters Detective,* September 1989.

Ryder, Bill. "The man who loved to kill people." *True Detective,* September 1986.

Salter, Jim. "Police think serial killer nabbed girls." *Oregonian,* December 11, 1993.

Salter, Jim. "Search for girl in pink results in tragedy." *Indianapolis Star,* December 10, 1993.

Sanchez, Sandra. "In St. Louis, child killer stalks by day." *USA Today,* December 10, 1993.

Sanchez, Sandra. "Terror, tears in St. Louis." *USA Today,* December 13, 1993.

Sanders, Ed. *The Family.* New York: Dutton, 1971.

Sifakis, Carl. *The Encyclopedia of American Crime.* New York: Facts on File, 1982.

Smith, Carlton. *Killing Season.* New York: Onyx, 1994.

Spinks, Sarah. *Cardiac Arrest: A True Account of Stolen Lives.* Toronto: Doubleday, 1985.

Squitieri, Tom. "Slayings of prostitutes linked." *USA Today,* March 15, 1990.

Stoddart, Charles. *Bible John.* Edinburgh: Paul Harris, 1980.

Terry, Maury. *The Ultimate Evil.* New York: Doubleday, 1987.

Thomas, Jamison. "Manhunt for the serial rape strangler." *Detective Dragnet,* August 1995.

Thomas, Jamison. "Tattooed giant who hog-tied women." *Startling Detective,* July 1991.

Thomas, Jerry. "Killer interrupts sanctity of Chatham, Avalon Park." *Chicago Tribune,* September 7, 1992.

Thompson, Duke. "Virginia serial slasher notches 10th kill!" *Headquarters Detective,* May 1996.

Tierney, Patrick. *The Highest Altar.* New York: Viking, 1989.

Tillman, Leroy. "Washington police arrest suspect in neighborhood slayings." Associated Press, January 29, 1998.

Tobias, Ronald. *They Shoot to Kill: A Psycho-Survey of Criminal Sniping.* Boulder, CO: Paladin Press, 1981.

Unatin, Don. "Can you help NYPD catch the cruising cabbie killer?" *Official Detective,* July 1991.

Unatin, Don. "The shocking rise of ritual murders!" *True Detective,* May 1987.

U.S. House of Representatives. *Issues at the Harry S. Truman V.A. Medical Center in Columbia, Mo.* Washington, D.C.: House of Representatives, Subcommittee on Hospitals and

Health Care, Committee of Veterans' Affairs (October 25, 1995).

Walton, Richard. "Is the psycho monster back?" *Detective Cases,* August 1992.

White, Ed. "'It eats at you' says mom who misses slain daughter." *Detroit News,* November 2, 1996.

White, Ed. "Murders scare prostitutes into different walk of life." *Detroit News,* November 3, 1996.

White, Ed. "Task force hunts possible serial killer of 11 women." *Los Angeles Times,* November 10, 1996.

Wilcox, Robert. *The Mysterious Deaths at Ann Arbor.* New York: Popular Library, 1977.

Wiley, John. "Four slayings in last weeks of '97 heighten concerns about serial killer." Associated Press, February 1, 1998.

Other Titles by Michael Newton:

☐ **34092 BLACK COLLAR CRIMES, An Encyclopedia of False Prophets and Unholy Orders, *by Michael Newton.*** This lexicon of lawlessness is truly astounding. Mail fraud, indecent exposure, theft, perjury, arson, assault with intent to kill, sexual abuse, contributing to the delinquency of a minor, bigamy, inciting a riot, public lewdness, manslaughter, sodomy, electronic eavesdropping, bankruptcy, fraud, obscenity, inflicting bodily harm, income tax evasion, child molestation... well, the list continues to astound pious readers! You'll never view clergy in the same way you do now, once you've read Newton's amazing expose of religious misconduct. ***1998, 5½ x 8½, 280 pp, soft cover.* $18.95.**

☐ **34050 HUNTING HUMANS, An Encyclopedia of Modern Serial Killers*, by Michael Newton.*** More than 500 detailed case histories of serial killers from the 20th Century. This disturbing book describes their lives and their exploits without any varnish or puffery — the chilling details speak for themselves. This huge book is an unforgettable chronicle of the world's most deranged homicidal maniacs. ***1990, 8½ x 11, 353 pp, illustrated, hard cover.* $34.95.**

Loompanics Unlimited
PO Box 1197
Port Townsend, WA 98368

SAL8

Please send me the books I have checked above. I have enclosed $__________ which includes $4.95 for shipping and handling of the first $20.00 ordered. Add an additional $1 shipping for each additional $20 ordered. Washington residents include 7.9% sales tax.

Name ______________________________

Address ______________________________

City/State/Zip ______________________________

VISA and MasterCard accepted. 1-800-380-2230 for credit card orders *only.*
8am to 4pm, PST, Monday through Friday.
www.loompanics.com